Microsoft Windows 2000 Network and Operating System Essentials

Microsoft Windows 2000 Network and Operating System Essentials

iUniverse.com, Inc.

San Jose   New York   Lincoln   Shanghai

Microsoft Windows 2000 Network and Operating System Essentials

Published by iUniverse.com, Inc.

For information address:
iUniverse.com, Inc.
5220 S 16th, Ste. 200
Lincoln, NE 68512
www.iuniverse.com

Cover Creation by Shay Jones

Graphic Production by Matt Bromley, Associate Consultant
Domhnall CGN Adams, Corporation Sole-http://www.dcgna.com
5721-10405 Jasper Avenue
Edmonton, Alberta, Canada T5J 3S2
(780) 416-2967
dcgna@yahoo.com

ISBN: 0-595-14814-X

Printed in the United States of America

Acknowledgments

We are pleased to acknowledge the following professionals for their important contributions in the creation of this study guide.

Technical Writer—Caleb Thompson, MSc, MCT, MCSE, MCP+I, A+, Network+

Supplemental Content—Loral Pritchett

Editor—Nina Gettler

Indexer—Loral Pritchett

Cover Creation, Text Conversion and Proofing—Shay Jones, AA, MCSE, MCP

Technical Reviewer—Steve Patrick, MCSE, Cisco, CCNA

Graphic Designer—Matt Bromley

V.P., Publishing and Courseware Development—Candace Sinclair

Course Prerequisites

The Microsoft Windows 2000 Network and Operating System Essentials study guide targets individuals who have the following skills:

- Proficiency using the Windows interface to locate, create, and manipulate folders and files and can configure the desktop environment

- General knowledge of computer hardware components, including memory, hard disks, and central processing units

- General knowledge of networking concepts, including network operating systems, client/server relationships, and local area network (LAN)

The Microsoft Windows 2000 Network and Operating System Essentials exam tests an individual's knowledge for identifying and implementing tasks involved in supporting Windows 2000 networks.

In addition, we recommend that you have a working knowledge of the English language, so that you are able to understand the technical words and concepts this study guide presents.

To feel confident about using this study guide, you should have the following knowledge or ability:

- The desire and drive to become an MCSE certified technician through our instructions, terminology, activities, quizzes, and study guide content

- Basic computer skills, which include using a mouse, keyboard, and viewing a monitor

- Basic networking knowledge including the fundamentals of working with Internet browsers, e-mail functionality, and search engines

- IP, remote connectivity and security

Hardware and Software Requirements

To apply the knowledge presented in this study guide, you will need the following minimum hardware:

- For Windows 2000 Professional, we recommend 64 megabytes of RAM (32 megabytes as a minimum) and a 1-gigabyte (GB) hard disk space.

- For Windows 2000 Server, we recommend a Pentium II or better processor, 128 megabytes of RAM (64 megabytes minimum), and a 2-GB hard drive. If you want to install Remote Installation Server with Windows 2000 Server, you should have at least two additional gigabytes of hard disk space available.

- CD-ROM drive

- Mouse

- VGA monitor and graphics card

- Internet connectivity

To apply the knowledge presented in this study guide, you will need the following minimum software installed on your computer:

- Microsoft Windows 2000

- Microsoft Internet Explorer or Netscape Communicator

Symbols Used in This Study Guide

To call your attention to various facts within our study guide content, we've included the following three symbols to help you prepare for the Microsoft Windows 2000 Network and Operating System Essentials exam.

Tip: The Tip identifies important information that you might see referenced in the certification exam.

Note: The Note enhances your understanding of the topic content.

Warning: The Warning describes circumstances that could be harmful to you and your computer system or network.

How to Use This Study Guide

Although you will develop and implement your own personal style of studying and preparing for the MCSE exam, we've taken the strategy of presenting the exam information in an easy-to-follow, ten-lesson format. Each lesson conforms to Microsoft's model for exam content preparation.

At the beginning of each lesson, we summarize the information that will be covered. At the end of each lesson we round out your studying experience by providing the following four ways to test and challenge what you've learned.

Vocabulary—Helps you review all the important terms discussed in the lesson.

In Brief—Reinforces your knowledge by presenting you with a problem and a possible solution.

Activities—Further tests what you have learned in the lesson by presenting ten activities that often require you to do more reading or research to understand the activity. In addition, we have provided the answers to each activity.

Lesson Quiz—To round out the knowledge you will gain after completing each lesson in this study guide, we have included ten sample exam questions and answers. This allows you to test your knowledge, and it gives you the reasons why the "answers" were either correct or incorrect. This, in itself, enhances your power to pass the exam.

You can also refer to the Glossary at the back of the book to review terminology. Furthermore, you can view the Index to find more content for individual terms and concepts.

Introduction to MCSE Certification

The Microsoft Certified Systems Engineer (MCSE) credential is the highest-ranked certification for professionals who analyze business requirements for system architecture, design solutions, deployment, installation, and configuration of architecture components, as well as troubleshooting system problems.

When you receive your MCSE certification, it proves your competence by having earned a nationally-recognized credential as an information technology professional who works in a typically complex computing environment of medium to large organizations. It is recommended that a Windows 2000 MCSE candidate should have at least one year of experience implementing and administering a network operating system environment.

The MCSE exams cover a vast range of vendor-independent hardware and software technologies, as well as basic Internet and Windows 2000 design knowledge, technical skills and best practice scenarios.

To help you bridge the gap between needing the knowledge and knowing the facts, this study guide presents Windows 2000 network and operating system essentials knowledge that will help you pass this exam.

 Note: This study guide presents technical content that should enable you to pass the Microsoft Windows 2000 Network and Operating System Essentials certification exam on the first try.

Microsoft Windows 2000 Network and Operating System Essentials Study Guide Objectives

Successful completion of this study guide is realized when you can competently understand, explain and identify the tasks involved in supporting Windows 2000 networks.

You must fully comprehend each of the following objectives and their related tasks to prepare for this certification exam:

- Read and understand scenario-based questions that are based on network and operating system essentials

- Describe the principal features of Windows 2000 and the basics of networking with Windows 2000

- Describe the types of user accounts and the primary security features of a Windows 2000 network.

- Identify the tools that perform various administrative tasks.

- Explain the features of common protocols used in a Windows 2000 network.

- Describe TCP/IP fundamentals, name resolution, routing, and IP addressing versus Classless Inter-Domain Routing (CIDR).

- Describe the network communication models found in a Windows 2000 network.

- Understand, explain and implement network architectures.

- Describe the common physical components used for network communication.

- Describe the concepts and protocols for remote access communication.

- Describe client/server technologies used when accessing Web services.

Figures

List of Tables

Contents

Lesson 2: Network Structure 39

Lesson 3: Network Protocols 97

Lesson 4: Introduction to TCP/IP 133

Lesson 5: IP Addresses and Subnets 179

Lesson 6:
Planning and Implementing TCP/IP 224

Lesson 7: Network Administration **269**

Lesson 8: Network Security 331

Lesson 10: Remote Access 433

Lesson 1: Introduction to Networking and Windows 2000

A network consists of two or more connected computers for the purpose of sharing tasks and information. Combining individual computers and resources (like printers) into one network benefits users and administrators. Networks provide users with quick and easy access to files and resources, and provide administrators with a centralized system for management.

Networking computers began in the 1970s. These early networks were cumbersome, difficult to upgrade or change, and often did not follow any uniform standards. From this less-than-glamorous beginning has emerged an international network of computers (the Internet) and standards (protocols) that define communication over networks. Only a few years ago, many businesses were reluctant to implement a network, citing high cost and lack of support. Now, the use of networks in business is common as organizations discover the ease and reliability with which they can communicate and share data, messages, graphics, printers, and other hardware resources.

One of the leaders in networking technologies and operating systems is Microsoft. Starting with Windows NT, Microsoft has developed a line of operating systems designed specifically to meet the needs of network users. The latest Microsoft Network Operating System (NOS) is Windows 2000.

This lesson gives you an understanding of networking fundamentals, and introduces you to the Windows 2000 family of products and their role in a networked environment.

After completing this lesson, you should have a better understanding of the following topics:

- Networking Basics

- Introduction to Windows 2000

- The Windows 2000 Network

Networking Basics

The concept of networking emerged from the need of stand-alone computers to share information with other users in a timely manner. Without a network, information must be either printed out or copied to floppy disks for others to copy information to their computers. Networking shares data and simplifies online communication among users. To accomplish this, a network utilizes a group of physically and logically connected computers, printers, and other devices to enable the sharing of files, printers, communication, and other resources.

Additional advantages of networking include the following:

- Maximization of communication and scheduling efficiencies

- Standardization of applications where all users have the same application and version

- Cost cuts through timely data and peripheral sharing

Understanding the Local Area Network (LAN)

A LAN consists of a limited number of computers connected together in a common area within a limited physical distance. For example, a small company or office located on a single floor of a building might use a LAN. Although there are no hard-and-fast rules about the size of a LAN, it is generally accepted that a LAN has fewer than 100 computers.

A LAN combines hardware and software technologies to allow users to share resources such as data, programs, storage devices, printers, and other peripherals. A LAN also enables users to collaborate and interact by sending messages and data to each other. Groupware applications that run on both the server computer and client workstations enable this collaboration.

LAN Communication

A LAN enables communication among network nodes that consists of workstations, hubs, repeaters, bridges, switches, routers, and servers. To facilitate communication, the networking hardware and software on LAN workstations, servers, and other devices must be compatible. This includes hardware such as network adapter cards, hubs (for linking network devices), and transmission media, as well as the software for server and workstation operating systems, application servers, and shared network devices. An example of LAN connectivity between a server and clients is shown in Figure 1.1.

Figure 1.1 LAN Servers and Client Connectivity

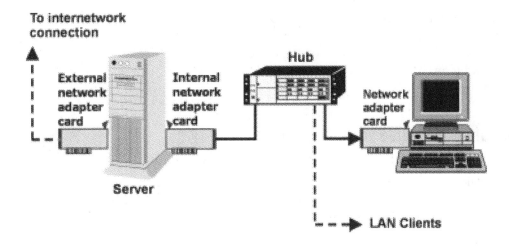

Network Access

When a LAN computer has data to send to another computer, it must have a way to access the network without interfering with other computers transmitting on the network. Different LAN topologies require different methods for computers to gain network access, but the goal of all access methods is to avoid data collisions by managing how and when computers transmit data.

Media

The transmission media used on a LAN depends on several factors, including the required data transmission rate, security needs, type of network adapter cards, and the physical deployment environment. LAN media must be compatible with network adapters, hubs, and other network devices or LAN communication can fail. Several types of transmission media include Unshielded Twisted Pair (UTP) cable, Shielded Twisted Pair (STP), coaxial cable (Thinnet and Thicknet), and fiber-optic cable. As technology increases and prices drop, wireless infrared LANs are becoming the more desirable and common transmission media.

Building an Internetwork

A network of one or more LANs connected by cable is called an internetwork. Like a LAN, there are no set rules regarding the size of an internetwork, but the term generally refers to a collection of two or more LANs located within the same building or campus. LANs are almost always connected by a physical cable, called a backbone that handles the network traffic carried between LANs. The less frequently used terms Metropolitan Area Network (MAN) and Campus Area Network (CAN) refer to internetworks of a specific size.

Expanding to a Wide Area Network (WAN)

When the infrastructure of a small business LAN or internetwork expands to include users located in different cities, states, or even countries, the network is called a WAN. A WAN can serve thousands of users and is often referred to as an enterprise network.

WANs consist of multiple LANs or internetworks that connect through leased lines from telephone carrier service providers, satellite links, microwave transceivers, or by radio transmission. Many companies are now building WANs using Virtual Private Network (VPN) technology, which sends encrypted communication over the Internet.

Exploring Networking Models

The networking model refers to the interrelationship of networked computers. Each computer on a network operates as either a client or server (although a computer can be both a client and server). A server is a computer that has a resource (like a file, a printer, or a Web page) to share on the network. A client is any computer that requests a resource from a server. The three types of network models (mainframe, peer-to-peer and client/server), each defines the interaction between clients and servers in different ways.

Centralized Processing Network

A network consists of one central server (the mainframe) that contains all the programs, performs all tasks, and maintains the databases. Workstations with minimal computing power access these resources on an as-needed basis. The original LANS were mainframe models. Most college campuses, for example, had one mainframe computer, and terminals throughout the campus. The terminals had no processing ability of their own, and could not function without the network connection to the mainframe. The advantages of mainframe networks (cheap terminals) became moot as the price of PCs dropped. Although it is rare to find any mainframe-based networks today, Terminal Services, a new technology in Windows 2000, may actually cause a resurgence of centralized computing.

Peer-to-Peer Network

A peer-to-peer network does not rely on a central server, but functions with workstations acting as equal peers for handling tasks, data storage, and security matters. A peer is a computer that acts as both server and client, providing shared resources on the network and requesting resources from other computers.

A peer-to-peer network usually meets the needs of small organizations or workgroups. However, a peer-to-peer network does not have any dedicated servers or computer hierarchy, as shown in Figure 1.2. Instead, each computer performs as an equal peer that functions as both client and server. This decentralizes data access and security control. In peer-to-peer networking, individual users perform certain administrative functions and decide which data to share on the network. Peer-to-peer networks are less secure than server-based networks because access control tools on local computers are limited.

Figure 1.2 Peer-to-Peer Network Model

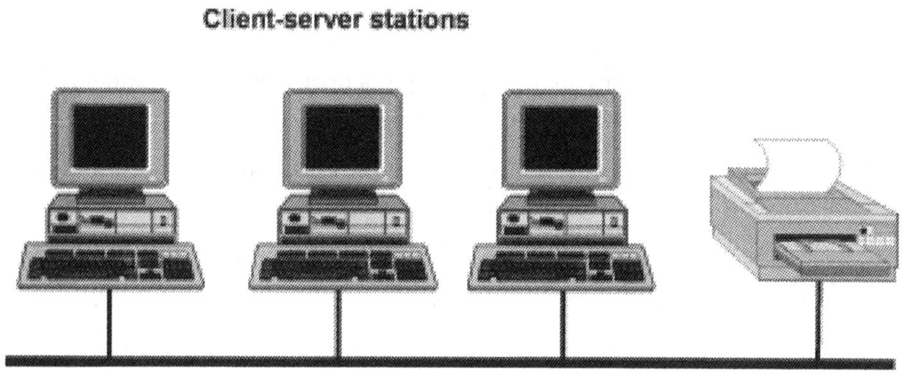

Client-server stations

Use a peer-to-peer network in the following situations:

- Organizational growth is limited to 10 or less network users

- Security and central administration are not important

- Users are capable of performing administrative tasks such as making resources available, data backup, and installing, maintaining, or upgrading application software

- The cost of a network server is prohibitive

Before implementing a peer-to-peer network, consider the following requirements:

- Peer-to-peer network users must share resources such as directories, printers, and modems

- When acting as a server, the workstation must support network resource access

---

 Note: Windows 2000 supports both peer-to-peer networks and client/server networks.

- The workstation must devote some of its resources to supporting network users

- Peer-to-peer network users set and track passwords for shared network resources. Since users set their own passwords and shares are not located on a dedicated server, centralized control is not possible, which results in minimal network security

- Before users can manage both user and administrator tasks, you should consider offering a training program for managing administrative tasks.

Client/Server Network

A client/server network has one or more central servers that manage users, data, security, and shared resource access. Unlike centralized processing (mainframe) networks, workstations share the processing load with the central server. The primary focus of this course is the client/server model.

When a user environment exceeds more than ten workstations, peer-to-peer networking is difficult to manage and quick access to network resources deteriorates. In this situation, most organizations deploy the client/server model (Figure 1.3) to take advantage of the speed, functionality, and security of a server-based network.

Figure 1.3 Client/Server Networking Model

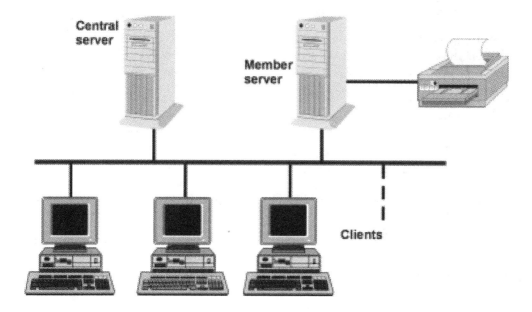

Servers manage the tasks of storing data, implementing network security, managing users, backing up critical data, sharing files, and providing access to shared resources. The server responds to service requests from network clients while also ensuring file and directory security. With a centrally managed server, it is easy to deploy fault-tolerance (the ability of a system to recover from failure) systems and plan for disaster recovery strategies.

Workstations connecting to the server receive a security logon prompt to enter user credentials (name and password). The logon defines their level of access to server/network resources based on assigned user rights and profile restrictions.

If the network becomes large enough, additional servers called member or stand-alone servers may be required. A member server handles special tasks on the network. The following describes several types of member servers represented in the client/server model:

File server—Manages user access and use of file resources. For example, you may store a group project file on a file server. The users can open the file from the server and edit the document locally using a word-processing application that runs on the workstation. When finished, the file is again saved on the file server where other users can access it.

Print server—Makes printers available to the network like a file server. A print server manages print jobs sent from the client. In large organizations, a dedicated print server expedites quick turnarounds for multiple simultaneous print jobs. Frequently, one server functions as both a file server and a printer server.

Database server—Maintains a database accessible by network client requests. The database always resides on the application server and only specific information related to the client request transmits to the client (instead of the entire database). The client sends requests through a local application like Microsoft Access to a database program such as Microsoft SQL Server.

Mail server—Manages e-mail services for network users. Mail servers carry a heavy processing load. Large organizations with many users communicating via e-mail require a dedicated server to handle the generation of heavy traffic.

Communication server—Handles the exchange of information among the network and remote computers and networks. Examples of communication servers are Remote Access Service (RAS) servers and fax servers. RAS allows users to connect to the network from remote locations, and fax servers allow users to send faxes through one central computer.

Client/Server Advantages

Following are the major advantages of the client/server environment:

Resource sharing—Central location of resources on servers allows central management and control for administrative support.

Note: Most networks utilize a combination of server-based and peer-to-peer networks with simultaneous client access to both server resources and other client workstation shares.

Security—A security policy can be centrally administered and applied from the server to every network user. This security aspect makes it a primary choice for the client/server-networking model.

Data backup—An organization can store critical data in one central location, making the backup process simpler and more reliable.

Fault-tolerance—An organization can store data on a single server, a fault-tolerance system, (the ability of a system to recover from failure) which uses data redundancy techniques and is easily implemented. An online backup copy of data replicates from the server and is retrievable if the server crashes.

User numbers—A server-based network supports many more users than a peer-to-peer network.

Client hardware minimized—Clients do not perform a server function, which reduces the requirement for client hardware resources such as RAM and hard disk space.

Choosing a Network Operating System (NOS)

When building a network, the operating system on each computer must have networking capabilities. The operating system on a computer is the program that boots the computer and allows you to run programs. You cannot run a computer without an operating system, and you cannot run a network of computers without a Network Operating System (NOS). Network operating systems vary greatly in capabilities, but they all provide the same basic services. Every NOS has the capability to perform the following functions:

*   Control network communication

*   Provide client computers access to resources

*   Ensure network security by using usernames and passwords

In the client/server network model, the NOS you choose runs on the servers. For example, if you choose Windows 2000 as your NOS, you load—at a minimum—Windows 2000 on each of your servers. You can also load Windows 2000 on each of the client computers, or you can use another operating system that Windows 2000 supports (including all Microsoft Windows products from Windows 3.11 through Windows 2000, UNIX/Linux computers, and Apple Macintosh computers).

Communicating Over a Network

All computers on a network must speak the same language. The language computers use on a network is called a network protocol. Like any language, a protocol sets the rules of communication: identifying yourself and others, using the same words and grammar, and not interrupting a current discussion. On networks, computers must identify themselves, use the same protocol to send information, and know how to send the information so that it does not collide with (interrupt) another communication. The network protocol defines all of this and more. For example, suppose you have a network of only three computers (Figure 1.4).

Figure 1.4 Simple Network Communications

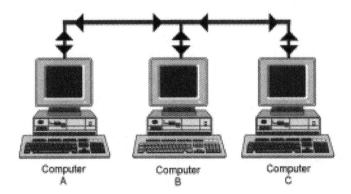

Suppose the user of Computer A wants to retrieve a file on Computer C. Computer A sends out a request for the resource. Both Computer B and Computer C receive the message. Computer B sees that the message is intended for another computer and ignores the message. Computer C reads the message, knows that it is the intended recipient of the message, and also knows the message came from Computer A.

Computer C responds to the message by sending back the requested file. Again, all computers on the network (in this case, just Computer B and Computer A) get the message. Computer B ignores the message, but Computer A keeps the file and makes it available to the user. It also sends a message back to Computer C, confirming receipt of the file.

This example is rather simplistic, but gives you an idea of what actually happens   in network communication. The network protocol is responsible for ensuring good communication among all computers on the network.

Introduction to Windows 2000

Windows 2000 is the newest Windows-based network operating system from Microsoft that builds upon their most popular network operating system, Windows NT 4.0. Windows NT 4.0 is known for its network security and relative stability, compared to other Microsoft operating systems. However, Windows NT 4.0 does not support many of the newer hardware devices, and does not fully support Plug and Play (PnP) technology. Windows 98, which is not at all secure, and not as stable, does support these newer technologies. Windows 2000 can be seen, in part, as a marriage of these two operating systems.

 Note: Stability in an operating system is achieved by limiting programs that run in that operating system. Windows NT 4.0 is stable in part because programs that try to directly access the hardware do not run.

The Windows 2000 operating system provides the following features:

Multitasking—Windows 2000 allows you to run more than one program at the same time. The number of programs that can run is limited only by the hardware in your computer.

Multiple processor support—Windows 2000 supports up to 32 Central Processing Units (CPUs), the brain of the computer in which all actions are processed, and uses Symmetric Multiprocessing (SMP) to allow programs to take advantage of the multiple processors. SMP is the architecture for computers where several processors share the same memory that has one copy of the operating system, applications, and data.

Plug and Play (PnP)—Windows 2000 fully supports PnP, which automatically detects hardware devices and handles all resource configuration.

Enhanced network security—Windows 2000 takes advantage of many of the newest security protocols (for example, Kerberos) to ensure a secure network.

Defining Windows 2000 Products

There are four different Windows 2000 products. Each product uses the Windows 2000 core structure, but has special enhanced features. Windows 2000 Professional has limited features for use as a network server, but has enhanced features as a client operating system. The three other Windows 2000 products are all members of the Windows 2000 Server family. They are designed specifically to run on server computers on different sized networks.

Windows 2000 Professional

Windows 2000 Professional is designed as the operating system for workstations, portable computers, and stand-alone computers. It is intended to replace Windows NT 4.0 Workstation. It is not designed to act as a file or application server. Although much of the user interface has not changed from Windows NT 4.0 or Windows 98, Windows 2000 Professional has a few enhancements that are designed to make the system easier to use, including enhanced features for mobile computer users.

Windows 2000 Server

Microsoft Windows 2000 Server, as the name implies, is designed as the operating system for your network servers. It includes all of the features and enhancements of Windows 2000 Professional, and supports the numerous server services unavailable on Windows 2000 Professional. Most important among these services is the Active Directory service. Active Directory is the new service that defines and supports the organization of your network. In Windows 2000, domain controllers are servers providing the Active Directory service.

Like Windows 2000 Professional, Windows 2000 Server makes use of the Microsoft Management Console (MMC) to centralize management tools. Any services running on the server are managed through the MMC, including the Domain Name System (DNS), Dynamic Host Configuration Protocol (DHCP), and Internet Information Services (IIS). Because the MMC is modular, allowing the addition of snap-ins (modules that run within the MMC and handle a different aspect of Windows 2000 management) at any time, other services that provide a snap-in are managed in this centralized way.

Another important feature of Windows 2000 Server is Remote Installation Services (RIS). RIS allows you to install Windows 2000 Professional on client computers across your network from a central server. RIS supports PnP hardware detection, allowing you to perform automatic installations on computers with different hardware.

Windows 2000 Advanced Server

Windows 2000 Advanced Server includes all of the features of Windows 2000 Server, but is much more scalable. Windows 2000 Advanced Server supports up to 8 GB of physical RAM on an Intel-based computer (32 GB on Alpha-based computers), and up to 8 processors. Furthermore, Windows 2000 Advanced Server supports Windows clustering. The Windows Cluster service allows you to join a group of servers to act as a single server and provides strong fault-tolerance and load balancing. If one of the servers in a cluster fails, another assumes the roles of the failed computer. Clustering distributes network demands to all of the servers in a cluster rather than to just one server.

Windows 2000 Advanced Server is the Windows 2000 version of Windows NT 4.0 Enterprise Server.

Tip: Windows Cluster service allows several servers to act as one server, providing load balancing and fault-tolerance.

Windows 2000 Datacenter Server

The most powerful member of the Windows 2000 family is Windows 2000 Datacenter Server that expands the features of Windows 2000 Advanced Server. Whereas Windows 2000 Advanced Server supports eight processors, Windows 2000 Datacenter Server supports up to 32 processors. It also supports up to 64 GB of physical memory on Intel-based computers (32 GB on Alpha-based servers). This is possible through Microsoft's implementation of Physical Address Extensions (PAEs) created by Intel. PAEs allow an operating system to take advantage of 36-bit memory addressing, rather than the 32-bit addressing that has been the standard for years.

The ability to support such large amounts of RAM and processing power makes Windows 2000 Datacenter Server an appropriate choice for the most demanding computing needs. Large data warehouses, e-commerce servers, and computers used for scientific and engineering modeling will benefit from running Windows 2000 Datacenter Server.

Comparing Windows 2000 Products

Matching your operating system choice to the demands of the computer on which it will run is an important task. Table 1.1 summarizes the features of each of the four Microsoft Windows 2000 products.

Table 1.1 Windows 2000 Key Features

Operating System	Description
Windows 2000 Professional	Designed as desktop operating system to replace Windows 95, Windows 98, and Windows NT 4.0.
Windows 2000 Server	Designed as the operating system for most servers in your network, and has all of the features of Windows 2000 Professional, plus support for server services (Active Directory, DHCP, DNS, and more).
Windows 2000 Advanced Server	Designed for servers in a large enterprise network, supports more RAM and CPUs, and contains all of the features of Windows 2000 Server
Windows 2000 Datacenter Server	The most powerful Windows 2000 product which is designed for the largest networks and data warehouses.

The Windows 2000 Network

This course concentrates on the Windows 2000 operating system and Windows 2000-based networks. The following provides a brief overview of the fundamental structure of Windows 2000 networks.

Exploring Active Directory

Windows 2000 provides a new directory service called Active Directory. Active Directory provides the foundation for all Windows 2000 networks. A directory service is a listing of all of the objects in the network, including computers, printers, and users. Based on a hierarchical structure, Active Directory provides flexible and expandable network architecture. This structure supports a variety of clients, including Windows 3.11, Windows 95/98, Windows NT 4.0, and even UNIX and Macintosh clients. In order to make migration (upgrading of a network from an older network operating system to a new one) as easy as possible for system administrators, Active Directory works in conjunction with the existing Windows NT 4.0 domain model. Nonetheless, there are many reasons to migrate to an Active Directory-based network.

Active Directory allows for a far more intuitive structuring of users, groups, and resources on the network. It permits the grouping of resources, rather than just the grouping of users. Using these groups, you can assign permissions and delegate administrative tasks based on resource allocation.

Active Directory requires the use of the Domain Name System (DNS), the hierarchical system where Internet hosts use both the domain name addresses and IP addresses. As a result, Microsoft has made DNS integration much easier to implement and maintain than in Windows NT 4.0. DNS now supports dynamic updates, eliminating the need to update the DNS table manually because DHCP automatically updates DNS. The integration of Active Directory and DNS also means that the incorporation of the Internet and Internet-based technologies is more intrinsic in Windows 2000-based networks.

Understanding Domains

Active Directory networks are based on a hierarchical structure. The basic unit of structure in Active Directory is the domain. A domain is a logical grouping of objects that share a common directory database. The directory database contains information about all of the objects within the domain. In any given domain, there is only one Active Directory database, although it may be stored on multiple computers.

Active Directory domains provide several benefits over the workgroup model of networking. Follow are the three main benefits of the domain structure:

Single account, single logon—A user only needs one user account to access any data resources on the network. In a workgroup, the user must have an account and password for each computer or resource.

Scalability—The domain structure works well for all sizes of networks from the small, 2-server LAN to the 1,000-server, multinational WAN.

Centralized management—All network resources (including user and computer accounts) are stored in one central directory database, greatly simplifying administration.

Domains are used for security and administrative purposes. An organization's network can consist of several domains, and the administrator for any given domain has administrative rights only for that domain (unless specifically granted rights to other domains). This allows the administrator to delegate control and administrative responsibility. In addition, every domain has its own security policies.

Domain Controllers

The Active Directory database for each domain stores on one or more domain controllers. A domain controller is a computer running Windows 2000 Server and Active Directory that makes the Active Directory available to other computers on the network. Domain controllers handle all network logons, comparing the username and password to the entries in the Active Directory, and then authenticating the user.

In Windows 2000 networks, multiple domain controllers in a domain provide fault- tolerance and load balancing. Fault-tolerance means that if one domain controller fails, the network is still accessible. Load balancing distributes the network demands on a domain controller to several computers, so that one computer does not cause a bottleneck, or the slowest place in the system, for the network.

All domain controllers are peers (they are equal). This is known as a multimaster replication model. Changes are made to the Active Directory database on any one of the controllers, and the changes replicate (copy) to the other domain controllers.

 Note: A domain controller is responsible for the Active Directory in only one domain.

Building Domain Organization

A collection of domains that share a common name is called a tree. In a tree, the first domain is called the root. All domains that branch from the root are called child domains. Child domains share part of the root domain's name, called the namespace. Namespace is the hierarchical structure of a domain tree where each layer of the tree shares a common DNS domain name.

For example, suppose you have a root domain named lightpointlearning.net. The namespace is lightpointlearning.net. You create a child domain named sales.lightpointlearning.net. Both domains share a similar namespace: lightpointlearning.net. These two domains form a tree (Figure 1.5).

Figure 1.5 Domain Tree

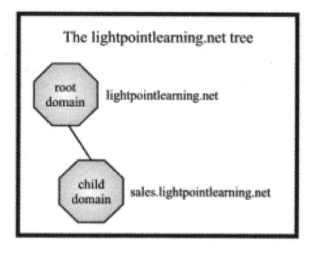

Tip: The highest-level domain (the root) must be the first domain you create in your network. Once you create the first domain, you cannot create a domain above it in the hierarchy; only child domains and other trees can be created.

In addition to creating a child domain under an existing domain, you can also create an independent domain that does not share the same namespace as the root. Although the two domains (or two domain trees, as the case may be) do not share a common namespace, they are both part of your organization. The term forest describes the situation when two or more trees exist that do not share a common namespace.

For example, suppose your company has one domain, named lightpointlearning.net. Your company joins forces with another company, also with one domain, named ibidpub.com. Rather than rebuilding either network, you leave both domains intact and implement trusts. Trusts allow you to share information between two trees. Both lightpointlearning.net and ibidpub.com are trees, and both are part of your organization, but they do not share a common name. The combination of these two trees is a forest (Figure 1.6).

Figure 1.6 Two Trees in a Forest

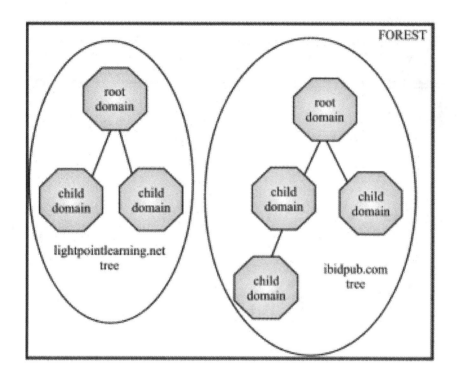

Logging on to a Windows 2000 Network

To access a Windows 2000 network, you must log on. All network users must log on to use any network resources. When you log on to a network, you provide a valid username and password. The username and password are sent to one of the domain controllers. The authenticating domain controller checks the Active Directory for a matching username, and then verifies the password.

Note: On a Windows 2000 workgroup, there are no domain controllers. You must provide a username and password each time you connect to a resource.

Using a Windows 2000 computer, you log on to the network by simultaneously pressing CTRL+ALT+DEL. From the Log On to Windows screen, enter a valid username and password, and then choose OK (Figure 1.7).

Figure 1.7 Log On to Windows 2000

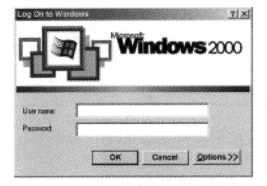

 Tip: If you have just installed Windows 2000 on a stand-alone computer, and have not yet created any usernames, log on using the Administrator account and the password you chose during the Windows 2000 setup.

Vocabulary

Review the following terms in preparation for the certification exam.

Term	Description
Active Directory	Defines and supports the organization of a network. In Windows 2000, domain controllers are servers providing the Active Directory service.
backbone	A physical cable called a ba ckbone handles network traffic carried between LANs.
bottleneck	The slowest component in a computer or network.
CAN	Campus Area Network is an infrequently used term for internetworks used in ca mpus-sized areas.
child domain	All domains that branch from the root are called child domains.
client	A client is any computer that requests a resource from a server.
client/server	A client/server network has one or more central servers that manage users, data, security, and shared resource access. Unlike centralized processing (mainframe) networks, workstations share the processing load with the central server.
clustering	Clustering distributes network demands to all of the servers in a cluster rather than to just one server.
CPU	The Central Processing Unit is the brain of the computer and processes all actions.

Term	Description
directory service	A directory service is a listing of all of the objects in the network, including computers, printers, and users.
DNS	A Domain Name System is the hierarchical system where Internet hosts use both the domain name addresses and Internet Protocol (IP) addresses.
domain	A domain is a logical grouping of objects that share a common directory database.
domain controller	A domain controller is a computer running Windows 2000 Server and Active Directory, and makes the Active Directory available to other computers on the network. Domain controllers handle all network logons by comparing the username and password to the entries in the Active Directory, and then authenticating the user.
fault-tolerance	The ability of a system to recover from failure.
forest	Two or more trees that do not share a common DNS namespace.
internetwork	A network of one or more LANs connected by cable is called an internetwork, and generally includes two or more LANs within the same building or campus.
LAN	A Local Area Network consists of a limited number of computers connected together in a common area within a limited physical distance.
load balancing	Load balancing distributes the network demands on a domain controller to several computers to avoid network bottlenecks.

Term	Description
mainframe	A central server that contains all the programs, performs all tasks, and maintains the databases.
MAN	Metropolitan Area Network is a less frequently used term for an internetwork used in a metropolitan area.
member server	If a network becomes large enough, additional servers called member or stand-alone servers may be required. A member server handles special tasks such as printing or file management on the network.
MMC	The Microsoft Management Console centralizes management tools in Windows 2000 and provides a common interface for these tools.
multimaster replication model	In a multimaster replication model, all domain controllers are peers (they are equal). Changes can be made to the Active Directory database on any one of the controllers, and the changes replicate (copy) to the other domain controller s.
namespace	The hierarchical structure of a domain tree where each layer of the tree shares a common DNS domain name.
network	A network consists of two or more connected computers that share tasks and information. Ne tworks provide users with quick and easy access to files and resources, and provide administrators with a centralized system for management.

Term	Description
network nodes	Groupings of workstations, hubs, repeaters, bridges, switches, routers, and servers.
network protocol	The language computers use on a network is called a network protocol.
networking model	The networking model refers to the interrelationship of networked computers. The three types of network models (mainframe or central server, peer -to-peer and client/server) each define the interaction between client s and servers in different ways.
NOS	The Network Operating System is the program that starts or boots the computer and allows you to run programs. You cannot run a computer without an operating system, and you cannot run a network of computers without a NOS.
PAEs	Physical Address Extensions allow an operating system to take advantage of 36-bit memory addressing, rather than the standard 32-bit addressing.
peer-to-peer network	A peer-to-peer network does not rely on a central server, but functions with workstations acting as equal peers for handling tasks, data storage, and security matters.
PnP	The Plug and Play technology automatically detects hardware devices and handles all resource configurations.
protocol	The set of rules that computers use to communicate over a network.

Term	Description
RIS	Remote Installation Services allows you to install Windows 2000 Professional on client computers across your network from a central server. RIS supports PnP hardware detection, which allows you to perform automatic installations on computers with different hardware.
root domain	In a tree, the first domain is called the root.
server	A computer that has a resource (like a file, a printer, or a Web page) to share on the network.
SMP	Symmetric Multiprocessing is the architecture for computers where several processors share the same memory that has one copy of the operating system, applications, and data.
snap-ins	Modules that run within the MMC; each snap-in handles a different aspect of Windows 2000 management.
VPN	Virtual Private Network technology allows sending encrypted communication over a public network such as the Internet.
WAN	Wide Area Networks are multiple LANs or internetworks that include users in a wide geographical area. A WAN can serve thousands of users and is often referred to as an enterprise network.
ytree	A collection of domains that share a common name is called a tree.

In Brief

If you want to...	Then do this...
Cut costs through timely data and peripheral sharing, standardize applications, and maximize efficient scheduling and communication	Implement a network.
Connect about 100 nodes (computers and printers) and share resources and information among users	Use a LAN with groupware applications that run on both the server computer and client workstations to enable users to collaborate and interact.
Connect two or more LANs within the same building or campus	Connect LANs by cable to create an internetwork.
Expand LANs to encompass users in different cities and states	Consider building WANs using VPN technology to use encrypted communication over the Internet.
Define the interaction between clients and servers	Consider three different networking models for your network or internetwork: central server, peer-to-peer, or client/server.
Build a network	Make sure each computer has networking capabilities with a NOS and its basic services and network protocols.
Support many of the newer hardware devices and the Plug and Play technology, run more than one program at the same time, use multiple processor support, and enhanced network security	Use the Windows 2000 core operating system structure in products such as Windows 2000 Professional, Windows 2000 Server, Windows 2000 Advanced Server, and Windows 2000 Datacenter Server.

If you want to...	Then do this...
Structure users, groups, and resources in an intuitive manner to more efficiently administer resource	Use the Active Directory directory service, which is new in Windows 2000.
Provide fault tolerance and load balancing in your network	Use Windows 2000 multiple domain controllers.
Create a forest	Create two domains that don't share the same namespace.
Log on to a windows 2000 network	Provide a valid username and password to the domain controller for verification.

Lesson 1 Activities

Complete the following activities to better prepare you for the certification exam.

1. Discuss some advantages networks provide.

2. List three types of networks and discuss their characteristics.

3. Explain the main goal of all network access methods.

4. List several types of transmission cable media.

5. Discuss the conditions and requirements to consider before implementing a peer-to-peer network.

6. When a client/server network becomes large, additional servers may be required. Describe these additional servers in the client server model.

7. List three basic services each NOS must perform.

8. Discuss three functions of network protocol, and describe how a simple network communicates.

9. Explain the major differences between the four Windows 2000 products.

10. Discuss the three biggest benefits of the Active Directory domains over the workgroup model of networking.

Answers to Lesson 1 Activities

1. Without a network, information must be either printed out or copied to floppy disks so others can copy information to their computers. With a network, sharing data and online communication among users is simplified. To accomplish this, a network utilizes a group of physically and logically connected computers, printers, and other devices to enable the sharing of files, printers, communication, and other resources. Additional advantages of networks include the following:

   - Maximization of communication and scheduling efficiencies

   - Standardization of applications where all users have the same application and version

   - Cost cuts through timely data and peripheral sharing

2. There are three types of networks: LANs, internetworks, and WANs. A LAN consists of a limited number of computers connected together in a common area within a limited distance and usually has fewer than 100 nodes (computers and printers).

   Internetworks are networks of one or more LANs connected by cable. An internetwork generally consists of a collection of two or more LANs within the same building or campus.

   WANs consist of multiple LANs or internetworks interconnected by leased lines from telephone carrier service providers, satellite links, microwave transceivers, or radio transmission. A WAN can serve thousands of users and is often referred to as an enterprise network.

3. When a LAN computer has data to send to another computer, it must have a way to access the network without interfering with other transmitting computers on the network. Different LAN topologies require different methods for computers to gain network access, but the goal of all access methods is to avoid data collisions by managing when and how computers transmit their data.

4. Several types of transmission media include Unshielded Twisted Pair (UTP) cable, Shielded Twisted Pair (STP) cable, coaxial cable (Thinnet and Thicknet), and fiber-optic cable. As the technology continues to increase and prices drop, wireless infrared LANs are becoming more common.

5. Before implementing a peer-to-peer network, you should consider the following requirements:

   - Peer-to-peer network users must share resources such as directories, printers, and modems.

   - When acting as a server, the workstation must support network resource access.

- The workstation must devote some of its resources to supporting network users.

- Peer-to-peer network users set and track passwords for shared network resources. Since users set their own passwords and shares are not located on a dedicated server, centralized control is not possible, which results in minimal network security.

- Before users can manage both user and administrator tasks, you should consider offering a training program for managing administrative tasks.

6. If the network becomes large enough, additional servers called member or stand-alone servers may be required. A member server handles special tasks on the network. The following describes several types of member servers in the client/server model:

File server-The file server manages user access and use of file resources. For example, you may store a group project file on a file server. The users can open the file from the server and edit the document locally using a word processor application running on the workstation. When finished, the file is again saved on the file server, where other users can access it.

Print server- A print server makes printers available to network users and manages print jobs sent from the client. In large organizations, a dedicated print server expedites multiple simultaneous print jobs. Often, one server serves as both a file server and a printer server.

Database server- Maintains a database that can be accessed by network client requests. The database always resides on the server in a database program such as Microsoft SQL Server and only specific information related to the client request is sent to the client (instead of the entire database).

Mail server-Manages e-mail services for network users. Mail servers carry a heavy processing load. In large organizations with many users communicating via e-mail, a dedicated server is needed to handle the heavy traffic generated.

Communication server-Handles the exchange of information between the network and remote computers and networks. Examples of communication servers are Remote Access Service (RAS) servers and fax servers. RAS allows users to connect to your network from remote locations, and fax servers allow users to send faxes through one central computer.

7. Network operating systems vary greatly in capabilities, but they all provide the same basic services. Every NOS must do the following:

    *   Control network communication

    *   Provide client computers access to resources

    *   Ensure network security by using usernames and passwords

8. On networks, computers must identify themselves, must use the same protocol to send information, and must know how to send the information so that it does not collide with (interrupt) another communication. The network protocol defines all of this, and more. For example, suppose you have a network of only three computers.

    Computer A wants to get a file on computer C. Computer A sends out a request for the resource. Both computer B and computer C receive the message. Computer B sees that the message is intended for another computer, and so ignores the message.

    Computer C reads the message, knows that it is the intended recipient of the message, and also knows the message came from computer A.Computer C responds to the message by sending the requested file back. Again, all computers on the network (in this case, just computer B and computer A) get the message. Computer B ignores the message, but computer A keeps the file and makes it available to the user. It also sends a message back to computer C, confirming receipt of the file.

9. There are four different Windows 2000 products. Each product uses the Windows 2000 core structure, but has special enhanced features.

    Windows 2000 Professional has been designed as the operating system for workstations, portable computers, and stand-alone computers. It is intended to replace Windows NT 4.0 Workstation. It is not designed to act as a file or application server.

    Microsoft Windows 2000 Server is designed as the operating system for network servers. It includes all of the features and enhancements of Windows 2000 Professional, and also supports the numerous server services unavailable on Windows 2000 Professional, including the Active Directory service.

Windows 2000 Advanced Server includes all of the features of Windows 2000 Server, but is more scalable. Windows 2000 Advanced Server supports up to 8 GB of physical RAM and up to 8 processors. Furthermore, Windows 2000 Advanced Server supports Windows clustering.

The most powerful member of the Windows 2000 family is Windows 2000 Datacenter Server. It expands the features of Windows 2000 Advanced Server. Windows 2000 Datacenter Server supports up to 32 processors and up to 64 GB of physical memory.

10. Active Directory domains provide several benefits over the workgroup model of networking. The three biggest benefits of the domain structure are as follows:

Single account, single logon-A user only needs one user account to access any of the resources on the network. In a workgroup, the user must have an account and password for each computer or resource.

Scalability-The domain structure works well for all sizes of networks, from the small, two-server LAN to the 1,000-server, multinational WAN.

Centralized management-All network resources (including user and computer accounts) are stored in one central directory database, greatly simplifying administration.

Lesson 1 Quiz

These questions test your knowledge of features, vocabulary, procedures, and syntax.

1. Which of the following media technologies will become more common as the technology matures and prices drop?

    A. Fiber optic

    B. Coaxial cable

    C. Infrared LANs

    D. UTP

2. What is the new Windows 2000 technology that may cause resurgence in centralized computing?

    A. Active Directory

    B. Web pages

    C. PCs

    D. Terminal Services

3. When is it appropriate to use a peer-to-peer network?

    A. When a user environment exceeds more than 10 workstations

    B. When organization growth is limited to 10 or less network users

    C. The cost of a network is prohibitive

    D. Security and central administration are not important

4. Which of the following are member servers in the client/server model?

    A. Communications

    B. File

    C. Database

    D. VPN

5.   Which of the following describes fault tolerance?

A. Fault-tolerance applies security policies from the server to every network user

B. Fault tolerance backs up critical company data in one central location

C. Fault tolerance replicates an online backup copy of data using data redundancy techniques

D. Fault tolerance reduces the need for more client hardware

6.   On which of the following is Windows 2000 Professional designed to operate?

A. Portable computers

B. Mainframes

C. Workstations

D. Stand-alone computers

7.   Which of the following is the most important server service available on Windows 2000 Server?

A. MMC

B. Active Directory

C. IIS

D. DHCP

8.   What Windows 2000 Advanced Server service distributes network demands to several servers, not just one?

A. Windows Fault

B. Windows Load balance

C. Windows RAM

D. Windows Cluster

9. Which of the following describe Windows 2000 Advanced Server?

    A. Designed for servers in a large enterprise

    B. Contains all of the features of Windows 2000 Server

    C. Supports more RAM and CPUs than Windows 2000 Server

    D. Designed for the largest networks and data warehouses, it the most powerful Windows 2000 product

10. Which of the following describes a collection of domains that share a common namespace?

    A. Tree

    B. Forest

    C. Child

    D. Root

Answers to Lesson 1 Quiz

1. Answers A and C are correct. Both Infrared technology and fiber-optic cable are expensive. LANs based on these technologies will become more common as the technology matures and prices drop.

   Answer B and D are incorrect. Coaxial cable and UTP are common-and very inexpensive-types of transmission media.

2. Answer D is correct. Terminal Services is the new Windows 2000 technology that may cause a resurgence in centralized computing.

   Answer A is incorrect. Although Active Directory is the new service that defines and supports the organization of your network, Terminal Services is more like the older mainframe centralized computing.

   Answers B and C are incorrect. PCs and Web pages may not cause resurgence in centralized computing.

3. Answer B is correct. It is appropriate to use a peer-to-peer network when organization growth is limited to 10 or less network users.

   Answer C is correct. It is appropriate to use a peer-to-peer network when the cost of a network is prohibitive.

   Answer D is correct. It is appropriate to use a peer-to-peer network when security and central administration are not important.

   Answer A is incorrect. When a user environment exceeds more than 10 workstations, peer-to-peer networking is difficult to manage and quick access to network resources deteriorates.

4. Answers A, B, and C are correct. Communications servers, file servers, and database servers are all member servers in the client/server model.

   Answer D is incorrect. A VPN is a Virtual Private Network used on larger internetworks and WANs for encryption purposes.

5. Answer C is correct. Fault tolerance replicates an online backup copy of data using data redundancy techniques.

    Answer A is incorrect. Security policies determine user accesses to network resources, but do not provide fault tolerance.

    Answer B is incorrect. Data backups provide a means for recovering lost data when a drive fails. Fault tolerance ensures that data is not lost in the first place.

    Answer D is incorrect. Client hardware is not affected by fault tolerance. The hardware on the fault-tolerant server usually needs to be enhanced to support fault tolerance.

6. Answers A, C, and D are correct. Windows 2000 Professional was designed to operate portable computers, workstations, and stand-alone computers.

    Answer B is incorrect. Windows 2000 Professional was not designed to operate mainframe computers.

7. Answer B is correct. Active Directory is the most important server service available on Windows 2000 Server. It defines and supports the organization of your network.

    Answer A is incorrect. MMC is the Microsoft Management Console, and is used to centralize tools in the Active Directory.

    Answers C and D are incorrect. IIS and DHCP are services running on the server, and can be managed through the MMC.

8. Answer D is correct. The Windows 2000 Advanced Server's Windows Cluster service distributes network demands to several servers, not just one.

    Answers A and B are incorrect. These answers are fictitious.

    Answer C is incorrect. This answer is fictitious. RAM is Random Access Memory, and not a Windows 2000 Advanced service.

9. Answers A, B, and C are correct. Windows 2000 Advanced Server was designed for servers in a large enterprise, contains all of the features of Windows 2000 Server, and supports more RAM and CPUs.

    Answer D is incorrect. Windows 2000 Datacenter Server is designed for the largest networks and data warehouses, and is the most powerful Windows 2000 product.

10. Answer A is correct. A collection of domains that share a common namespace is called a Tree.

    Answer B is incorrect. A forest is two or more trees that do not share a common namespace.

    Answer C is incorrect. A child is a domain that branches from the root domain.

    Answer D is incorrect. A root is the first domain in a tree.

Lesson 2: Network Structure

On the most basic level, networks are made up of computers connected by a cable, each running a Network Operating System (NOS). The two main components of a network are hardware and software. The NOS, together with protocols, make up the software. Hardware includes the cable, the Network Interface Cards (NICs) that attach computers to the cable, and other devices that help traffic information. This hardware is independent of the NOS—using the same hardware, you could run a Microsoft Windows 2000 network or a Novell NetWare network.

This lesson reviews the hardware that is the foundation of networks. The arrangement of these devices in a network is called a topology, and there are five network topologies with which you need to be familiar.

Every network has rules that define how computers communicate without creating data collisions (like interruptions in a conversation). These network access rules combine with network topologies to define the network architecture. The lesson concludes with a summary of five different network architectures.

After completing this lesson, you should have a better understanding of the following topics:

- Network Components
- Network Topology
- Network Architecture

Network Components

Network components are devices that facilitate and manipulate data transfer from the source to destination. During data transfer, network components perform the following crucial functions:

- Provide signal distribution and connectivity within the LAN or out to other networks

- Modify, condition, or convert data

- Route data over the best available path

- Expand the network or segment traffic

This section describes the following devices: NICs, network cables, wireless devices, and several other devices used to build and expand a network.

Choosing a Network Interface Card (NIC)

A Network Interface Card (NIC), also known as a network adapter, is a device that connects a computer to a LAN by accepting the physical connection to the network media (Figure 2.1). The network adapter negotiates the demands of the computer and the network architecture with its rules for accessing the shared network media.

When handling data, the NIC performs the following basic functions:

- Converts the data format for transmission across the physical network media

- Controls data flow onto the physical media

- Sends the data to other devices

- Accepts incoming data and converts it to a format recognized by the receiving computer

Figure 2.1 NIC

Data Conversion

Internal computer circuits move data on buses in a parallel fashion to accommodate rapid processing. A bus is an internal signal path that passes binary information. Early computers used 8 bits of data, 1 bit moving on each of 8 parallel-running buses. Today's computers are constructed using 16- and 32-bit parallel buses.

Data travels through the network media in a single stream, known as serial transmission. To transmit data from a computer onto the network media, the NIC converts data from a parallel to serial data format (Figure 2.2).

Figure 2.2 Parallel to Serial Conversion

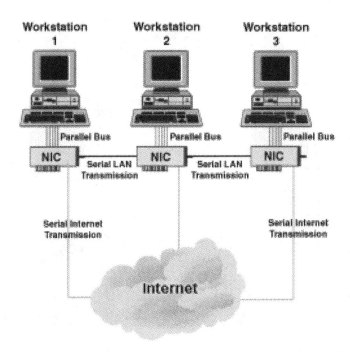

NIC Requirements

Although each computer on your network may have a different brand or model of NIC, each NIC must meet some specific criteria. The criteria for the NIC are as follows:

- The NIC must physically fit in the computer (and match the computer's bus type)

- The NIC must support the cable type used on your network

- The NIC must be supported by the computer's operating system

A NIC must match the data bus architecture of the computer in which it is installed. The following are four different types of data bus architectures:

Industry Standard Architecture (ISA)—ISA architecture has either an 8-bit or 16-bit expansion slot and is used on IBM PCs.

Extended Industry Standard Architecture (EISA)—An extension of ISA architecture that utilizes a 32-bit expansion slot. EISA architecture was introduced in 1988 but rarely used today.

Micro Channel Architecture (MCA)—An IBM proprietary architecture incompatible with ISA buses, functioning as either a 16- or 32-bit bus.

Peripheral Component Interconnect (PCI)—A 32-bit architecture used in most PCs and Macintosh computers. Many current implementations of PCI are Plug and Play (PnP) compatible, meaning that devices installed in this architecture require minimal user assistance to configure computer changes.

The NIC connectors must support the physical characteristics of the network media in use, such as coaxial, twisted-pair, or fiber-optic cable. Some typical NIC types are RJ-45, BNC, and AUI. Some NICs have a combination of connector types.

Finally, the operating system must support the NIC. In most cases, the NIC ships with its own drivers, providing support for most major operating systems. If Windows 2000, for example, does not have drivers for your new NIC, the NIC probably has drivers that work with Windows 2000.

Understanding Network Cable Types

Network cables provide a physical path over which data travels to reach specified destinations. Certain characteristics of the network media have an impact on how fast and efficiently the data can travel from source to destination.

You need to understand the various cable properties regarding the characteristics of your network to ensure compatibility before implementation.

Coaxial Cable

Coaxial cable is a widely used network cabling that transmits voice, data, and video information over relatively long distance with reasonable security. Coaxial cable is constructed of a solid copper inner conductor surrounded by a braided wire-mesh layer of Teflon shielding, encased in an outer layer of nonconductive material such as rubber (Figure 2.3).

Figure 2.3 Coaxial Cable Layers

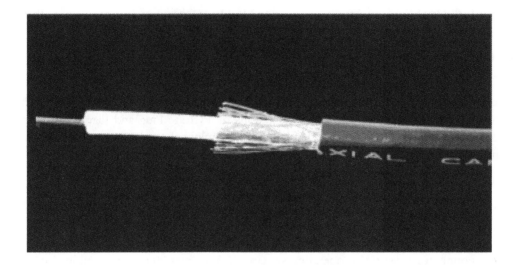

In coaxial cable, data signals travel through the copper inner conductor while the shielding, normally grounded, prevents outside noise, crosstalk, or Electromagnetic Interference (EMI)(the disruption of electrical performance), from reaching the inner conduction path and interfering with the data.

 Note: With unshielded cables, crosstalk and EMI can be a problem. Crosstalk occurs when data radiates across adjacent unshielded cable and sends energy onto other data paths.

For coaxial cable to function properly, the inner conductor and braided shielding must not make contact, or data signals short to the ground and never reach their destination.

The following are types of coaxial cables and connectors you can use on a LAN:

Thinnet—Thin, flexible coaxial cable in the RG-58 family of cables that is ¼-inch thick with a 50-ohm impedance. Thinnet is also known as 10BASE2 cable.

Following are the two 10Base2 cable types:

*   RG-58/U that has a solid inner conductor

*   RG-58 A/U that has a braided inner conductor

Thinnet carries a signal for approximately 185 meters before attenuation results in data loss. Attenuation is signal loss through media.

Tip: The conversion factor between meters and feet is 3.28. For example, 185 meters x 3.28 = 606.8 feet.

Thicknet—Thick, rigid coaxial cable sometimes referred to as standard Ethernet or 10Base5. It is similar to Thinnet coaxial cable, but has a thickness of ½-inch, and carries signals farther before attenuation occurs¾the typical cable distance where attenuation occurs is 500 meters (1,640 feet).

Since Thicknet transfers data over longer distances, it is often used as a LAN backbone segment with smaller Thinnet-based networks connecting to the backbone through transceivers. The transceiver to NIC connections is made with a transceiver cable attaching to a Attachment Unit Interface (AUI) port or DB-15 connector on the NIC.

Coax connectors—Thinnet and Thicknet both use a standard coaxial cable connector called the British Naval Connector (BNC) to connect cables and computers (Figure 2.4).

Figure 2.4 BNC Connector

Twisted-Pair Cable

Twisted-pair cable consists of several pairs of insulated copper wires twisted around each other. The cable twists prevent unwanted signals from other twisted pairs, and reduces crosstalk and other interference. Twisted-pair cable is also referred to as 10BaseT cable.

The following describes unshielded and shielded twisted-pair cable characteristics:

Unshielded Twisted Pair (UTP)—UTP consists of two wires twisted around each other with no shielding (Figure 2.5) and is the most common cable type in LANs. UTP is commonly used for telephone installations and already exists in many buildings, making it advantageous for networks that can utilize the characteristics of UTP.

Figure 2.5 UTP Cable

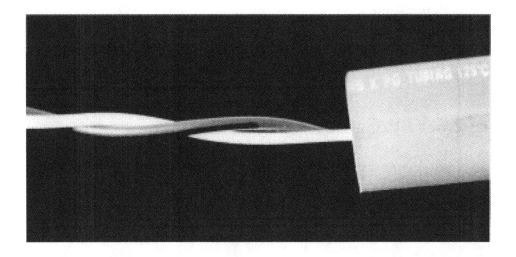

UTP has a maximum cable length of 100 meters (328 feet) before significant attenuation occurs. There are five UTP standards, as follows:

Category 1—Standard telephone cable that supports voice only.

Category 2—Four twisted pairs that handle data transmission rates up to 4 Mbps.

Category 3—Four twisted pairs with three twists per foot to support transmission rates up to 10 Mbps.

Category 4—Four twisted pairs that support data transmission rates up to 16 Mbps.

Category 5—Four twisted pairs that support data rates up to 100 Mbps. This is the most popular version of UTP.

 Tip: To plan for future network upgrades, install Category 5 UTP to accommodate enhanced data transmission rates up to 100 Mbps.

UTP utilizes RJ-45 connectors, which are similar to RJ-11 telephone connectors, except they are larger and contain eight wires instead of four. RJ-45 and RJ-11 connectors are not compatible.

Shielded Twisted Pair (STP)—STP and UTP both use internally twisted-wire pairs, but STP uses foil and braided mesh for ground shielding (Figure 2.6). The shielding captures any unwanted noise or electromagnetic energy radiating near the STP cable run and grounds it to prevent interference. Shielding also prevents the signals on the cable from radiating out to other cables and creating crosstalk.

Figure 2.6 STP Cable

Fiber-Optic Cable

Fiber-optic cable, made of glass or plastic fibers, carry digital data signals using light pulses. Since only light waves traverse the fiber-optic medium instead of electrical signals, the cable is highly efficient, resistant to extraneous noise and EMI, and cannot be tapped like a copper-based cable. This means fiber-optic is a very secure transmission media suitable for high-speed, high-capacity data transmissions over long distance with little attenuation.

A fiber-optic cable assembly is constructed of a central optical fiber (a thin cylindrical glass core) surrounded by a concentric layer of glass cladding with an outer reinforced layer of plastic (Figure 2.7). Optical fibers carry light signals in one direction only. Therefore, a fiber-optic cable assembly must have two fibers—one to transmit data and one to receive.

Figure 2.7 Fiber-Optic Cable

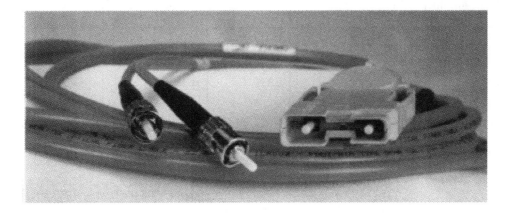

Fiber-optic transmission rates are very fast, typically in excess of 100 Mbps with a distance capability of 2 kilometers (6,562 feet).

Cable Comparisons

When deciding the cable type to use on a network, use the following table to compare the relative benefits and downfalls of each (Table 2.1).

Table 2.1 Connection Media Characteristics

Feature	Thinnet	Thicknet	Twisted Pair	Fiber-Optic
Distance	185 meters	500 meters	100 meters	2 kilometers
Relative Cost	2	3	1 (least expensive)	4 (most expensive)
Transmission rate	10 Mbps	10 Mbps	4 to 100 Mbps	100 Mbps to 1 Gbps
Noise and EMI susceptibility	Good	Good	Poor	None
Preferred uses	Medium-to-large networks with high security	Backbones connecting two or more LANs	Any LAN where computers are less than 100m apart from each other	Any size installation requiring high speed, data integrity, and security

Using Wireless Devices

Although the vast majority of LANs use cables to transmit network data, there is an increasing use of wireless technologies. A wireless network provides greater flexibility and mobility for users, and may be the only option in older buildings and historic sites where running cable through a wall is impractical or impossible. For LANs, there are two primary wireless technologies in use: infrared and radio.

Infrared transmission

An infrared light beam carries network data over relatively short distances. The distance between the transmitting computer and the receiving computer must be unobstructed and in a straight line. Ideally, transmissions should occur away from direct sunlight, since sunlight includes the infrared spectrum. The infrared waves from sunlight interfere with infrared transmissions.

Narrowband Radio

Radio waves, unlike infrared, travel through walls. In a network connection using narrowband radio, the transmitter and receiver do not need to be within a line of sight. However, radio signals are more susceptible to interference from metal in walls (like steel supports and rebar), and you must subscribe to a radio service to use this technology.

Building a Network

Most networks consist of more than one or two computers. In fact, many networks far exceed the physical limitations of the cables. For example, a network using UTP cable, which has a maximum length of 100 meters, cannot have more than a few computers within close proximity. However, you can use network devices such as repeaters, hubs, switches, bridges, routers, and brouters to build and extend networks.

Repeaters

A repeater is a network device that restores and repeats a digital signal. LAN data traffic consists of digital signals with discrete voltages and durations. As a digital signal traverses the network medium, it sustains transmission losses and distortion that impairs the ability of a destination node to recognize it as valid digital data (Figure 2.8).

Figure 2.8 Digital Signal Restoration

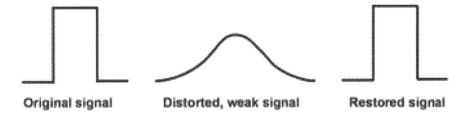

Original signal   Distorted, weak signal   Restored signal

Hubs

A hub is a central point of connectivity for network devices that distributes computer signals and data. A hub is also called a multi-port repeater because it repeats its input signal to all devices or segments connected to the other ports. Hubs expand a network and increase the number of computers in a LAN.

Hubs typically have anywhere from 4 to 24 ports using female RJ-45 connectors (used with UTP and STP cables). Many hubs also have a BNC connector for coaxial cable.

Understanding Switches

A switch is a multi-port device that segments (separates) a large network into smaller segments to reduce network traffic, increase bandwidth, and reduce collisions. Each port on a switch services a separate network because the switch only repeats data to the destination port. In contrast, a hub repeats data to all its ports.

Bridges

You can use a bridge, like a switch, to divide a network and isolate traffic. Segmenting a network with a bridge is a good strategy for expanding a LAN and relieving traffic congestion. However, when using a bridge to separate an overburdened LAN into two linked segments (Figure 2.9), you must follow guidelines to avoid inter-LAN bottlenecks. This requires deciding what devices to place on each side of the bridge so that 80% of the traffic on each LAN segment remains local, and 20% or less of the traffic requires bridge processing and forwarding.

Figure 2.9 Implementing LAN Segmentation with a Bridge

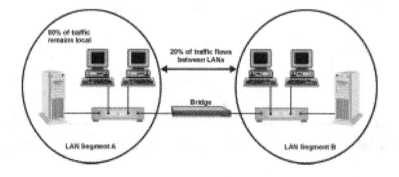

The following situations can provide solutions when using a bridge:

Dividing a network to isolate and filter traffic—Bridges alleviate traffic bottlenecks by segmenting the network into separate networks with reduced traffic on each segment.

Joining LAN segments—Bridges allow connecting two or more LANs to form one larger network while managing and filtering traffic to each segment.

Expanding segment distances—Bridges provide a convenient way to add a group of computers onto an isolated segment.

Linking media—Bridges accept different media, such as coaxial and UTP cable.

Connecting networks—Bridges allow connecting different frame types, such as Ethernet and token ring, and forwarding packets between them (depending on the software).

Routers

A router is a sophisticated network component that allows you to logically interconnect complex network environments having several network segments with varied protocols and architectures. A router can provide the following functions:

- Connect networks using multiple redundant paths

- Separate administrative domains

- Limit unnecessary traffic

- Prioritize packet processing

- Provide security

 Note: Routers only work with certain protocols. TCP/IP, for example, is a routable protocol, whereas NetBEUI is not.

Brouter

A brouter combines the best features of the bridge and router. A brouter provides more cost effective and manageable internetworking than you can achieve with separate bridges and routers. A brouter acts as a router for one protocol and bridges all others. A brouter handles routable and non-routable protocols by routing selected routable protocols, and bridging non-routable protocols.

 Note: Most routers today have bridging capabilities.

Network Topology

Network topology is the shape (or design) of a network. There are many ways to connect all computers on a network, and the result is a variety of network design configurations. Some topologies are restricted by cable type; others provide fault tolerance.

 Note: Decide upon a network topology before installing and configuring network components. Mapping the physical and logical environment in advance saves time and effort during network implementation.

Most network designs are built upon on one of four fundamental topologies: bus, star, ring, and mesh. Networks can be a combination of two or more of these topologies.

Understanding Bus Topology

A bus topology is a simple design that uses a single cable to connect network devices. The single cable, sometimes called a trunk or backbone, connects devices along a linear segment (Figure 2.10).

Communication in a bus topology involves sending data across the backbone from the source to destination computer. The data consists of streams of electronic pulses that travel in both directions on the cable to all connected computers. However, only the computer with the intended address accepts the message. The other computers and devices ignore the message.

Only one computer at a time transmits data in a bus topology network while the other computers wait for the network to clear. As a result, with many computers connected in a bus topology configuration, network traffic quickly becomes congested. The more computers you have waiting to place data on the bus results in a network that runs slower.

Figure 2.10 Bus Topology

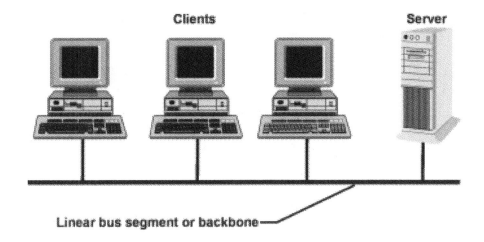

After the destination computer receives the data, the original data transmission continues to travel over the cable. All bus topology networks require a terminator on both ends of the cable. The terminator stops the signal as soon as it reaches the end of the cable, preventing the signal from bouncing back and colliding with other transmissions.

Bus topology is a passive technology because each computer on the network listens for transmitted data, and checks the data's destination address. However, only the computer to which the data is addressed responds; the other computers do not respond. If the message isn't intended for Computer A, Computer A simply ignores the message. It does not repackage and resend the message. The advantage of this configuration is that if one computer on the network fails, the other computers can still send and receive data. Data transmission does not rely on any intermediary computers between the transmitting and receiving computers.

Building a Star Topology

The star topology network consists of computers, printers, and other devices connected by cable segments to a central hub in a configuration that resembles a star (Figure 2.11).

Figure 2.11 Star Topology

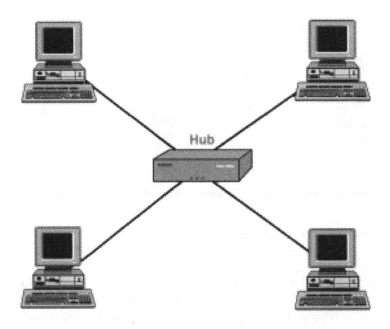

Data transmits in a star topology network from the sending computer to a hub where the signal repeats to all computers on the network (Figure 2.12). Like bus topology, star topology is passive. All computers receive the data, but only the intended computer accepts the message.

Figure 2.12 Star Topology Data Transmission

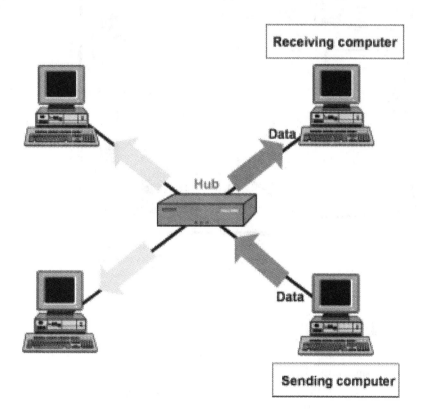

The primary advantage to the star topology is that if a single computer malfunctions or a cable breaks, the network remains fully operational (except for the one failed component). The disadvantage of star topology is that the network depends upon the hub, and if the hub fails, the network is unusable until the hub is replaced. Star topology also uses significantly more cable than a bus (Figure 2.13).

Figure 2.13 Star and Bus Topology Cable

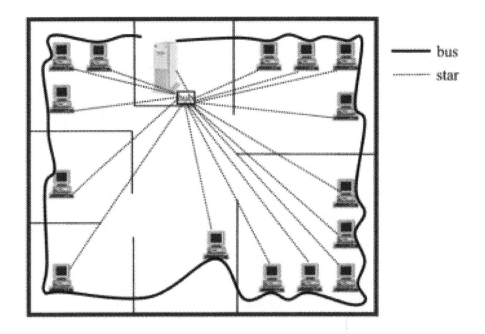

Designing a Ring Topology

Ring topology connects all computers on a single physical circle of cable with no terminated ends (Figure 2.14). The data signal travels around the loop in one direction and passes through each computer. Since each computer on the network regenerates the data signal, ring topology is considered an active network. Consequently, in a ring topology network, the entire network goes down if one computer fails.

Figure 2.14 Ring Topology

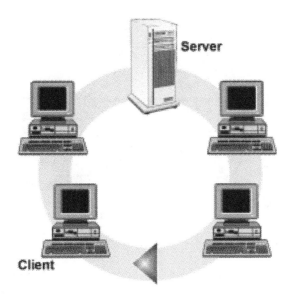

The most common implementation of the ring topology is the token-ring network. It utilizes an electronic token to manage client computer network access. The token is a predefined 24-bit code that enables only the computer possessing the token to put data on the network.

Understanding Mesh Topology

Mesh topology has multiple redundant paths that interconnect network devices (Figure 2.15). Multiple communication paths to a destination allow you to select the best network route at any given time. Mesh topology is commonly used in a WAN. The most complex example of a mesh topology is the Internet, where data can travel on many different paths between the same source and destination.

Figure 2.15 Mesh Topology

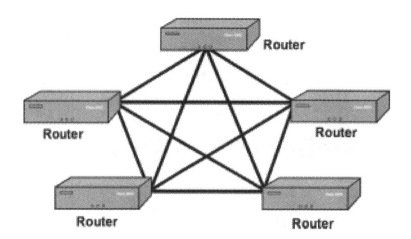

The major advantage to mesh topology is its strong fault tolerance. If one network segment fails—for any reason—all computers continue to communicate. Similar to a highway system, if one road in under construction, you must travel to your destination by taking another path. The route may be longer, but you still get there. The major disadvantage to the mesh topology is its expense. The amount of cable needed to provide this kind of fault tolerance could be very expensive.

Combining Topologies

It is very common for a network to combine the use of more than one type of topology. One topology may be appropriate for part of your network, but inappropriate for the entire network. Two of the more common hybrid topologies are star-bus and star-ring.

Star-Bus Topology

Star-bus topology combines the simplicity of bus topology with the point-to-point connections of star topology. The star-bus topology has several star networks linked together with linear bus trunks (Figure 2.16). Star-bus networks are common in office buildings. Each floor of an office building may be wired in the shape of a star with a single central backbone connecting each floor. Unlike a traditional bus topology, each node on the bus, instead of just a single computer, is actually a star network.

Figure 2.16 Star-Bus Topology

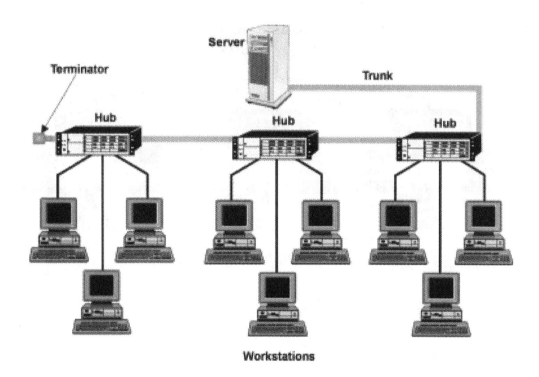

If one computer fails in the star-bus configuration, other network computers continue to transmit and receive data. If one hub goes down, the computers on that hub can no longer communicate on the network.

Star-Ring Topology

In a star-ring topology, star networks connect not by a backbone (as in a star-bus network), but by a ring topology. In a ring network, a computer failure brings down the network. In a star-ring, the failure of one computer does not affect the remainder of the network since the computers are not part of the ring. Only the hubs are part of the ring, so a hub failure causes network failure (Figure 2.17).

Figure 2.17 Star-Ring Topology

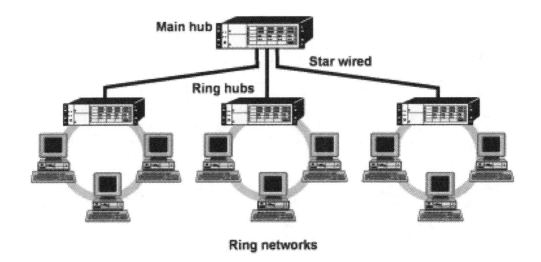

Network Architecture

Network architecture defines the overall structure of a network and its components, including hardware and software that make a network functional. The standard network architecture models discussed in this section are Ethernet, token ring, frame relay, Asynchronous Transfer Mode (ATM), and Fiber Distributed Data Interface (FDDI). All network architecture models have certain elements in common that are applicable to the standard and high-speed models described in this section.

Understanding Network Access Methods

In an unregulated network, multiple users can simultaneously place data onto the network cable. If two signals are placed on the cable at the same time, data collisions occur (Figure 2.18). A data collision can cause a loss of data, and requires both computers to retransmit. Even on a network consisting of three computers, collisions can bring the network to a standstill, where no data successfully transmits.

Figure 2.18 Data Collision

Data packets   Data packets

Therefore, it is necessary to implement controls (access methods) that organize when and how users gain access to the network. The four common network access methods are as follows:

- Carrier Sense Multiple Access with Collision Detection (CSMA/CD)

- Carrier Sense Multiple Access with Collision Avoidance (CSMA/CA)

- Token passing

- Demand priority

CSMA/CD

CMSA/CD is the most common access method used on all Ethernet networks. Using CSMA/CD, a computer first checks the network cable for the presence of a signal (a Carrier Sense Multiple Access (CSMA)). If no signal is detected, the computer assumes it is safe to send data (Figure 2.19).

Figure 2.19 CSMA/CD

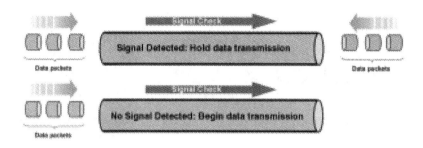

CSMA/CD prevents most, but not all collisions. If two computers transmit at exactly the same time, the data collides. CSMA/CD is very inexpensive to implement and provides relative fast communications on smaller networks, however it is not the preferred choice for very large networks.

CSMA/CA

CSMA/CA also uses Carrier Sense Multiple Access. Like CSMA/CD, computers using CSMA/CA first check the cable for data. If they do not detect any transmissions, the computer sends out an intent-to-transmit message. Each computer on the network receives this intent to transmit and waits until the originating computer transmits its data. Although this method causes fewer collisions than CSMA/CD, it is much slower. Usually two transmissions occur during each data transmission: the intent to send, and then the send. Due to a significant decrease in network performance, few networks use CSMA/CA. The only major network type that still uses CSMA/CA is AppleTalk.

Token Passing

Token passing is a network access method that does not cause data collisions. Significantly more overhead is involved with token passing, but the absolute avoidance of collisions means that data rarely needs to be resent.

With token passing, a digital token (a special bit pattern) systematically passes to each computer on the network in a pre-defined order. A computer with data to send waits until it receives the token, attaches its data to the token, and passes it on. The data travels to each computer in order until it arrives at the destination. The receiving computer removes the data, attaches confirmation of receipt to the token, and sends the token back to the original sending computer. This original computer strips the token and sends back onto the network without data. The next computer in line then sends the data, which starts the process over again (Figure 2.20).

Figure 2.20 Token Passing

Token passing ensures that all computers on the network have equal access and equal rights to send data, unlike CSMA/CD and CSMA/CA.

Demand Priority

Demand priority is a newer access method that allows certain computers priority over others regarding transmitting data. For example, you may wish to give priority to file servers that send files out to many clients. Demand priority is used solely with 100VG-AnyLAN networks, which are proprietary networks based on Hewlett- Packard technology.

Access Methods Comparison

Table 2.2 lists the advantages and disadvantages of four network access methods.

Table 2.2 Network Access Methods

Access Method	Advantages	Disadvantages
CSMA/CD	Inexpensive and fast on small networks.	Slow in larger networks and does not support priority.
CSMA/CA	Inexpensive and very easy to implement.	Very slow.
Token passing	Gives all computers equal access and fast on larger networks.	Slower than CSMA/CD on smaller networks and is more expensive.
Demand priority	Supports priority assignments and is fast.	Proprietary and is expensive.

Defining Network Architectures

A network architecture defines the combination of a network topology and an access method. In this section, you will learn the characteristics of five network architectures, including Ethernet, token ring, frame relay, ATM, and FDDI.

 Note: The Institute of Electrical and Electronics Engineers (IEEE) developed a model that clearly defines many of the network models. Developed in February of 1980, the standards received the name 802. Many people refer to the network architecture by its 802 name.

Ethernet

Ethernet is the most popular network architecture. The IEEE 802.3 Ethernet specification uses the CSMA/CD network access method, and can use the bus or star topology, depending on the cable type used. The original 802.3 specification defines Ethernet transmission rates of 10 Mbps. More common today are Ethernet networks that support 100-Mbps Ethernet, and Gigabit Ethernet, which supports 1,000-Mbps transmission rates. Table 2.3 summarizes the Ethernet architecture.

Table 2.3 Ethernet Network Specifications

Network Element	IEEE 802.3 Specification
Topology	Bus, star, or star-bus
Access method	CSMA/CD
Data transfer speed	10 Mbps, 100 Mbps, or 1,000 Mbps
Cable types	Thicknet (10Base5), Thinnet (10Base2), UTP (10BaseT), or fiber-optic (10BaseF)

Ethernet implementations consist of 10Base2, 10Base5, 10BaseT, and 10BaseF.

10Base2—10Base2 uses Thinnet cable on a bus topology and uses a 10-Mbps data rate (Table 2.4).

Table 2.4 10Base2 Specifications

Feature	Description
Topology	Bus
Access method	CSMA/CD
Data rate and transmission type	10 Mbps
Cabling	Thinnet coax
Maximum cable segment length	185 meters; up to 925 meters with repeaters
Maximum computers per segment	30

 Note: The Thinnet network uses a 5-4-3 rule. The 5-4-3 rule specifies that a Thinnet network can contain up to five cable segments, separated by four repeaters, and only three of the segments can have devices.

10Base5—10Base5 uses Thicknet cable on a bus topology and achieves a 10-Mbps data rate (Table 2.5). It also adheres to the 5-4-3 rule.

Table 2.5 10Base5 Specifications

Feature	Description
Topology	Bus
Access method	CSMA/CD
Data rate and transmission type	10 Mbps
Cabling	Thicknet coaxial
Maximum cable segment (backbone) length	500 meters; up to 2,500 meters with repeaters
Maximum computer to transceiver segment length	50 meters
Maximum nodes (computers, repeaters, devices) per backbone segment	100

10BaseT—10BaseT Ethernet uses twisted-pair cable on a star topology to achieve a 10-Mbps data rate (Table 2.6).

Table 2.6 10BaseT Specifications

Feature	Description
Topology	Star with multi-port hub
Access method	CSMA/CD
Data rate and transmission type	10 or 100 Mbps
Cabling	Category 3, 4, and 5 Unshielded Twisted Pair (UTP) or Shielded Twisted Pair (STP)
Maximum cable segment length (network adapter card to hub)	100 meters
Maximum number of computers in a 10BaseT LAN	1,024

 Note: Most installations of 10BaseT networks use Category 5 cable that supports both 10-Mbps and 100-Mbps transmission rates.

10BaseF—10BaseF uses fiber-optic cable on a star or bus topology for 10-and 100-Mbps data rate. Although 10BaseF does not use the bandwidth capabilities of fiber-optic cable to the fullest, the fiber-optic cable allows you to carry an Ethernet signal up to 2 kilometers away (Table 2.7).

Table 2.7 10BaseF Specifications

Feature	Description
Topology	Star or bus
Access method	CSMA/CD
Data rate and transmission type	10 or 100 Mbps
Cabling	Fiber optic
Maximum cable segment length (NIC to hub)	2,000 meters (2 kilometers)
Maximum number of computers in a 10BaseT LAN	1,024

Token Ring

Token-ring architecture (IEEE 802.5) uses token passing on a ring topology. The network may physically be wired as a star, but the central hub is called a Multiple Access Unit (MAU). The wiring inside the MAU forms a ring, and data traveling across the network travels on this ring. Table 2.8 describes token-ring features.

Table 2.8 Token-Ring Specifications

Feature	Description
Topology	Ring (wired as a star)
Access method	Token passing
Data rates and transmission type	4 and 16 Mbps
Cabling	STP and UTP
Maximum STP cable segment length (MAU to computer)	100 meters
Maximum computers per ring with STP	260

Frame Relay

Frame relay is typically used over WAN connections. The frame relay architecture sends data packets of variable sizes over many different cable types and lines, usually leased from a telephone company. By using the telephone company's fiber-optic and other digital cables, a Permanent Virtual Circuit (PVC) is established. PVC acts as a single cable connection between two end points, and data may travel over many different cables to its destination.

 Note: Frame relay uses the point-to-point access method where a computer sends data packets directly to another computer without other computers receiving or acting upon the data.

Asynchronous Transfer Mode (ATM)

ATM uses the point-to-point access method to send fixed-length packets over a switched network. Like frame relay, ATM is generally used for WANs and uses leased lines from the telephone company. Unlike frame relay, ATM uses fixed-length packets that increases network speed and bandwidth.

 Note: ATM supports data transmissions up 622 Mbps, making it a suitable medium for transmitting data, voice, and real-time audio and video.

Fiber Distributed Data Interface (FDDI) Architecture

FDDI uses fiber-optic cable wired as a ring to transmit data. Devices access an FDDI network using token-passing methods. Unlike token ring that is wired like a star, FDDI is wired as a ring with two fiber-optic cables. Each cable transmits data in the opposite direction, providing fault-tolerance (Figure 2.21).

Figure 2.21 FDDI Network

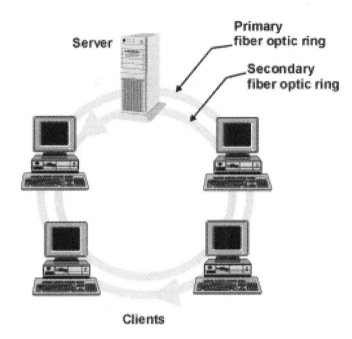

Data is carried on one cable (the primary ring) exclusively until that cable breaks. Data then travels along the second cable (the secondary ring) in the opposite direction until it reaches its intended destination.

FDDI is most commonly used as a backbone for other LANs. Most major metropolitan areas now have one or more FDDI rings. Companies can lease access to the FDDI and use it to link two or more office buildings. Because FDDI uses fiber-optic cable, high-data transmission rates and distances of up to 100 kilometers (62 miles) are possible. Some university and college campuses use this technology as well. Table 2.9 summarizes the FDDI specifications.

Table 2.9 FDDI Specifications

Feature	Description
Topology	Ring
Access method	Token passing
Data transmission rate	100 Mbps
Network media	Fiber-optic cable
Maximum ring distance	200 kilometers
Maximum number of devices on the ring	500

Vocabulary

Review the following terms in preparation for the certification exam.

Term	Description
10Base2 cable	A thin, flexible coaxial cable with a 50 -ohm impedance sometimes referred to as Thinnet cable .
10Base5 cable	A thick, rigid coaxial cable sometimes referred to as standard Ethernet or Thicknet cable .
10BaseF cable	Uses fiber-optic cable on a star bus topology and can carry an Ethernet signal up to 2 kilometers away.
10BaseT cable	Several pairs of copper wires (twisted-pair cable) twisted around each other that reduce crosstalk and other interference.
ATM	Asynchronous Transfer Mode is a standard architecture that uses the point-to-point access method and uses fixed length data packets for increased network speed and bandwidth.
attenuation	Attenuation is signal loss through media and typically occurs at a distance of about 500 meters (1,640 feet).
BNC	The British Naval Connector is a hardware connector used between Thinnet and Thicknet cables and computers.
bridge	A network device that works like a switch. It divides a network and isolates traffic, with 80% of the traffic on each LAN segment remaining local. The other 20% or less of the traffic requires bridge processing and forwarding.

Term	Description
brouter	A brouter is a network device that acts as a router for selected routable protocols, and bridges non-routable protocols.
bus	A bus is an internal signal path that passes binary information. Today's computers use 16- and 32-bit parallel buses.
bus topology	A simple network design that uses a single cable, also called a trunk or backbone, to connect network devices in a single line.
CMSA/CD	Carrier Sense Multiple Access/Collision Detection is the most common access method used on all Ethernet networks. A CSMA/DC computer checks the network cable for signals. If there is no signal, the computer assumes it is safe to send data.
coaxial cable	A widely used network cable that transmits voice, data, and video information over relatively long distance with reasonable security.
crosstalk	Interference that occurs when data radiates across adjacent unshielded cable and sends energy onto other data paths.
CSMA/CA	Carrier Sense Multiple Access/Collision Avoidance is a common access method. A computer checks network cable for data. When no transmissions are detected, it sends an intent-to-transmit message. Each computer receives the message and waits to receive the data.
data collision	A loss of data that occurs when two signals are placed on the cable at the same time.

Term	Description
demand priority	A new access method for 100VG-AnyLAN networks that give certain computers data transmission priority over others.
EISA	Extended Industry Standard Architecture is an extension of ISA architecture that utilizes a 32-bit expansion slot.
EMI	Electromagnetic Interference is the disruption of electrical performance.
Ethernet	The most popular network architecture, this IEEE 802.3 Ethernet specification uses the CSMA/CD network access method, and can use the bus or star topology, depending on its cable type.
FDDI	Fiber Distributed Data Interface architecture uses fiber-optic cable, wired as a ring, to transmit data.
fiber-optic	Cable made of glass or plastic fibers that transmit digital data signals using light pulses.
frame relay	An architecture that is used in WAN connections that sends data packets with the point-to-point access method.
hardware	Any component on a network that includes cable or NICs that attach computers to the cable, and other devices that help traffic information.
hub	A central connection point for network devices that distributes signals and data, expands networks, and increases the number of computers in a LAN.

Term	Description
IEEE 802.3	The Institute of Electrical and Electronics Engineers 802.3 is a standard Ethernet specification that uses CSMA/CD network access and can use bus or star topology. Ethernet networks today can support 1,000-Mbps transmission rates.
infrared	A light beam that carries network data over short distances and is used as a primary wireless technology for LANs.
ISA	Industry Standard Architecture is a data bus architecture for IBM PCs with either an 8- or 16-bit expansion slot.
MAU	A Multiple Access Unit is the central hub in a token-ring architecture. The wiring inside the MAU forms a ring on which data travels.
MCA	Micro Channel Architecture is an IBM proprietary bus architecture incompatible with ISA buses, and functions as either a 16- or 32-bit bus.
mesh topology	Multiple redundant paths interconnect network devices in mesh topology. These multiple communication paths to a destination allow selecting the best network route at any time. The topology is commonly used on WANs and the Internet.
multi-port repeater	Also called a hub, this repeater repeats its input signal to all devices or segments that connect to other ports.
network access method	Controls that organize when and how users gain access to a network. Four common network access methods are CSMA/CD, CSMA/CA, token passing, and demand priority.

Term	Description
network architecture	The overall structure of a network and its components, including hardware and software that make a network functional.
network components	Devices that facilitate and manipulate data transfer from its source to its destination.
network software	NOS together with protocols make up the network software.
NIC	A Network Interface Card, also called a network adapter, is a device that connects a computer to a LAN by accepting the physical connection to the network media. The NIC converts data from a parallel to serial data format
NOS	The Network Operating System is the program that starts or boots the computer and allows you to run programs. You cannot run a computer without an operating system, and you cannot run a network of computers without a NOS.
passive technology	Bus topology is an example of passive technology where each network computer listens for transmitted data, checks the destination address, but never actively resends the data.
PCI	Peripheral Component Interconnect is a 32-bit bus architecture found in most PCs and Macintosh computers. Many implementations of PCI are Plug and Play (PnP) compatible that requires minimal user configuration.
point-to-point	This access method sends data packets directly to another computer without other computers receiving or acting upon the data.

Term	Description
PVC	Permanent Virtual Circuit acts as a single cable connection between two end points although it uses many different cables.
radio	A primary wireless LAN technology obtained through a radio service subscription.
repeater	A network device used to build and extend networks, a repeater restores and repeats a digital signal.
ring topology	A ring topology connects all computers on a single physical circle of cable with no end terminations. The data signal travels the loop in one direction and passes through each computer.
router	A sophisticated network device that logically interconnects complex network environments on several segments having differing protocols and architectures.
serial transmission	A type of transmission where data travels through the network media in a single stream.
shielding	A protective layer, such as the braided wire-mesh and outer layer of nonconductive material on coaxial cables, that captures and grounds radiating noise, crosstalk, or electromagnetic energy to prevent interference.
star topology	The star topology network consists of computers, printers, and other devices connected by cable segments to a central hub in a configuration that resembles a star.
star-bus topology	A topology that combines several star networks linked together with linear bus trunks. A single central backbone connects each star.

Term	Description
star-ring topology	Star networks are not connected by a backbone as in a star-bus network, but by a ring topology.
STP	Shielded Twisted Pair cable consists of two wire s twisted around each other with foil and braided mesh for ground shielding.
switch	A multi-port device that segments a large network into smaller segments to reduce network traffic, increase bandwidth, and reduce collisions.
Thicknet	Thick, rigid coaxial cable referred to as standard Ethernet or 10Base5 that transfers data over longer distances and is often used as a LAN backbone segment with smaller Thinnet.
Thinnet	Thin, flexible coaxial cable, als o known as 10BASE2 cable that carries a signal for approximately 185 meters before attenuation causes data loss.
token passing	A network access method that causes no data collisions and ensures all network computers have equal acces s rights to send data.
token ring	An IEEE 802.5 standard architecture model that uses token passing on a ring topology, which may be wired as a star, but uses a MAU.
topology	The arrangement of hardware that forms th e framework of the network.
twisted-pair cable	Several pairs of insulated copper wires twisted around each other. The cable twists prevent unwanted signals from other twisted pairs, and reduces crosstalk and other interference . Twisted-pair cable is also referred to as 10BaseT cable.

Term	Description
UTP	Unshielded Twisted Pair cable consists of two wires twisted around each other with no shielding. It is the most common LAN cable type, and is used for land telephone installations.

In Brief

If you want to...	Then do this...
Build and expand a network	Use network adapters, network cables, wireless devices, and several other devices.
Choose a NIC	Make sure it matches the data bus architecture in the computer in which it is installed.
Ensure compatibility of network cable with the characteristics of a proposed network	Understand the various types, categories and uses for coaxial cable, twisted-pair cable, fiber-optic cable, and their connectors.
Use network cabling that transmits voice, data and video information over long distance with reasonable security	Use Thinnet coaxial cable to carry a signal for 185 meters before attenuation occurs, and Thicknet to carry signals to 500 meters before attenuation occurs.
Decide which cable type to use on a network	Consider the benefits and downfalls of the Thinnet, Thicknet, twisted-pair and fiber-optic cable types regarding distance, relative cost, transmission rates, noise and EMI susceptibility, and preferred uses.
Network with cables	Consider using wireless technologies such as infrared and narrowband radio transmissions for carrying network data over relatively short distances.

If you want to...	Then do this...
Build and extend your network	Use devices such as repeaters, hubs, switches, bridges, routers, and brouters to, among many functions, strengthen digital signals, reduce collisions and traffic, and interconnect your network.
Decide upon a network topology before installing and configuring network components	Map the physical and logical environment to decide which of the following topologies is best for you: bus, star, ring, mesh, star-bus, or star-ring.
Prevent data collision on your network	Implement controls or access methods that organize when and how users gain access to the network, such as CSMA/CD, CSMA/CA, token passing, and demand priority.
Define the combination of a network topology and an access method for your network	Choose among five network architectures, including Ethernet, token ring, frame relay, Asynchronous Transfer Mode (ATM), and Fiber Distributed Data Interface (FDDI) network architectures.

Lesson 2 Activities

Complete the following activities to better prepare you for the certification exam.

1.   Discuss the purpose and functions of a NIC, and list three criteria each NIC must meet to properly work on your network.

2.   List and describe four types of data bus architectures.

3.   Devise a table that compares relative benefits and downfalls of each major cable type regarding distance, relative cost, transmission rate, noise and EMI susceptibility, and preferred uses.

4.   Explain several situations where a bridge might provide a solution to network problems.

5.   Explain the simple bus topology and how it relates to passive technology.

6.   Describe the differences between a ring topology and a mesh topology.

7.   List two types of combination network topologies, and discuss their advantages and disadvantages.

8.   Explain why it is important to implement network controls and list four common network access methods.

9.   Network architecture defines the combination of a network topology and an access method. Compare and contrast access methods by listing advantages and disadvantages of each.

10.   Ethernet is the most popular network architecture. List four Ethernet implementations of the IEEE 802.3 specifications.

Answers to Lesson 2 Activities

1. A NIC, also known as a network adapter, is a device that connects a computer to a LAN by accepting the physical connection to the network media. The network adapter mediates the demands of the computer on one side and the network architecture, with its rules for accessing the shared network media, on the other. When handling data, the network adapter performs the following basic functions:

*   Converts the data format for transmission across the physical network media

*   Controls data flow onto the physical media

*   Sends the data to other devices

*   Accepts incoming data and converts it to a format recognized by the receiving computer

    Although each computer on a network may have a different brand or model of NIC, each NIC must meet some specific criteria. These criteria are listed and described below:

*   The NIC must physically fit in the computer (and match the computer's bus type).

*   The NIC must support the cable type used on your network.

*   The NIC must be supported by the computer's operating system.

2. A network adapter card must match the data bus architecture in the computer in which it is installed. The following are four different types of data bus architectures:

    Industry Standard Architecture (ISA)-ISA architecture has either an 8-bit or 16-bit expansion slot and is used on IBM PCs.

    Extended Industry Standard Architecture (EISA)-An extension of ISA architecture that utilizes a 32-bit expansion slot. EISA architecture was introduced in 1988 but is rarely used today.

    Micro Channel Architecture (MCA)-An IBM proprietary architecture incompatible with ISA buses, functioning as either a 16- or 32-bit bus.

    Peripheral Component Interconnect (PCI)-PCI is a 32-bit architecture used in most PCs and Macintosh computers. Current implementations of PCI are PnP-compatible, meaning that devices installed in this architecture require minimal user assistance to configure computer changes.

3.   Your table should look something like this:

Feature	Thinnet	Thicknet	Twisted pair	Fiber optic
Distance	185 meters	500 meters	100 meters	2 kilometers
Relative Cost	2	3	1 (least expensive)	4 (most expensive)
Transmission rate	10 Mbps	10 Mbps	4 to 100 Mbps	100 Mbps to 1 Gbps
Noise and EMI susceptibility	Good	Good	Fair	None
Preferred uses	Small to Medium networks.	Backbones connecting two ore more LANs.	Any LAN where computers are less than 100 meters apart from each other.	Any size installation requiring high speed, data integrity, and security.

4.   The following are examples of how you might use a bridge:

Dividing a network to isolate and filter traffic-Bridges can alleviate traffic bottlenecks by segmenting the network into separate networks with reduced traffic on each segment.

Joining LAN segments-Bridges allow connecting two or more LANs to form one larger network while managing and filtering traffic to each segment.

Expanding segment distances-Bridges provide a convenient way to add a group of computers onto an isolated segment.

Linking media-Bridges accept different media, such as coaxial and UTP cable.

Connecting networks-Bridges allow connecting different frame types, such as Ethernet and token ring, and forwarding packets between them (depending on the software).

5. In a bus topology network, each computer is attached to a single cable (called a backbone). The bus topology is a passive network type-computers attached to the network are not responsible for regenerating the data signals. When a computer sends data, every other computer on the network receives the data. Only the intended recipient acts upon the data. All other computers simply ignore the signal. They do not regenerate it or pass it on to the recipient.

    The advantage of a passive network is clear: if one computer on the network fails, the other computers can still send and receive data. Data transmission does not rely on any intermediaries between the transmitting and receiving computers.

6. The ring topology connects all computers on a single physical circle of cable with no terminated ends. The data signal travels around the loop in one direction and passes through each computer. Since each computer regenerates the data signal, ring topology is considered an active network. In a ring topology network, if one computer fails, the entire network goes down. The most common implementation of the ring topology is the token-ring network. It utilizes an electronic token to manage client computer network access. The token is a predefined 24-bit code that enables only the computer possessing the token to put data on the network.

    In a mesh topology, there are multiple redundant paths that interconnect network devices. Multiple communication paths to a destination allow for selecting the best network route at any time. It is common to use mesh topology in a WAN. The largest example of a mesh topology is the Internet, where data can travel on many different paths between the same source and destination. The major advantage to mesh topology is strong fault tolerance. If one network segment fails-for any reason-all computers can continue to communicate. Much like highway system, if one road is under construction, you can reach your destination by taking another path. It may be a longer path, but you will get there. The major disadvantage to the mesh topology is expense. The amount of cable needed to provide such fault tolerance can be very expensive.

7. Two types of combined network topologies are Star-bus and Star-ring topologies.

    Star-bus topology combines the simplicity of bus topology with the point-to-point connections of star topology. The star-bus topology has several star networks linked together with linear bus trunks. Star-bus networks are common in office buildings. Each floor of an office building may be wired as a star, but a single central backbone connects each floor. Unlike a traditional bus topology, each node on the bus is actually a star network (instead of a single computer). If one computer fails in the star bus configuration, other network computers are unaffected and continue to transmit and receive data. If one hub goes down, the computers on that hub can no longer communicate on the network.

In a star-ring topology, star networks are connected not by a backbone (as in a star-bus network), but by a ring topology. In a ring network, a computer failure brings down the network. In a star-ring, the failure of one computer does not affect the remainder of the network, since the computers are not part of the ring. Only the hubs are part of the ring, so a hub failure will cause network failure.

8.   A data collision causes loss of data, and both computers must retransmit. Even on a network consisting of three computers, collisions could bring the network down to a standstill, with no data successfully transmitted. For this reason, it is necessary to implement controls (access methods) that organize when and how users gain access to the network. There are four common network access methods, as follows:

- Carrier Sense Multiple Access with Collision Detection (CSMA/CD)

- Carrier Sense Multiple Access with Collision Avoidance (CSMA/CA)

- Token passing

- Demand priority

9.   Your table should look something like this example:

Access Method	Advantages	Disadvantages
CSMA/CD	Inexpensive. Fast on small networks.	Slow in larger networks. Does not support priority.
CSMA/CA	Inexpensive. Very easy to implement.	Very slow.
Token Passing	All computers have equal access. Fast on larger networks.	Slower than CSMA/CD on smaller networks. More expensive.
Demand Priority	Supports priority assignments. Fast.	Proprietary. Expensive.

10.   Four Ethernet implementations of the IEEE 802.3 specifications are:

10Base2—10Base2 uses thinnet cable on a bus topology and has a 10-Mbps data rate. Adheres to the 5-4-3 rule.

10Base5—10Base5 uses Thicknet cable on a bus topology and achieves a 10Mbps data rate. It also adheres to the 5-4-3 rule.

10BaseT—10BaseT Ethernet uses twisted-pair cable on a star topology to achieve a 10 Mbps data rate.

10BaseF—10BaseF uses fiber-optic cable on a star or bus topology for 10-and 100-Mbps data rate. Although 10BaseF does not use the bandwidth capabilities of fiber-optic cable to the fullest, the fiber-optic cable allows you to carry an Ethernet signal up to 2 kilometers.

Lesson 2 Quiz

These questions test your knowledge of features, vocabulary, procedures, and syntax.

1.   What does a NIC have to do to transfer data from a computer onto the network media?

   A. Fit in the computer

   B. Convert data from a parallel to serial data format

   C. Support the network cable type

   D. Be supported by the computer's operating system

2.   Which of the following describe a brouter?

   A. Acts as a router for one protocol and bridges all others

   B. Handles routable protocols

   C. Handles non-routable protocols

   D. More expensive than a router or a bridge

3.   Which of the following repeats its input signal?

   A. Repeater

   B. Hub

   C. Multi-port repeater

   D. Switch

4.   How fast does a fiber-optic cable transmit?

   A. 4 to 100 Mbps

   B. 10 Mbps

   C. 100 Mbps to 1 Gbps

   D. 2 Mbps

5. Which of the following is a advantage of a passive network?

    A. If one computer on the network fails, they all do

    B. If one computer on the network fails, the others continue to work

    C. Data transmission doesn't rely on intermediaries between transmitting and receiving computers.

    D. Data transmission relies on intermediaries to continue transmission

6. Which of the following is a major advantage of mesh topology?

    A. Multiple communication paths

    B. Strong fault tolerance

    C. Affordable

    D. Electronic tokens

7. Which of following are hybrid topologies?

    A. Internet

    B. Bus

    C. Star-bus

    D. Star-ring

8. Which of the following are access methods?

    A. CSMA/CD

    B. CSMA/CA

    C. Token passing

    D. Demand priority

9.   Which of the following network architectures is wired like a ring with two fiber-optic cables?

   A. ATM

   B. FDDI

   C. Category 5

   D. PnP

10. Which of the following represents the rule for thinnet cable that defines the number of segments, repeaters, and segments with devices?

   A. 1-2-3

   B. 2-4-6

   C. 3-6-9

   D. 5-4-3

Answers to Lesson 2 Quiz

1. Answer A is correct. To transfer data from a computer onto the network media, a NIC must physically fit in the computer and match the computer's bus type.

    Answer B is correct. To transfer data from a computer onto the network media, a NIC must convert data from a parallel to serial data format.

    Answer C is correct. To transfer data from a computer onto the network media, a NIC must Support the network cable type.

    Answer D is correct. The NIC must be supported by the computer's operating system in order to work.

2. Answer A is correct. A brouter acts as a router for one protocol and bridges all others.

    Answer B is correct. A brouter handles routable protocols.

    Answer C is correct. A brouter handles non-routable protocols.

    Answer D is incorrect. A brouter is more cost effective and manages internetworking better than separate bridges and routers.

3. Answer A is correct. Repeaters restore and repeat an input signal.

    Answer B is correct. A hub repeats the input signal to all devices or segments connected to other ports.

    Answer C is correct. A multi-port repeater is another name for a hub. It repeats its input signal to all devices or segments connected to other ports.

    Answer D is correct. A switch repeats data to the destination port.

4. Answer C is correct. A fiber-optic cable transmits at 100 Mbps to 1 Gbps.

    Answers A, B, and D are incorrect. Twisted pair coaxial transmits at 4 to 100 Mbps. Thicknet transmits at 10 Mbps. Fiber-optic cable travels up to 2 Kilometers at 100 Mbps to 1 Gbps.

5.   Answer B is correct. The clear advantage of a passive network is that if one computer on the network fails, the others continue to send and receive data.

Answer C is correct. A clear advantage of a passive network is that data transmission doesn't rely on intermediaries between transmitting and receiving computers.

Answer A is incorrect. A passive network does not fail when one computer on the network fails.

Answer D is incorrect. Passive network data transmissions do not rely on intermediaries to continue transmission.

6.   Answers A and B are correct. Strong fault tolerance is a major advantage of mesh topology. If one network segment fails for any reason, all computers can continue to communicate. Multiple communication paths provide this fault tolerance.

Answers C and D are incorrect. Mesh topologies are very expensive. Electronic tokens are characteristic of ring topologies, not mesh topologies.

7.   Answer C is correct. Star-bus is a hybrid topology that combines the simplicity of bus topology with the point-to-point connections of star topology.

Answer D is correct. Star-ring is a hybrid topology where star networks are connected by rings and not a backbone.

Answers A and B are incorrect. The Internet is the largest example of mesh topology, and a bus topology is the basic and most simple topology.

8.   Answers A, B, C, and D are correct. CSMA/CD, CSMA/CA, token passing and demand priority are all network access methods.

9.   Answer B is correct. FDDI network architectures are wired like a ring with two fiber-optic cables.

Answer A is incorrect. ATM network architecture is generally used for WANs and uses leased lines from the telephone company.

Answers C and D are incorrect. Category 5 and PnP are not network architectures.

10.   Answer D is correct. The 5-4-3 rule specifies that a thinnet network can contain up to 5 cable segments, separated by 4 repeaters, and only 3 of the segments can have devices.

Answers A, B, and C are incorrect. These titles are fictitious.

Lesson 3: Network Protocols

All network devices use the same network protocol. A protocol is similar to a language because it defines the rules that allow computers to exchange information with a minimal amount of interruption. Network protocols establish standards that determine how data transmits over cable, how devices determine the data destination, and how devices reply to received data.

Devices on a network may use more than one protocol, but there must be at least one common protocol among all devices. On a network, protocol defines how data transmits over the cable, how devices determine the intended destination for the data, and how the device replies to the data received.

The International Organization for Standardization (ISO) designed the Open Systems Interconnection (OSI) network model. This seven-layer model establishes the foundation for all network communication. Each layer is responsible for one part of network communication, from placement of the data on a cable, or destination address assignment, to data compression.

There are four common network protocols in use today: TCP/IP, IPX/SPX, NetBEUI/NetBIOS, and AppleTalk. Each protocol builds upon the definitions set forth in the OSI model, and Windows 2000 supports all four of these network protocols.

After completing this lesson, you should have a better understanding of the following topics:

*   Open Systems Interconnection (OSI) Model

*   Common Network Protocols

*   Data Transmission

Open Systems Interconnection (OSI) Model

The International Organization for Standardization (ISO), an international organization that creates universal standards for exchange of information, saw the need to standardize network communications. While networks were still in their infancy, the ISO created a seven-layer model upon which to design network protocols. This model, called the Open Systems Interconnection (OSI) model, serves as a framework for protocols. Each layer in the OSI model addresses one specific role in network communication.

Understanding the Seven OSI Layers

The OSI model is drawn as a stack of seven layers. These seven layers address all functions of data exchange on a network. Each layer handles only one aspect of communication, and relies on the layer immediately above and the layer immediately below it on the stack. The seven layers of the OSI model (from bottom to top) are as follows: Physical, Data Link, Network, Transport, Session, Presentation, and Application (Figure 3.1).

 Note: Each layer of the OSI model has a name and a number according to its level in the stack. The Physical Layer is at the bottom of the stack and is Layer 1; the Application Layer is at the top of the stack and is Layer 7.

Figure 3.1 OSI Model

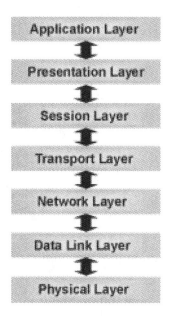

All network communication travels from the top of the OSI stack on one computer, down through all seven layers, across the network cable, and up through all seven layers on the destination computer. This is an important concept. No one layer by itself is able to handle the complexities of network communication, and each layer relies upon the layers above and below to get the message to its final destination (Figure 3.2).

Physical Layer (Layer 1)

The Physical Layer, as the name implies, addresses the physical connections between a computer and the network. Data inside the computer moves across multiple parallel paths (called parallel transmission). When this data transmits over a network, it converts into a single stream of data (called serial transmission). The Physical Layer defines this conversion from parallel to serial, placing data on the network, and then converting serial to parallel data on the receiving computer. The Physical Layer knows nothing about the actual data, its contents, or destination.

Figure 3.2 Network Communications

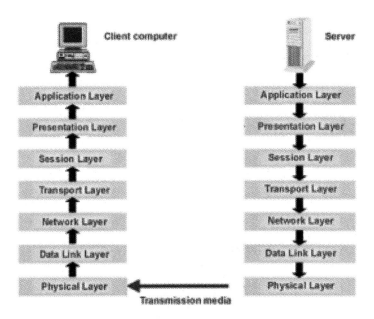

Data Link Layer (Layer 2)

The Data Link Layer defines the network access method. The network access method specifies how each device sends information without causing data collisions. Examples of network access methods include Carrier Sense Multiple Access/Collision Detection (CSMA/CD), which is the most common access method that is used on all Ethernet networks, and token passing. Network access methods are assigned numbers beginning with 802. The 802 Specifications define subsets of the Data Link Layer. For example, 802.3 refers to Ethernet using CSMA/CD and 802.5 defines token ring using token passing. The Data Link Layer relies upon the Physical Layer to get the data onto the network, and relies on the Network Layer to address the data.

Network Layer (Layer 3)

The Network Layer makes sure data gets to its intended location. The mailroom of the network, it addresses messages and determines the best route for data to arrive at its intended destination. In some protocols, the address is a number (like an IP address); in others, it is a name (like a computer name). The Network Layer only handles data addressing, but does not know how to put data on the network or have knowledge about network access methods. The lower layers of the OSI handle these tasks.

Transport Layer (Layer 4)

The Transport Layer ensures error-free delivery of the data and handles data flow control. On the sending computer, the Transport layer adds information to the data that allows the recipient to check the data for errors before processing, and handles the flow of data by breaking the data into smaller pieces. Data sent in smaller pieces is more likely to arrive error-free (and less likely to cause a data collision). The Transport Layer reassembles the pieces of data on the receiving computer and checks the error information.

The Transport Layer does not care about the destination address. Likewise, it does not know about the contents of the data. It receives data from the Session Layer, repackages the data, and hands it off to the Network Layer.

Session Layer (Layer 5)

The Session Layer establishes communication between two computers. This on-going communication is called a session. It is important to remember that network communication normally uses all seven layers and that the Session Layer on one computer requires the lower layers to communicate with the Session Layer on another computer. However, a session is often referred to as communication between Session Layers. This is called virtual communication because it appears as though only the two Session Layers are establishing communication, when, in fact, the Transport, Network, Data Link, and Physical layers are equally involved in establishing the session (Figure 3.3).

Figure 3.3 Virtual Communication

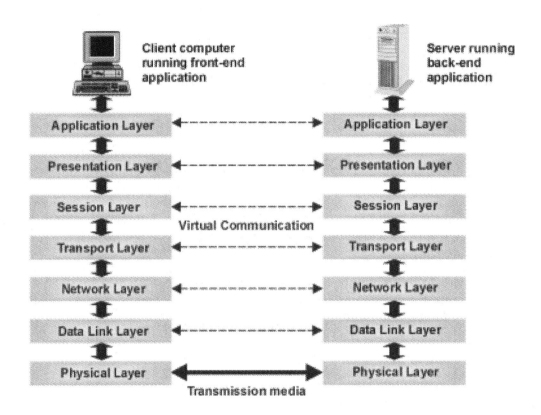

Presentation Layer (Layer 6)

The Presentation Layer prepares the data for network transmission on the sending computer by converting it from its original form into a generic form. The Presentation Layer may also encrypt the data (scramble it for security) and compress it. The Presentation Layer decrypts and decompresses the data on the receiving computer, and then converts the data to the format needed by the Application Layer. Because the Presentation Layer is able to convert data, it can also convert data from one protocol to another.

Note: A gateway, which is used to transfer data from one network type to another, works at the Presentation Layer, converting data from one protocol to another, and then resending the data.

Application Layer (Layer 7)

The Application Layer provides the interface between user applications and the network, but does not include the actual applications (like a Web browser, for example). This top layer of the OSI model receives information from an application, and passes it on the Presentation Layer.

Using the OSI Model with Protocols

The greatest strength of the OSI model is its organization. Each layer is responsible for only one aspect of the network. This clearly defined structure makes new network design and protocol creation possible. Although you may never actually design a network protocol, the following scenario shows the importance of the OSI model.

Suppose you created a fast, efficient, and secure protocol for your company based on the OSI model. When you first created the protocol, your company used an ARCNet network, an old network architecture rarely used today. When your company switched from ARCNet to Ethernet, they wanted to continue to use your clever protocol, but ARCNet and Ethernet use very different cable types and cable access methods. This situation makes the benefits of using the OSI model clear. Rather than having to rewrite the entire protocol, you only need to change the bottom two layers—the Physical Layer and the Data Link layer—because they are the only layers that address cable types and network access methods. Most of your protocol remains unchanged because you used the OSI model as a reference. Otherwise, you would have to rewrite the entire protocol every time your company upgrades the network.

Protocol Suites

Often a protocol addresses only one part of the OSI model (one layer or a group of layers), but does not contain all of the features needed to support full network communication. You may combine several protocols into a protocol suite (or protocol stack). For example, the Transmission Control Protocol (TCP) combines with the Internet Protocol (IP) and several other protocols to form the TCP/IP protocol suite.

Common Network Protocols

Windows 2000 supports many network protocols. Each protocol has strengths and weaknesses, making the appropriate choice for each network relative. The four most common network protocols (or protocol suites) that Windows 2000 supports are Transmission Control Protocol/Internet Protocol (TCP/IP), Internetwork Packet Exchange/Sequenced Packet Exchange (IPX/SPX), NetBIOS Extended User Interface (NetBEUI), and AppleTalk.

Examining TCP/IP

TCP/IP is the single most important network protocol. Every computer in the world uses TCP/IP for connecting to the Internet, and many Local Area Networks (LANs) use the TCP/IP protocol suite as well. Created in 1970s, the TCP/IP protocol is fast, efficient, and reliable. Features of TCP/IP include the following:

- Uses numeric IP addresses to identify the sending and receiving computers

- Is routable, allowing data to be sent from one network segment to another

- Ensures reliable delivery transmission, even over less-than-perfect public lines

- Is supported by every major computer operating system, including UNIX and Linux, MacOS, Novell Netware, and Windows 2000

Tip: TCP/IP is a protocol suite that includes many protocols—TCP, UDP, IP, DNS, WINS, ARP, FTP, Telnet, RIP, OSPF, among others.

TCP/IP and the OSI Model

The TCP/IP protocol suite includes components from the Network, Transport, Session, Presentation, and Application layers of the OSI model (Figure 3.4).

Figure 3.4 TCP/IP and OSI

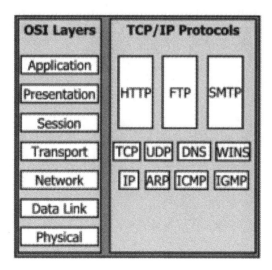

TCP/IP does not have a Data Link Layer or Physical Layer component. It is designed to work with multiple Data Link Layer protocols to enable TCP/IP for use on Ethernet networks, token-ring networks, the Internet, and even AppleTalk networks.

 Note: The modularity of the OSI model allows using one protocol for multiple network architectures.

Exploring IPX/SPX

The Internet Packet Exchange/Sequenced packet Exchange (IPX/SPX) protocol suite, like the TCP/IP suite, is a routable protocol that uses numeric addresses to identify computers. Novell designed IPX/SPX for exclusive use on a NetWare network. In the IPX/SPX suite, IPX is a Network Layer protocol that provides addressing and routing information, and SPX works at the Transport Layer to provide reliable transmission of data (Figure 3.5).

Figure 3.5 IPX/SPX and OSI

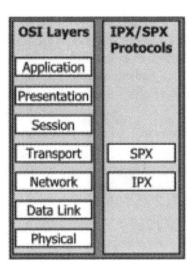

Microsoft wanted Windows NT 4.0 to support adding a Windows NT server to an existing Novell network. However, Microsoft could not include the IPX/SPX protocol with Windows NT 4.0 because Novell owns this proprietary protocol. As a solution to the problem of making Windows NT compatible with the popular Novell network, Microsoft created the NWLink protocol that is fully compatible with IPX/SPX. Therefore, if you want to use the IPX/SPX protocol in Windows 2000, load the NWLink protocol.

Note: NWLink stands for NetWare Link. The sole purpose of NWLink is to link Windows-based computers to Novell NetWare networks. You can use NWLink only on a Windows network.

Using NetBEUI and NetBIOS

NetBIOS Enhanced User Interface (NetBEUI) was originally designed as part of a protocol suite with the Network Basic Input/Output System (NetBIOS). It is a proprietary Microsoft protocol. NetBIOS uses friendly names (called NetBIOS names or WINS names) to identify computers on the network. Combined with NetBEUI, this protocol suite provides a fast, small network protocol that is very easy to implement. A network administrator only needs to assign each computer a unique NetBIOS name to begin using the network.

However, there are two major drawbacks to NetBEUI. First, it is only Microsoft-based computers support NetBEUI (those running MS-DOS and any Windows product). Second, NetBEUI is not routable. It does not carry data from one network segment to another, which all but the smallest networks require.

NetBIOS is a Session Layer protocol in the OSI model. NetBEUI is a Transport and Network Layer protocol. However, the Network Layer component does not support routing or addressing (Figure 3.6).

Following the OSI model when designing a protocol suite is very important. If the NetBIOS and NetBEUI protocols did not conform to the OSI model, the disadvantages of NetBEUI would negate the conveniences of NetBIOS. However, the modular, layered nature of the OSI model allows programmers to redesign NetBIOS so that it works with the routable protocol TCP/IP. NetBIOS names are usable on a segmented network.

 Note: The implementation of NetBIOS and TCP/IP is called NBT, or NetBIOS over TCP.

Figure 3.6 NetBEUI/NetBIOS and OSI

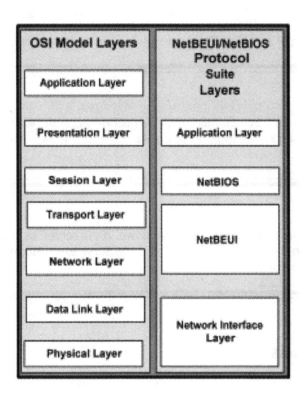

Working with AppleTalk

Apple Computer designed the AppleTalk protocol for Macintosh-based networks. Of the four protocols discussed here, AppleTalk is the easiest to implement. Each Macintosh computer generates its own network number when attached to the network cable. The administrator only needs to attach computers to the cable to use the network.

Note: Like TCP/IP and IPX/SPX, AppleTalk is a routable protocol.

You can install and use the AppleTalk protocol on Windows 2000 computers. When you install AppleTalk on a Windows 2000 Server, Macintosh clients can access the server as if it were an Apple server. Likewise, Windows 2000 computers can use the AppleTalk protocol to access Apple servers.

Tip: Macintosh clients can use a Windows 2000 server as file or printer server by installing the AppleTalk Protocol and File Services for Macintosh or printer Services for Macintosh.

Using Other Protocols

In addition to the four protocols discussed, Windows 2000 also supports several other protocols. These protocols are not widely used, but are gaining popularity. You should be familiar with the Asynchronous Transfer Mode (ATM), Data Link Control (DLC), and Infrared Data Association (IrDA) protocols.

Asynchronous Transfer Mode (ATM)

ATM is high-speed network architecture that uses the ATM protocol over various cable types to simultaneously transmit data, telephone, and real-time audio and video. ATM is a connection-oriented (point-to-point) protocol that uses multiple channels to connect two devices. The point-to-point access method sends data packets directly to another computer, without other computers receiving or acting upon the data. Data transmits in discrete packages of a fixed length.

Data Link Control (DLC)

The DLC protocol has two purposes: It accesses older mainframe computers (specifically, those made by IBM); it communicates with printers. You can connect some printers directly to the network (as compared to connecting them to a computer with a network connection), and can establish a connection to these printers using the DLC protocol.

 Note: Only the print server needs to have DLC. All other computers can send print jobs to the server using any protocol, and the print server uses DLC to communicate directly with the printer.

Infrared Data Association (IrDA)

Wireless devices and laptops have lead to an increase in the use of Infrared as a network medium. The IrDA sets the standards for Infrared use with computers and networks. The IrDA protocol suite is used to transfer information between a computer and peripheral devices (like digital cameras, a cordless mouse or keyboard), and Personal Digital Assistants (PDAs). The IrDA protocol is also used to transfer information between a computer (typically a portable computer) and the network.

Following are the four IrDA standards:

Serial IrDA (IrDA-SIR)—Supports data transmissions up to a maximum of 115,000 bps (bits per second).

Fast IrDA (IrDA-FIR)—Supports communication at speeds up to 4 Mbps (megabits per second).

IrLPT—Uses the infrared port on the computer as a printer port, and sends information to the printer through this infrared port.

IrTran-P—Allows a Windows 2000 computer to receive digital images from a digital camera or other digital imaging devices.

Data Transmission

Data that transmits across the network may be sent from one computer to another, to multiple computers, or to all computers on the network. Messages intended for every device on the network can cause significant bottlenecks and decrease network bandwidth. At the same time, such messages may be necessary for particular network functions.

Understanding Unicast Transmissions

In a unicast transmission (or directed transmission), the data transmits from one computer to another. If there is more than one intended recipient, each computer receives its own copy of the data that is sent separately. For example, suppose two different clients on a network request the default home page from your company's Web server. Even if these requests could arrive at the Web server at exactly the same time (which they cannot), the Web server would issue the home page data in two separate transmissions, one to each requesting computer (Figure 3.7).

Figure 3.7 Unicast Transmissions

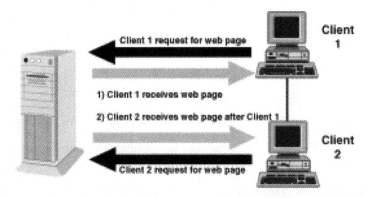

Note: Unicast transmissions are the most efficient when data is being sent to a few computers. When sending data to many computers, unicast transmission is inappropriate.

Understanding Broadcasts

Broadcast transmission simultaneously sends data to all computers on the network segment. Broadcasts are the most efficient way to transfer a single copy of the data to multiple computers (Figure 3.8).

Figure 3.8 Broadcast Transmissions

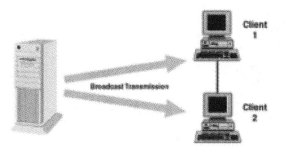

Broadcast messages cannot be carried across routers. Routers, which are used to segment a network, only pass on data transmissions that have a specific destination address. Since a broadcast transmission has no specific destination address, routers fail to forward them. Only computers on the same segment as the sending computer receive the broadcast (Figure 3.9).

Tip: Because broadcasts are not routable, they do not work on the Internet. A broadcast transmission sent over the Internet will not reach any computers beyond the
local segment.

Figure 3.9 Broadcasts and Routers

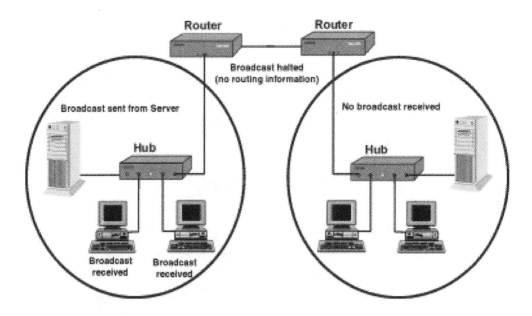

Understanding Multicasts

A multicast transmission sends a single copy of the data to multiple computers, but only to those computers that request the data. For example, suppose you work for a radio station. You want your Web server to provide live streaming audio to users who request it. From the Web page, they may choose a link to begin receiving the audio feed. The Web server sends the data in a multicast so that it arrives at all requesting computers (Figure 3.10).

Figure 3.10 Multicast Transmission

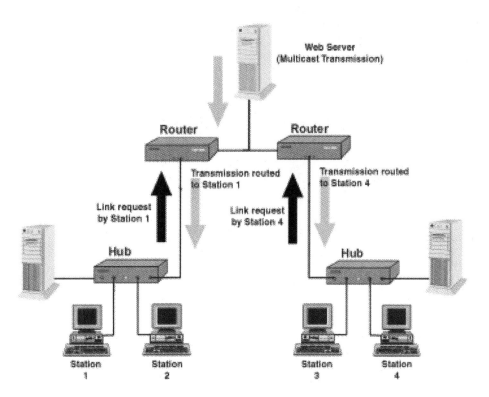

Since multicast transmissions use specific destination addresses, they are fully routable. Routers handle the multicast transmissions like unicast transmissions.

Vocabulary

Review the following terms in preparation for the certification exam.

Term	Description
802 Specifications	The 802 Specifications define subsets of the Data Link Layer of the OSI model. For example, 802.3 refers to Ethernet using CSMA/CD, and 802.5 defines token ring using token passing.
AppleTalk	A routable protocol for Macintosh-based networks. Macintoshes generate their own network number up on attachment to the network cable.
Application Layer	The layer of OSI that provides interface among user applications and the network, and passes applications information to the Presentation Layer.
ATM	Asynchronous Transfer Mode is a high-speed network architecture that uses the ATM protocol, a point-to-point protocol that uses multiple channels to connect two devices.
broadcasts	A broadcast transmission simultaneously sends data to all computers on the network segment.
CSMA/CD	Carrier Sense Multiple Access/Collision Detection is the most common access method, and is used on all Ethernet networks.
Data Link Layer	The layer of the OSI that defines network access methods. It relies on the Physical Layer to get data onto the network, and relies on the Network Layer to address the data.

Term	Description
DLC	Data Link Control is a protocol is used to access older IBM mainframe computers and to directly communicate with printers.
gateway	A gateway works at the Presentation Layer, con verts data from one network type or protocol to another, and then resends the data.
IPX/SPX	Internetwork Packet Exchange/Sequenced Packet Exchange is a protocol suite designed by Novell exclusively for NetWare networks. IPX is a Network Layer routable protocol that uses numeric addresses to identify computers. The SPX Transport Layer protocol provides reliable data transmission .
IrDA	Infrared Data Association sets the standards for infrared use with computers and networks. The IrDA protocol is used to transfer information between a co mputer (typically a portable computer) and the network.
IrDA-FIR	One of the four IrDA infrared standards that support communication at speeds up to 4 Mbps.
IrDA-SIR	One of the four IrDA infrared standards that support communication at speeds up to a maximum of 115,000 bps.
IrLPT	One of the four IrDA infrared standards that uses the infrared port on the computer as a printer port, and sends information to the printer through this infrared port.
IrTran-P	One of the four IrDA infrared standards that allows a Windows 2000 computer to receive digital images fr om a digital camera or other digital imaging devices.

Term	Description
IrTran-P	One of the four IrDA infrared standards that allows a Windows 2000 computer to receive digital images from a digital camera or other digital imaging devices.
ISO	The International Organization for Standardization is an international organization that creates standards, and designed the seven-layer OSI model from which network protocols are designed.
multicasts	A multicast transmission sends a single copy of the data to multiple computers that request the data.
NBT	The implementation of NetBIOS and TCP/IP is called NBT, or NetBIOS over TCP.
NetBEUI/NetBIOS	NetBIOS Extended User Interface (NetBEUI)/NetBIOS is a proprietary Microsoft protocol suite. NetBIOS uses friendly names (called NetBIOS names or WINS names) to identify computers on the network. Combined with NetBEUI, this protocol suite provides a fast, small network protocol that is easy to implement.
network access method	The network access method specifies how each network device sends information without causing data collisions. Network access methods are assigned numbers beginning with 802.
Network Layer	The layer of the OSI primarily responsible for getting data to its intended location, and handles data addressing.
NWLink	A Microsoft protocol fully compatible with IPX/SPX and usable in Windows 2000.
OSI	The Open Systems Interconnection network model is a seven-layer model that provides a foundation for all network communication. Each layer is responsible for and addresses one part of network communication.

Term	Description
Physical Layer	The layer of the OSI that defines the data transmission conversion from parallel to serial, placement of data on the network, and the conversion of serial to para llel data on the destination computer.
point-to-point	The point-to-point or connection-oriented access method sends data packets directly to another computer without other computers receiving or acting upon the data.
Presentation Layer	The layer of the OSI that prepares, converts, encrypts, compresses, decrypts, and decompresses data for network transmission. It also converts data from one protocol to another.
protocol	A network protocol is a set of rules that defines how data transmits on the cable, how devices determine the intended destination for the data, and how the device replies to data transmissions. Devices on a network may use more than one protocol, but must share at least one common protocol.
protocol suite	Several protocols combined together are called a protocol suite or protocol stack.
routable protocol	A protocol that uses numeric addresses to identify computers.
routers	Routers segment networks and pass on data transmission s that have destination addresses.
Session Layer	The layer of the OSI that establishes communication between two computers.

Term	Description
TCP/IP	Transmission Control Protocol (TCP) combines with the Internet Protocol (IP) and several other protocols to create the TCP/IP protocol suite. It includes components from the Network, Transport, Session, Presentation, and Application layers of the OSI model.
Transport Layer	The layer of the OSI that ensures error-free data delivery and handles flow control. It receives data from the Session Layer, repackages it, and sends it to the Network Layer.
unicast	A directed transmission where data transmits from one computer to another, and is most efficient when data transmits to only a few computers.

In Brief

If you want to...	Then do this...
Understand the framework for protocols and standardized network communication and refer to each layer by its name or number in the stack	Learn the structure of the Open Systems Interconnection OSI model and the purpose and functions of its seven layers from the bottom to the top: Physical Layer, Layer 1 Data Link Layer, Layer 2 Network Layer, Layer 3 Transport Layer, Layer 4 Session Layer, Layer 5 Presentation Layer, Layer 6 Application Layer, Layer 7
Understand the OSI network communication path	Consider this important concept: All network communication travels from the top of the OSI stack on one computer, down through all seven layers, across the network cable, and up through all seven layers on the destination computer. No one layer can handle the complexities of network communication, and each layer relies upon the layers above and below to get the message to its destination.
Design a network protocol	Use the OSI model as a reference for modular programming, which allows maintenance of layer modules rather than having to rewrite th e entire protocol.
Use several protocols which address full network communication	Use protocol suites, which are several protocols combined together in a protocol stack , such as TCP/IP or IPX/SPX, NetBEUI, or AppleTalk.

If you want to…	Then do this…
Use the IPX/SPX protocol in Windows 2000	Load NWLink to use the IPX/SPX protocol in Windows 2000.
Use NetBIOS with TCP/IP and use NetBIOS names on segmented networks	Implement NetBIOS over TCP or NBT to use NetBIOS names over segmented networks.
Macintosh clients to access the server as if it were an Apple server	Install and use the AppleTalk protocol on Windows 2000 servers
Send a single copy of data to all computers on the network segment, but not over the Internet	Use the broadcast transmission to send data simultaneously to all computers on the network segment, but not through routers
Send a single copy of data to multiple computers, but only to those computers that request the data	Use multicasts to send a single copy of data to many computers that request it.

Lesson 3 Activities

Complete the following activities to better prepare you for the certification exam.

1. Explain the important concept of how all network communication travels through the OSI stack.

2. Explain the basic premise the OSI model addresses, and list the aspects of communication it addresses.

3. Discuss the function of protocol suites or stacks, and give the most common protocols that Windows 2000 supports.

4. List four features of the most globally important network protocol.

5. Explain the origins of NWLink.

6. Explain why NetBIOS names can now be used on a segmented network.

7. The IrDA protocol suite is used to transfer information between computers and peripherals. List and discuss four IrDA standards.

8. Name one of the easiest protocols to implement and explain why it is easy to implement.

9. Name two uses for the DLC protocol.

10. List three types of data transmission and the purpose of each.

Answers to Lesson 3 Activities

1. All network communication travels from the top of the OSI stack on one computer, down through all seven layers, across the network cable, and up through all seven layers on the destination computer. This is an important concept. No one layer can handle the complexities of network communication, and each layer relies upon the layers above and below to get the message to its destination.

2. ISO created a seven-layer model upon which network protocols could be designed. This model, called the Open Systems Interconnection (OSI) model, serves as a framework for protocols. Each layer in the OSI model addresses one specific role in network communication.

    The OSI model is depicted as a stack of seven layers. Combined, these seven layers address all functions of data movement on a network. Individually, each layer handles only one aspect of communication, and relies on the layer immediately above and the layer immediately below.

    The seven layers of the OSI model are named for the aspects that they address, and are as follows (from the bottom of the stack to the top): Physical, Data Link, Network, Transport, Session, Presentation, and Application.

3. Often a protocol addresses only one part of the OSI model (perhaps one layer, or a group of layers). A protocol may not contain all of the features you need to support full network communication. Several protocols may be combined together into a protocol suite (or protocol stack). For example, the Transmission Control Protocol (TCP) combines with the Internet Protocol (IP) and several other protocols to create the TCP/IP protocol suite.

    Windows 2000 supports many network protocols. Each protocol has its strengths and weaknesses, and each is the best choice in some network situations. The four most common network protocols (or protocol suites) supported by Windows 2000 are Transmission Control Protocol/Internet Protocol (TCP/IP), Internetwork Packet Exchange/Sequenced Packet Exchange (IPX/SPX), NetBIOS Extended User Interface (NetBEUI), and AppleTalk.

4. TCP/IP is the single most important network protocol. Features of TCP/IP include the following:

    - TCP/IP uses numeric IP addresses to identify the sending and receiving computers

    - TCP/IP is routable, allowing data to be sent from one network segment to another

- TCP/IP ensures reliable delivery transmission, even over less-than-perfect public lines

- TCP/IP is supported by every major computer operating system, including UNIX and Linux, MacOS, Novell Netware, and Windows 2000

5. When Microsoft released Windows NT 4.0, they wanted to provide support for adding a Windows NT 4.0 server to an existing Novell network. Novell networks were (and still are) very popular, and Microsoft wanted to ensure compatibility. Microsoft could not include the IPX/SPX protocol with Windows NT 4.0, because it is a proprietary protocol owned by Novell. So Microsoft created the NWLink protocol, which is fully compatible with IPX/SPX. If you want to use the IPX/SPX protocol in Windows 2000, load NWLink.

6. There are two major drawbacks to NetBEUI. First, it is only supported by Microsoft-based computers (those running MS-DOS and any Windows product). Second, NetBEUI is not routable. It cannot be used to carry data from one network segment to another (which is a necessity on all but the smallest networks). However, the layered nature of the OSI model has allowed programmers to redesign NetBIOS to work with TCP/IP, a routable protocol. The implementation of NetBIOS and TCP/IP is called NBT, or NetBIOS over TCP.

7. There are four IrDA standards, as follows:

   Serial IrDA (IrDA-SIR)— Supports data transmissions up to a maximum of 115,000 bps (bits per second).

   Fast IrDA (IrDA-FIR)—Supports communication at speeds up to 4 Mbps (Megabits per second).

   IrLPT—Uses the infrared port on the computer as a printer port, and sends information to the printer through this infrared port.

   IrTran-P—Allows a Windows 2000 computer to receive digital images from a digital camera or other digital imaging devices.

8. Of the four protocols discussed here, AppleTalk is the easiest to implement. Each Macintosh computer generates its own network number when attached to the network cable. The administrator only needs to attach computers to the cable to use the network.

   You can install and use the AppleTalk protocol on Windows 2000 computers. When you install AppleTalk on a Windows 2000 Server, Macintosh clients can access the server as if it were an Apple server. Likewise, Windows 2000 computers can use the AppleTalk protocol to access Apple servers.

9. The DLC protocol is used for two purposes. It is used to access older mainframe computers (specifically, those made by IBM). It is also used to communicate with printers. You can connect some printers directly to the network (as opposed to connecting them to a computer with a network connection), and can establish a connection to these printers using the DLC protocol.

10. Three types of data transmissions are unicast, broadcast, and multicast transmissions. Unicast transmissions send data from one computer to another. Broadcast transmissions simultaneously send data to all computers on the network segment. Multicast transmissions send a single coy of data to multiple computers, but only to those computers that request the data.

Lesson 3 Quiz

These questions test your knowledge of features, vocabulary, procedures, and syntax.

1. Which of the following occurs in the Physical Layer (Layer 1)?

    A. Converts data from parallel to serial

    B. Converts data from serial to parallel

    C. Places data on the network

    D. Determines the best route data should travel

2. Which of the following are standard access methods in the Data Link Layer?

    A. DLC

    B. CSMA/CD

    C. Token passing

    D. ATM

3. What are the primary responsibilities of the Network Layer?

    A. To put data on the network

    B. To define access methods

    C. To handle data addressing

    D. To determine the best route data should travel to its destination

4. Which OSI layer checks data for errors?

    A. Session Layer

    B. Application Layer

    C. Presentation Layer

    D. Transport Layer

5.   What is a virtual communication?

   A. When two computers pretend to share information

   B. When it appears as though two session layers establish communication

   C. When the Transport, Network, Data Link, and Physical layers are involved in session establishment

   D. When ongoing communication occurs between two computers

6.   Which OSI model layer allows data conversion and converts data from one protocol to another?

   A. Data Link

   B. Transport

   C. Presentation

   D. Physical

7.   Which of the following sets of layers in the OSI model does the TCP/IP protocol suite include?

   A. Network, Transport, Presentation, Application

   B. Session, Data Link, and Physical

   C. Physical, Data Link, Application

   D. Transport, Session, Data Link, Presentation

8.   Which of the following is a Novell proprietary protocol?

   A. TCP/IP

   B. IPX/SPX

   C. NWLink

   D. AppleTalk

9.   Which IrDA standard uses the infrared port on the computer as a printer port, and sends information to the printer through this infrared port?

A. IrDA-SIR

B. IrDA-FIR

C. IrLPT

D. IrTran-P

10. Which type of data transmission best supports streaming audio?

A. Multicast transmission

B. Broadcast transmission

C. Unicast transmission

D. Directed transmission

Answers to Lesson 3 Quiz

1. Answers A, B, and C are correct. The Physical Layer is responsible for converting data transmissions to and from serial and parallel and is responsible for placing the data on the network.

    Answer D is incorrect. The Network Layer determines the best route data should travel.

2. Answers B and C are correct. CSMA/CD and token passing are examples of network access methods defined in the Data Link Layer of the OSI model.

    Answers A and D are incorrect. DLC is a protocol, not an access method, and ATM is a high-speed network and protocol, and not an access method defined in the Data Link Layer.

3. Answers C and D are correct. The network layer is responsible for addressing data and determining the best route data should travel to its destination.

    Answers A and B are incorrect. The lower layers handle the responsibilities of putting data on the network and defining access methods.

4. Answer D is correct. The Transport Layer is responsible for ensuring error-free delivery of the data and handling flow control.

    Answers A, B, and C are incorrect. The Session, Application, and Presentation Layers are not responsible for data error checks or flow control.

5. Answer B is correct. Virtual communication appears as though Session layers are communicating directly with each other. However, the sending and receiving network communication must use all seven layers (in most cases) to establish a session.

    Answer A is incorrect. Computers don't pretend.

    Answer C is incorrect. All network communication involves the Transport, Network, Data Link, and Physical layers for session establishment.

    Answer D is incorrect. When ongoing communication occurs between two computers, the occurrence is called a session.

6.   Answer C is correct. The Presentation Layer allows data conversion and conversion of data from one protocol to another.

Answers A, B, and D are incorrect. The Data Link, Transport, and Physical Layers prepare data for the network transmission but don't provide protocol conversion.

7.   Answer A is correct. The Network, Transport, Presentation, and Application layers in the OSI model are included in the TCP/IP protocol suite.

Answers B, C, and D are incorrect. TCP/IP does not have a Data Link or Physical Layer component. It is designed to work with multiple Data Link layer protocols so TCP/IP can work with Ethernet, Token Ring, and AppleTalk networks and the Internet.

8.   Answer B is correct. IPX/SPX is a Novell proprietary protocol

Answers A, C, and D are incorrect. TCP/IP is non-proprietary, Microsoft developed NWLink, and Apple developed AppleTalk.

9.   Answer C is correct. The IrLPT standard uses the infrared port on the computer as a printer port, and sends information to the printer through this infrared port.

Answer A is incorrect. The IrDA-SIR standard supports data transmissions up to a maximum of 115,000 bps (bits per second).

Answer B is incorrect. IrDA-FIR supports communication at speeds up to 4 Mbps (Megabits per second).

Answer D is incorrect. IrTran-P allows a Windows 2000 computer to receive digital images from a digital camera or other digital imaging devices.

10.   Answer A is correct Multicast data transmission best supports streaming audio. It sends a single copy of the data to many computers that request it.

Answers B, C, and D are incorrect. Broadcasts are not routable and don't work on the Internet, and unicast or directed transmissions would be inefficient because each computer gets its own copy, sent individually.

Lesson 4: Introduction to TCP/IP

The Transmission Control Protocol/Internet Protocol (TCP/IP) is the protocol of the Internet—all computers that attach to the Internet use the TCP/IP protocol. It is also the default Windows 2000 protocol. Several strengths of TCP/IP include the following:

- Supports all major operating systems

- Is routable

- Accommodates all sizes of networks

- Provides reliability and speed

TCP/IP is actually a protocol suite—a collection of many protocols that work together. Each protocol works at one or more layers of the Open System Interconnection (OSI) model. Each layer of the OSI model defines a very specific set of tasks the protocol performs.

TCP/IP uses numbers (IP addresses) to identify devices on the network. Every device (or host) on the network has a unique IP address. However, these addresses are difficult to remember. Two services that run on Windows 2000 servers—the Domain Name System (DNS) and Windows Internet Name Service (WINS)—provide you the option of user-friendly names on a TCP/IP network by converting names to IP addresses as needed.

After completing this lesson, you should have a better understanding of the following topics:

- TCP/IP Overview

- Data Transfer Using TCP/IP

- Name Resolution

TCP/IP Overview

The TCP/IP protocol suite follows the Open System Interconnection (OSI) model, and is a layered suite (or stack) of protocols. Individual protocols operate at one or more of the OSI layers. Microsoft often describes the TCP/IP stack in its own layered structure that closely matches the OSI model. Both models are described in this section.

In addition to the protocols that make up the TCP/IP suite, TCP/IP for Windows 2000 includes several utilities that work with specific TCP/IP protocols. These utilities help diagnosing problems on a TCP/IP network, and you should become familiar with them.

Using the Open System Interconnection (OSI) Model

The OSI model is an open standard that defines the way network protocols work. The model divides into seven layers where each layer performs one or two specific tasks regarding network communication. This layered structure allows you to make a protocol (like TCP/IP) work on many different network types and on multiple operating systems. The TCP/IP protocol suite also includes numerous smaller protocols that map to specific layers in the OSI model (Figure 4.1).

The TCP/IP suite does not include components for the first two layers (Physical Layer and Data Link Layer) of the OSI model. This allows using TCP/IP on many different network types, which are defined in the Data Link Layer, as well as a multitude of Network Interface Cards (NICs), which are defined in the Physical Layer. The protocols are described here in order from the bottom layer of the OSI stack to the top layer.

Figure 4.1 OSI and TCP/IP

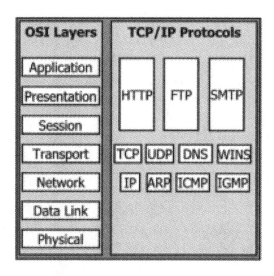

Internet Protocol (IP)

At the Network Layer (Layer 3), IP assigns every object on the network an address. The IP address must be unique as it identifies the source and destination computers for every data transmission. IP also provides routing information, ensuring data reaches its destination, even if the destination is on a different network segment than the source.

 Note: IP is a connectionless protocol. Like all connectionless protocols, it is fast but unreliable and assumes other protocols in the suite will ensure reliable delivery.

Internet Control Message Protocol (ICMP)

ICMP sends control messages for diagnosing the unsuccessful delivery of data. The **PING** utility uses ICMP to verify a connection to a remote computer. To do so, run the **PING** command from a command prompt followed by an IP address (for example, **PING 216.219.146.170**). Your computer sends four ICMP packets to the destination computer asking for a reply, and the PING utility displays the results of the four ICMP requests (Figure 4.2).

Figure 4.2 PING Utility

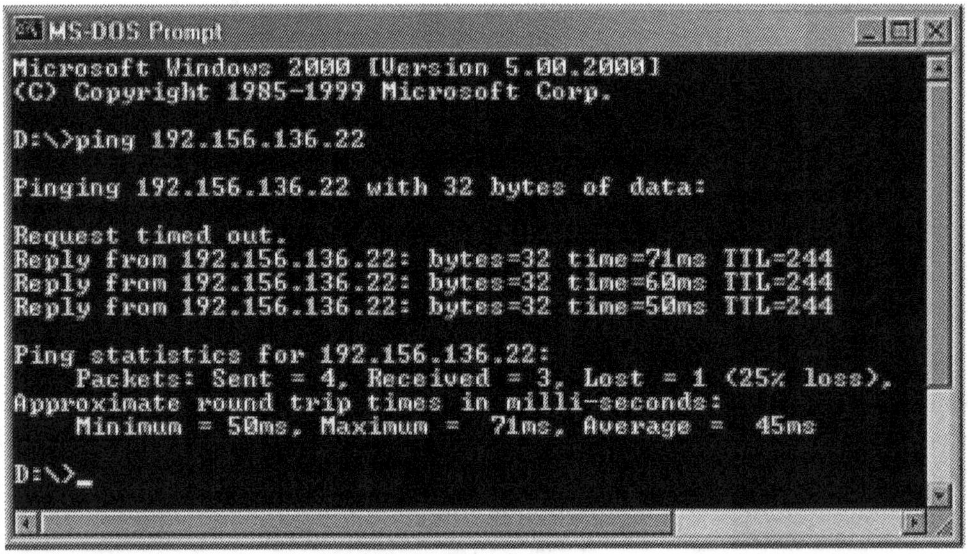

```
MS-DOS Prompt                                          _ □ X
Microsoft Windows 2000 [Version 5.00.2000]
(C) Copyright 1985-1999 Microsoft Corp.

D:\>ping 192.156.136.22

Pinging 192.156.136.22 with 32 bytes of data:

Request timed out.
Reply from 192.156.136.22: bytes=32 time=71ms TTL=244
Reply from 192.156.136.22: bytes=32 time=60ms TTL=244
Reply from 192.156.136.22: bytes=32 time=50ms TTL=244

Ping statistics for 192.156.136.22:
    Packets: Sent = 4, Received = 3, Lost = 1 (25% loss),
Approximate round trip times in milli-seconds:
    Minimum = 50ms, Maximum =  71ms, Average =  45ms

D:\>_
```

Tip: The PING utility—which installs when you install TCP/IP—is one of the best tools to use when troubleshooting a TCP/IP network. If you can successfully ping another computer, you know that you have a good physical connection and that TCP/IP is installed and working properly on both machines.

Internet Group Management Protocol (IGMP)

IGMP does multicasting. Multicasting is the process of sending one copy of data to multiple computers at the same time. It differs from broadcast messages in two ways:

- Multicast messages are only sent to computers that request the information

- Multicast messages are routable while broadcasts are not

Address Resolution Protocol (ARP)

Every Network Interface Card (NIC) is assigned a Media Access Control (MAC) address. This address is burned into the NIC at the factory, cannot be changed, and is guaranteed as universally unique. The MAC address identifies each object on the network, and is used at the Data Link Layer for sending and receiving data. ARP is the TCP/IP protocol that converts IP addresses to MAC addresses and vice versa.

When your computer sends data to another computer, the TCP/IP stack addresses the data to an IP address that may looks like this: 216.219.146.170. However, when the data reaches the Data Link Layer, a physical address (MAC address) is required. To accommodate this request, an ARP broadcast transmits to convert the IP address into a MAC address. This conversion is a MAC address that is a series of hexadecimal numbers (For example, 00-B0-64-1B-0E-30). This MAC address actually sends the data.

Note: ARP uses broadcast transmissions.

Transmission Control Protocol (TCP)

TCP works at the Transport Layer of the OSI model to ensure reliable delivery of data. TCP takes data from the Session Layer on the transmitting computer and breaks it into smaller pieces. It then repackages the data, passing it down to IP for addressing. TCP then reassembles the data on the receiving computer and passes it up to the Session Layer.

 Note: Unlike IP, TCP is a connection-oriented protocol that ensures all sent data arrives at their destination. If some data does not arrive, TCP resends the lost packets.

User Datagram Protocol (UDP)

UDP is a connectionless protocol that works at the Transport Layer of the OSI model. UDP converts and sends data but does not confirm receipt of the data at the final destination. Although UDP can cause some data loss, it is a much faster protocol than TCP that facilitates real-time transmissions over the Internet.

Maintaining a balance between faster transmission and more reliable delivery must be weighed carefully. For most data, reliable delivery using TCP is of primary importance. However, for some applications, like live-streaming audio, speed is the more important factor.

Note: Live-streaming audio is sent on the Internet using UDP. This protocol reduces overhead and keeps data flowing as quickly as possible. A few seconds of music data loss has no major negative effect.

Domain Name System (DNS)

DNS, a Transport Layer protocol, resolves IP addresses to hostnames. Hostnames identify computers on a TCP/IP network. Anyone who uses the World Wide Web (WWW) is familiar with entering a hostname into the Web browser. Names like www.lightpointlearning.net and www.microsoft.com are hostnames.

Because data transmissions must be sent using IP addresses that ultimately convert into MAC addresses, the TCP/IP suite must be able to resolve hostnames to IP addresses. DNS provides this service.

Windows Internet Name service (WINS)

Like DNS, WINS is a resolution protocol that works at the Transport Layer. WINS resolves NetBIOS names to IP addresses. NetBIOS is a Microsoft-proprietary protocol, originally designed to work with NetBEUI, that uses common names to identify computers. With the popularity of TCP/IP, NetBIOS was rewritten to work with TCP/IP. The WINS service converts NetBIOS names to IP addresses.

Hypertext Transfer Protocol (HTTP)

The HTTP protocol transfers files written in HyperText Markup Language (HTML) At the Session, Presentation, and Application layers, WWW files are written in HTML, and so HTTP is the protocol that transfers Web pages.

File Transfer Protocol (FTP)

FTP is the primary file transfer protocol spanning the Session, Presentation, and Application layers. WWW files are written in HTML, and so HTTP is the protocol that transfers Web files. For files not written in HTML, FTP downloads (copies files from a server to a client over the Internet) and uploads files. FTP provides basic directory and file management. You can use FTP to create directories, copy and delete files, and request directory listings.

Simple Mail Transfer Protocol (SMTP)

Like HTTP and FTP, SMTP works at the Session, Presentation, and Application layers of the OSI model to provide file transfer services. However, SMTP files consist of   e-mail messages and their attachments.

Using TCP/IP Layers

Although mapping TCP/IP protocols to OSI layers provides a better comparison between the TCP/IP protocol suite and other protocol suites, the TCP/IP stack has also been divided into its own three-layer model for simplicity (Figure 4.3).

Figure 4.3 TCP/IP Layer Model

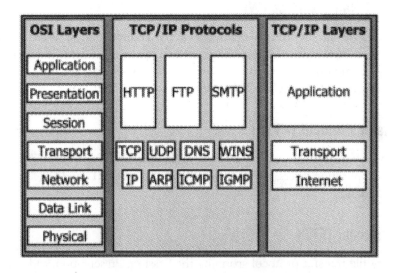

Following are the three layers of the TCP/IP model:

Application Layer—Corresponds with the top three layers of the OSI model (Application, Presentation, and Session layers). The FTP, HTTP, and SNMP protocols are members of the Application Layer.

Transport Layer—Maps directly to the Transport Layer (Layer 4) of the OSI model and includes TCP, UDP, DNS, and WINS.

Internet Layer—Matches OSI Layer 3, the Network Layer, and includes IP, ICMP, IGMP, and ARP.

Using TCP/IP Utilities

When you install the TCP/IP protocol in Windows 2000, you also install numerous utilities. These utilities work at various layers of the OSI model. Some are designed to help you diagnose problems, while others enhance TCP/IP connectivity.

 Note: Many of the TCP/IP utilities and the TCP/IP protocols share the same name. The utilities are not protocols, but are user interfaces that allow you to use the protocols.

Table 4.1 describes the TCP/IP utilities included with Windows 2000. To use any of these utilities, type the name of the utility at a command prompt.

Table 4.1 TCP/IP Utilities

Category	TCP/IP Utility	Description
Connectivity	Telnet	Allows remotely accessing a server with a command -line-like interface.
	FTP	File Transfer Protocol uses TCP for file transfers.
	TFTP	Trivial File Transfer Protocol uses UDP to transfer files.
Diagnostic	ARP	Displays the contents of the Address Resolution Protocol cache (the table of MAC and IP addresses).
	Ipconfig	Displays the current TCP/IP configuration information, including the IP address and hostname.
	Nbtstat	Displays currently active NetBIOS over TCP/IP sessions.
	Netstat	Displays currently active TCP/IP connections.
	Ping	Sends ICMP requests to another computer, and verifies a good connection.
	Route	Displays the local routing table.
	Tracert	Displays the routers through which data travels to reach the destination computer.

 Note: The **NETDIAG** utility simultaneously runs many of the TCP/IP diagnostic utilities. It is not loaded when you install the TCP/IP protocol, but can be found on the Windows 2000 CD-ROM in the \Support\Tools directory.

Data Transfer Using TCP/IP

Data transfers among computers in the form of discrete packets. Packets are addressed using IP addresses, ports, and sockets. The IP address is a unique number assigned to each object on the network that works at the Network Layer. Ports and sockets differentiate different TCP/IP data transmissions occurring simultaneously on the same computer.

Examining TCP/IP Packets

Data transmitting across a TCP/IP network divides into smaller pieces called packets. The primary advantages of breaking data into smaller packets are as follows:

- Smaller packets travel faster over the network than undivided data, reducing the likelihood of a collision

- The likelihood of delays on the network lessen using smaller packets

- In the event of a data collision, less data is lost or has to be resent with smaller packets

A TCP/IP packet has three parts: the header, the data, and the trailer (Figure 4.4).

Figure 4.4 TCP/IP Packet

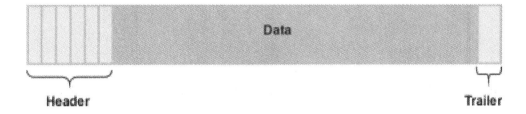

Packet Header

The packet header contains the source address, the destination address, and an alert signal that indicates that data is being sent.

As the packet moves down through the OSI model, different headers add to the raw data (Figure 4.5). At the Transport Layer, TCP or UDP adds a header with segmentation information. At the Network

Layer, IP adds the source and destination IP addresses, and at the Data Link Layer, ARP adds the source and destination MAC addresses.

 Note: As the data travels down through the OSI layers, the name changes. A segment is TCP data at the Transport Layer. A message is UDP data at the Transport Layer. When the data reaches IP, it is called an IP Datagram, and by the time the message reaches the Data Link Layer, it is called a frame.

Figure 4.5 Data Packet Header

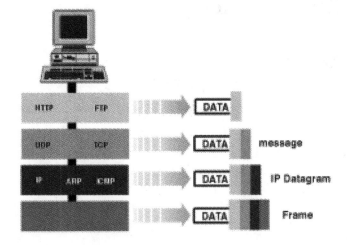

Packet Data

The middle section of the data packet contains the actual data that is sent. The size of the data in each packet varies, depending on the type of network. In general, data size ranges from 500 bytes to 4 kilobytes (KB).

Packet Trailer

The trailer in a TCP/IP packet contains error-checking code. The Cyclical Redundancy Check (CRC) is a mathematical calculation of the data. A number calculates at the source, and this CRC number adds in the trailer. Once at the receiving computer, the same mathematical function takes place on the packet. The receiving computer checks its calculated CRC number to that calculated in the trailer. If the numbers match, the data is considered valid. If the numbers do not match, the data is resent.

Understanding IP Addressing

Like all other network protocols, TCP/IP has a method for identifying each object on a network. Every object or host (a computer or printer, for example) has a unique IP address. The current version of IP (Version 4 IPv4) uses 32-bit IP addresses that allow for 2^{32} IP addresses (about 4.3 billion addresses). The next release of IP (Version 5 IPv6) will support 128-bit addressing, for a maximum of 2^{128}, or about 3.4×10^{38} IP addresses.

Currently, an IP address is a 32-bit number that is written as four octets separated by decimals, such as 194.168.25.1. The actual IP address is a series of 32 bits (binary digits or 0s and 1s). The IP address 194.168.25.1 looks like this to a computer:

11000010101010000001100100000001

Tip: Each number in an IP address is called an octet because it represents exactly 8 bits of data.

These IP addresses are the only way to locate and access hosts on the network. All transactions between computers are based on the IP addresses of the sending and receiving computers. When developing a TCP/IP-based network, you must make sure to assign a unique IP address to each host on the network. IP addressing is a very important part of Windows 2000 networking.

 Note: Each host on a TCP/IP network must have a unique IP address in order to avoid network conflicts.

Understanding Sockets and Ports

A computer attached to a TCP/IP network can have several TCP/IP concurrent transmissions. TCP/IP needs a way to differentiate among TCP/IP streams of data. An application can open a socket, which is a software object that connects that application to an application on the destination computer.

 Tip: Picture a socket as the endpoint of a communication. Just like a network cable ends in a physical socket, a TCP/IP transmission ends in a software socket.

A port identifies individual applications within a computer. Each port is assigned a number from 0 to 65,535 and may contain multiple sockets (Figure 4.6). There are TCP ports and UDP ports.

Figure 4.6 TCP Port with Multiple Sockets

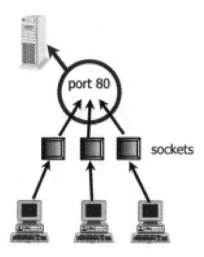

When you browse the Internet using a Web browser, you receive data carried by the TCP/IP protocol. Data passes through a port (the default for Web pages is Port 80). If you open multiple Web pages, each page passes through Port 80, but uses its own socket (Figure 4.7).

Figure 4.7 Web Pages with Unique Sockets

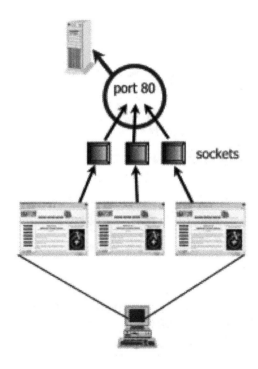

 Note: Several ports are pre-defined for TCP/IP applications. For example, FTP uses Port 20 and Port 21; HTTP uses Port 80, and Telnet uses Port 23.

Routing Data

One of the strengths of TCP/IP is that it is a routable protocol. A routable protocol carries data across different network segments. A network is broken into segments for administrative reasons and to reduce network traffic. When a network is segmented, routers perform the role of directing traffic (Figure 4.8).

Figure 4.8 Segmented Network with Routers

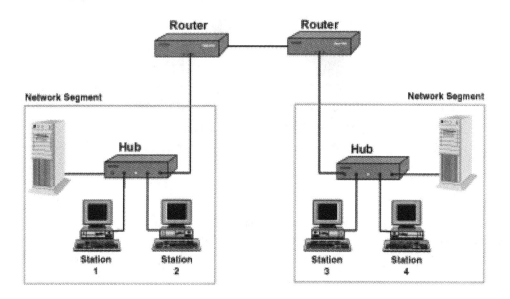

Data transmissions are simple on a single-segment network. The sending computer sends out a broadcast for the destination computer's MAC address, and then sends the data to that address (Figure 4.9).

Figure 4.9 Data Transmission on Single-Segment Network

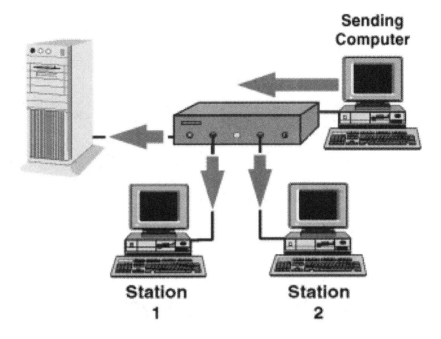

However, broadcasts are not routable. A router that receives a broadcast message (like a request for a MAC address) does not forward the message on to any other segments (Figure 4.10).

Figure 4.10 Router Stopping a Broadcast

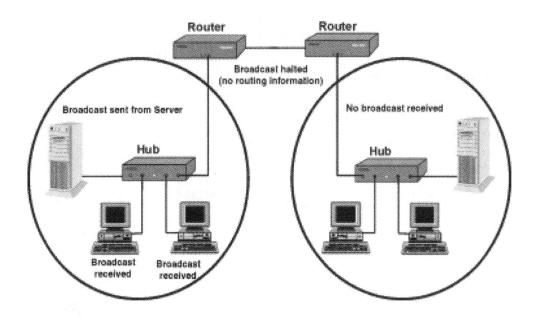

Data transmits either of the following two ways on a segmented network:

Direct—If the destination is located on the same segment as the source, the IP datagram encapsulates with the destination computer's MAC address, and the data goes directly to the destination computer.

Indirect—If the destination is located on a different segment than the source, the IP datagram encapsulates with the router's MAC address. The makes the router responsible for re-encapsulating the IP datagram for transmission to the proper segment.

Each router contains a routing table. This table is either manually or dynamically updated, and contains a list of computers with their IP addresses. The router uses this table for information to redirect messages to the correct segment.

Note: Of all TCP/IP protocols, IP plays the most important role in routing. IP is a Network Layer protocol in the OSI that handles all addressing and routing capabilities.

The steps in the packet routing procedure (Figure 4.11) when a router receives a TCP/IP packet are as follows:

Figure 4.11 Packet Routing Procedure

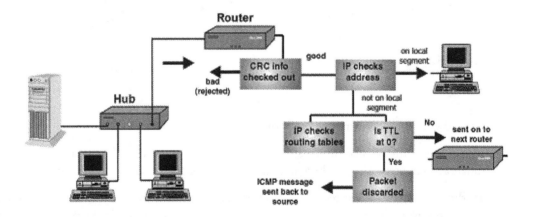

1.   The CRC information is checked. If the CRC is bad, the data is rejected.

2.   If the CRC is good, the IP protocol on the router checks the destination IP address.

      If the IP address is located on one of the segments to which the router is attached, the router re-encapsulates the data with the destination's MAC address and sends the data.

If the destination IP address is not located on one of the segments to which the router is attached, the router checks the routing table for the best route, re-encapsulates the data, and then and sends it to the next router along the route.

3. Before sending the packet to another router, the router decreases the Time to Live (TTL) indicator by 1.

    If the TTL is 0, the router discards the packet and sends an ICMP message to the source computer indicating the failure.

4. The process repeats for each router until the packet arrives at a router on the destination's segment. The packet is then sent to the destination computer.

 Note: TTL defines how many hops (through how many routers) a packet travels before it is no longer valid.

Name Resolution

As you have seen, TCP/IP uses IP addresses to identify all objects on the network. These 32-bit numbers are necessary but difficult to remember. It is easier to remember names rather than numbers, which is why name-based protocols like NetBIOS and AppleTalk are so popular.

A 32-bit IP addresses is cumbersome. If users had to remember the 32-bit IP address of each computer on their network in order to send or receive information, the network would not be very user friendly. The transition toward 128-bit addresses in Ipv6 is not going to improve this situation. Imagine having to remember the address of your favorite Web page as the following IP address:

0110110001101100111001010011010011011000110010011001100110010101010
1011000110110011100101001101001101100011001001100110011010101

or even this

`192.168.12.5.20.12.7.46.33.17.8.211.18.31.100.50`

The following is an example of how the IPv6 address appears in the hexadecimal format in which they will most likely be written:

`4A3F:AE67:F418:DC55:3412:A9F2:0340:EA1D`

In order to make TCP/IP more user-friendly, you can assign names to computers. These names convert into their IP addresses when data transmits.

Understanding Different Computer Names

The following two types of computer names are used with TCP/IP:

Hostnames—Hostnames identify every host (object) on the network. Hostnames can be a single name like Server1 or a full domain name, like server1.lightpointlearning.com, and can be up to 255 characters long.

NetBIOS names—NetBIOS names are used on networks running NetBIOS over NetBEUI or TCP/IP. Many older Windows-based clients require the presence of NetBIOS names to find resources on a LAN. NetBIOS names may be up to 15 characters long.

 Note: You can only assign a hostname to a computer in Windows 2000. Windows 2000 automatically creates the NetBIOS name from the first 15 characters of the hostname. You cannot alter this NetBIOS name.

Because there are two different computer names, there are two different services for resolving the names to IP addresses. DNS resolves hostnames to IP addresses, and WINS resolves NetBIOS names to IP addresses.

Resolving Hostnames

Hostnames and IP addresses are resolved by referring to a static table (called the Hosts file) or by using DNS.

Hosts File

The Hosts file is a standard text file that must be updated manually. The Hosts file contains a listing of hostnames with their associated IP addresses (Figure 4.12).

Figure 4.12 Typical Hosts File

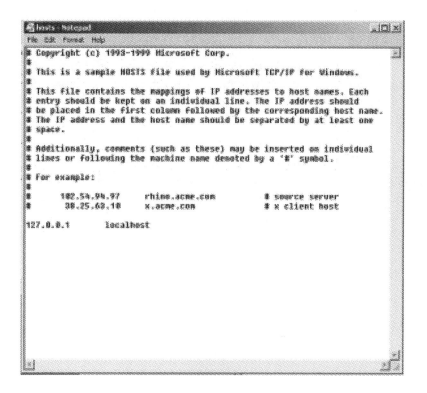

Tip: You can view the Hosts file on your Windows 2000 computer using any text editor (like Notepad). The file is found in the c:\winnt\system32\drivers\etc\ directory.

The Hosts file is cumbersome because it is manually created and is updated with every change in the network. The sole benefit of the Hosts file is its ability to customize an alias. Aliases allow a user to type in a name other than the hostname that resolves to the proper IP address. For example, if you create an alias GoodSite that maps to the address 216.219.146.170, entering GoodSite into your Web browser's address bar brings up the Web page at 216.219.146.170.

Domain Name System (DNS)

DNS converts IP addresses into hostnames users are more likely to remember, and also reconverts the names back into IP addresses as necessary. In many ways, it functions like a phonebook. You can find someone's phone number by looking up the name, and reverse phonebooks allow you to look up a number to find a person.

DNS uses a hierarchical naming structure (called a namespace) so all computers within a domain share a common domain name. For example, in the lightpointlearning.com domain, all hostnames end with lightpointlearning.com (Figure 4.13). Even computers that are several domains down the hierarchy share that common namespace.

Figure 4.13 Hierarchical Domain Namespace

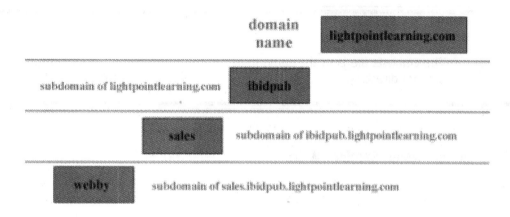

This hierarchical structure enables DNS servers to only keep track of a few computers. Every DNS server needs to know the IP addresses for the computers within its namespace, but for addresses beyond the namespace, the DNS server refers to other DNS servers for resolution. Without this structure, each DNS server would need to have a list of every host on the Internet and its corresponding IP address.

Resolving NetBIOS Names

Like hostnames, NetBIOS names is resolved using a static file (called the Lmhosts file), or through using the dynamic WINS service.

Lmhosts File

The Lmhosts file contains IP addresses and NetBIOS names. It is a standard text file that requires manual updating. NetBEUI networks exchange all information through broadcasts, which means NetBIOS names are not usable across routers, and, therefore, are not usable on segmented networks.

Using the Lmhosts file, you can map a NetBIOS name to an IP address on another segment. On networks using NetBIOS over TCP/IP, this is a moot point, since IP packets are routable.

Tip: The Lmhosts file is in the same folder as the Hosts file, c:\winnt\system32\drivers\etc\ directory.

Windows Internet Name Service (WINS)

WINS provides a dynamic way to map IP addresses to NetBIOS names. Like a DNS server, a WINS server provides a client computer with the appropriate IP address to use, based on the requested NetBIOS name. You can use WINS servers to resolve NetBIOS names on other segments as well.

Once a prominent features in Windows-based networks, WINS now plays a minor role next to DNS. Since most networking is done on TCP/IP-based networks using hostnames, WINS servers primarily support older Windows-based clients that require NetBIOS names.

Understanding Windows 2000 Name Resolution

When you enter a name into a network application, the application determines whether the name is a hostname or NetBIOS name. If it is a hostname, the computer uses the Hosts file and DNS to resolve the name. If the name is a NetBIOS, the computers uses the Lmhosts file or WINS. If the computer is resolving a hostname but fails to do so using the Hosts file or DNS, a Windows 2000 computer also checks the Lmhosts file and WINS.

A Windows 2000 computer goes through a series of steps to resolve a hostname (Figure 4.14). These steps are defined in the following example where Client1 refers to the hostname of a client computer, and Server1 refers to a server on the same network:

Figure 4.14 Hostname Resolution

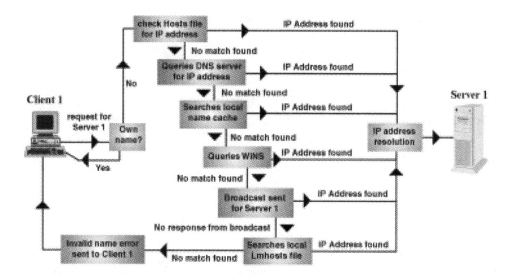

1. A user on Client1 enters the user-friendly name Server1 into a Web browser.

2. Computer1 makes sure the name is not its own hostname. In this case, Server1 is not the hostname for Client1.

3. Client1 checks the Hosts file to see if there is an entry for Server1. If there is an entry, it resolves the name to the IP address that also lists in the Hosts file.

4. Client1 queries the default DNS server to resolve the name Server1 to an IP address. The DNS server either returns an IP address or an error message that no address could be resolved.

5. If an error message is returned, Client1 searches its local name cache for a match. If a match for Server1 is found in the cache, the IP address is resolved.

6. Client1 queries the WINS server for resolution of the name.

7.   If the WINS server does not contain a record for the name Server1, a broadcast is sent out to see if any computer responds to the name Server1.

8.   If the broadcast fails, Client1 checks its local Lmhosts file. If no match is found, the name is considered invalid and an error message returns to the user.

Following are the steps for resolving a NetBIOS name:

1.   The NetBIOS name cache is checked.

2.   The WINS server is queried. If no default WINS server is configured on the client, Step 3 occurs before this step.

3.   A broadcast message is sent out on the local segment.

4.   The Lmhosts file is checked.

5.   The Hosts file is checked.

6.   The DNS server is queried.

 Note: During NetBIOS name resolution, the Lmhosts file is not checked until after the broadcast message has been sent and fails.

Vocabulary

Review the following terms in preparation for the certification exam.

Term	Description
ARP	Address Resolution Protocol is the TCP/IP protocol that resolves or converts IP addresses to MAC addresses, and vice versa.
ARP utility	The TCP/IP diagnostic utility ARP displays the contents of the Address Resolution Protocol cache (the table of MAC and IP addresses).
connectionless	Data transmission that doesn't require network nodes to be directly connected. Data packets with addresses pass through nodes until delivery.
CRC	The Cyclical Redundancy Check is a mathematical calculation of the data portion of a packet. The calculated number adds to the packet trailer for error-checking purposes.
DNS	The Domain Name System is a Transport Layer protocol that resolves IP addresses to friendly names called hostnames.
frame	Data is called a frame when it reaches the Data Link Layer.
FTP	File Transfer Protocol spans the OSI Application, Presentation, and Session layers of the OSI model and is the primary file transfer protocol for HTTP and other files.

Term	Description
FTP utility	The TCP/IP connectivity utility File Transfer Protocol uses TCP for file transfers.
hops	Hops represent steps or instances through which packets travel from a router to another router.
hostnames	Identify every host (object) on a network. The names are friendly and can be up to 255 characters long; hostnames are entered in World Wide Web browsers.
Hosts file	The Hosts file is a static table of Hostnames and IP addresses. It's a standard text file that must be manually updated, and is used to resolve two different computer names.
HTML	HyperText Markup Language is the programming language of the WWW.
HTTP	HyperText Transfer Protocol, among the OSI Session, Presentation, and Application layers, transfers files written in HTML. WWW files are written in HTML, and HTTP transfers Web pages.
ICMP	The Internet Control Message Protocol sends control messages used for diagnosis of unsuccessful data delivery. Additionally, the PING utility uses ICMP to verify a connection to a remote computer.
IGMP	The Internet Group Management Protocol performs multicasting, which simultaneously sends one copy of data to multiple computers.
IP	Internet Protocol is a connectionless protocol on the OSI Network Layer that assigns addresses objects on the network and provides routing information to ensure network data delivery.

Term	Description
IP address	The Internet Protocol address is a unique 32-bit number written as four octets separated by decimals that identifies each device (object or host) on the network.
IP datagram	The name applied to data as it travels through the OSI layers when it reaches the Internet Protocol.
Ipconfig utility	The TCP/IP diagnostic utility that displays the current TCP/IP configuration information, including the IP address and hostname.
Lmhosts	The Lmhosts file is a static table of NetBIOS names and IP addresses that must be manually updated.
MAC address	A unique Media Access Control address number is burned into the NIC and cannot be changed. This number identifies each object on the network, working at the Data Link Layer to send and receive data.
message	A message is UDP data at the Transport layer.
multicasting	The process of simultaneously sending one copy of data to multiple requesting computers. Multicasting messages are routable.
namespace	The hierarchical naming structure that allows all computers within a domain to share a common domain name.
Nbstat utility	The TCP/IP diagnostic utility Nbstat that displays currently active NetBIOS over TCP/IP sessions.

Term	Description
NetBIOS	A Microsoft-proprietary protocol, originally designed to work with NetBEUI, which uses common names to identify computers. It was rewritten to work with TCP /IP.
NetBIOS names	Names used on networks running NetBIOS over NetBEUI or TCP/IP that can contain up to 15 characters.
Network Layer	The layer of the OSI primarily responsible for getting data to its intended location, and handles data addressing
NIC	The Network Interface Card, also called network adapter, is a hardware device inside a computer that allows a c omputer to access a network, and is manufactured with a MAC address .
octets	Each number in an IP address is called an octet because it represents exactly 8 bits of data.
OSI	The Open Systems Interconnection network model is a seven-layer model that provides a foundation for all network communication. Each layer is responsible for and addresses one part of network communication.
packet data	The middle section of the TCP /IP packet that contains the actual data being sent.
packet header	The front section of the TCP/IP packet that contains the source address, destination address, and an alert signal.
packet trailer	The end part of the TCP /IP packet that contains error-checking code.

Term	Description
packets	Units of data divide into smaller pieces when the data is sent across a TCP/IP network. Packets include three parts: the header, the data, and the trailer.
PING utility	The **PING** utility installs with TCP/IP and works with ICMP to verify the network's remote physical connections by using IP addresses.
port	Ports for TCP and UDP identify individual applications within a computer, and may contain multiple sockets.
routable protocol	A protocol is that carries data across different network segments.
Route utility	The TCP/IP diagnostic utility Route displays the local routing table.
router table	A table that lists computers and their IP addresses the router accesses to redirect messages to the correct segment.
routers	A device that segments networks and passes on data transmissions that have destination addresses.
segment	In data transfer using TCP/IP, a segment is what TCP data is called at the Transport layer.
SMTP	Simple Mail Transfer Protocol works at OSI layers 5, 6, and 7 to provide file transfer services for e-mail message and attachment files.
socket	A software object that connects an application to another application on a destination computer. Sockets differentiate TCP/IP streams of data; transmissions end in a software socket.

Term	Description
TCP	Transmission Control Protocol TCP is a connection-oriented protocol that works at the Transport Layer of the OSI to ensure data arrives at its destination. If data does not arrive, TCP resends lost packets.
TCP/IP	Transmission Control Protocol/Internet Protocol is a protocol suite—a collection of many protocols designed to work together. Each protocol works at one or more layers of the OSI model. Each layer of the OSI model defines a very specific set of tasks the protocol should perform.
TCP/IP Application Layer	This layer corresponds with the Application, Presentation, and Session layers of the OSI model.
TCP/IP Internet Layer	This layer matches the Network Layer of the OSI, and includes IP, ICMP, IGMP, and ARP.
TCP/IP Layer Model	The TCP/IP stack divides into its own three-layer model (Application, Transport, and Internet layers), and maps these layers to the OSI model.
TCP/IP protocol suite	The TCP/IP protocol suite includes numerous smaller protocols that map to specific layers in the OSI model.
TCP/IP Transport Layer	This layer maps directly to the Transport Layer of the OSI model and includes TCP, UDP, DNS, and WINS.
Telnet utility	A TCP/IP connectivity utility that remotely accesses a server with a command-line-like interface.
TFTP utility	The TCP/IP connectivity utility Trivial File Transfer Protocol uses UDP to transfer files.
Tracert	The TCP/IP diagnostic utility Tracert displays the routers through which data travels to reach the destination computer.

Term	Description
TTL	Time To Live defines how many hops (through how many routers) a packet travels before it is no longer valid.
UDP	The User Datagram Protocol is connectionless and works at the Transport Layer of the OSI. It is faster than TCP, reduces overhead, and is often used for Internet real-time transmissions.
utilities	Many of the TCP/IP utilities share the same name as TCP/IP protocols. TCP/IP utilities are user interfaces that allow using the protocols.
WINS	The Windows Internet Name Service works at the OSI Transport Layer, and resolves NetBIOS names to IP addresses. WINS servers support older Windows-based clients that require NetBIOS names.
WWW	The World Wide Web is a complex system of servers that accommodates displaying and linking Web pages written in HTML, and accommodates a variety of files in a variety of formats that may include text, graphics, video and audio files.

In Brief

If you want to...	Then do this...
Implement the default Windows 2000 transmission and Internet protocols	Use TCP/IP suite for fast, reliable, routable data transmission on all sizes of networks supported by major operating systems.
Make a protocol that works on many different network types and can be used on multiple operating systems	Use the OSI seven-layer model to structure your protocol for a standard method that defines the way network protocols work.
Diagnose a TCP/IP network	Use the Windows 2000 utilities that work with specific TCP/IP protocols.
Send data through a fast, connectionless but unreliable protocol that identifies the source and destination for every transmission	Use the IP protocol with UDP.
Diagnose unsuccessful data delivery	Use the ICMP protocol with the PING utility to diagnose physical network problems and to verify remote computer connections.
Send one copy of data to multiple requesting computers over routers	Use the IGMP protocol for multicasting, which sends one copy of data to multiple requesting computers over routers.
Send data with reliability	Use the TCP connection-oriented protocol, which ensures all data arrives at the destination and resends it if it doesn't arrive.

If you want to...	Then do this...
Send or receive live-streaming audio over the Internet with fast data flow	Use the UDP protocol for fast but less reliable data transmission for less critical data transmissions such as music.
Transfer HTML Web pages	Use the HTTP protocol.
Copy files between a server and client over the Internet	Use the File Transfer Protocol (FTP), and its utility, also called FTP, to download and upload files.
Use TCP/IP diagnostic utilities	Use the ARP, Ipconfig, NBstat, Netstat, PING, Route, and Tracert utilities for diagnosis tasks at the command prompt.
Develop a TCP/IP-based network that locates and accesses hosts on the network	Make IP addressing an important part of your Windows 2000 network development project, and assign a unique IP address to every host on the network.
Make TCP/IP more user-friendly	Assign friendly hostnames to computers, or use the automatically assigned Windows 2000 NetBIOS name, to make TCP/IP more user-friendly.
Resolve hostnames and NetBIOS names to IP addresses	Use DNS to resolve hostnames to IP addresses and WINS to resolve NetBIOS names to IP addresses.

Lesson 4 Activities

Complete the following activities to better prepare you for the certification exam.

1. List four major strengths of TCP/IP protocol.

2. Discuss the differences between the OSI model and the TCP/IP model.

3. List the three layers of the TCP/IP model and explain how the components relate to the OSI model.

4. List the TCP/IP connectivity and diagnostic utilities and explain their uses.

5. List and describe the three sections of a data packet.

6. Give the name for data at each layer of the OSI model.

7. Define IP addressing and explain its major importance in a network.

8. Explain why a server on a different network segment won't receive broadcast messages sent from your computer.

9. List and explain the two types of TCP/IP computer names.

10. Describe the general steps in Windows 2000 name resolution.

Answers to Lesson 4 Activities

1. The four major strengths of the Windows 2000 default protocol TCP/IP are as follows:¡ Supported by all major operating systems

    • Is routable

    • Accommodates all sizes of networks

    • Provides reliability and speed

2. The TCP/IP suite does not include components for the Physical and the Data Link layers of the OSI model. This allows TCP/IP to work on many different network types (defined in the Data Link Layer) and a multitude of NICs, which are defined in the Physical Layer. Although mapping TCP/IP protocols to OSI layers provides a better comparison between the TCP/IP protocol suite and other protocol suites, the TCP/IP stack divides into its own three-layer model for simplicity.

3. The three layers of the TCP/IP model are as follows:

    Application Layer-Corresponds with the top three layers of the OSI model (the Application, Presentation, and Session layers). The FTP, HTTP, and SNMP protocols are members of the Application Layer.

    Transport Layer-Maps directly to the Transport Layer of the OSI model and includes TCP, UDP, DNS, and WINS.

    Internet Layer-Matches OSI Network Layer, and includes IP, ICMP, IGMP, and ARP.

4. TCP/IP connectivity and diagnostic utilities are as follows:

    Telnet accesses remote servers with a command line interface.

    FTP (File Transfer Protocol) uses TCP for file transfers.

    TFTP (Trivial File Transfer Protocol) uses UDP to transfer files.

    ARP displays the contents of the Address Resolution Protocol cache (the table of MAC and IP addresses).

    Ipconfig displays the current TCP/IP configuration information, including the IP address and hostname.

Nbtstat displays currently active NetBIOS over TCP/IP sessions.

Netstat displays currently active TCP/IP connections.

PING sends ICMP requests to another computer, and verifies a good connection.

Route displays the local routing table.

Tracert displays the routers through which data travels to reach the destination computer.

5.   The three sections of a TCP/IP data packet are the header, the data, and the trailer.

The packet header contains the source address, the destination address, and an alert signal. The alert signal indicates that data is being sent.

The packet data is the middle section of the data packet, which contains the actual data. The amount of data that can be sent in each packet varies and depends on the network type. In general, data sizes range from 500 bytes to 4 kilobytes (KB).

The packet trailer contains error-checking code. The Cyclical Redundancy Check (CRC) is a mathematical calculation of the data. A calculation occurs at the source, and the resulting CRC number is added in the trailer. On the receiving computer, the same calculation is performed on the packet. The receiving computer checks its resulting CRC number to that in the trailer. If the numbers match, the data is assumed good. If not, the data is resent.

6.   As the data travels down through the OSI layers, the name changes. A segment is TCP data at the Transport layer. A message is UDP data at the Transport layer. When the data reaches IP, it is called an IP Datagram, and by the time the message reaches the Data Link layer, it is called a frame.

7.   An IP address is (currently) a 32-bit number that is written as four octets separated by decimals, such as 192.168.25.1. The major importance of IP addressing is that it is the only way that computers can locate and access hosts on the network. All transactions between computers are based on the IP addresses of the sending and receiving computers. As you develop a TCP/IP-based network, you must make sure to assign a unique IP address to each host on the network.

8.   Routers direct traffic over network segments. Routers only pass on messages that contain a valid IP address for the destination computer. If a router receives a broadcast message, it will not forward the message on to any other segments, because broadcast messages do not use a valid host IP address.

9. Two types of computer names used with TCP/IP are hostnames and NetBIOS names. Hostnames identify every host (object) on the network and can be a single name like Server1 or a full domain name, like server1.lightpointlearning.net. Hostnames can be up to 255 characters long.NetBIOS names are used on networks running

    NetBIOS over NetBEUI or TCP/IP. Many older Windows-based clients require the presence of NetBIOS names to find resources on a LAN. NetBIOS names are up to 15 characters long.

10. When you enter a name into a network application, the application determines whether the name is a hostname or NetBIOS name. If it is a hostname, the computer uses the Hosts file and DNS to resolve the name. If the name is a NetBIOS, the Lmhosts file or WINS resolves the name. If the computer is resolving a hostname, and fails to do so with the Hosts file or DNS, a Windows 2000 computer also checks the Lmhosts file and WINS.

Lesson 4 Quiz

These questions test your knowledge of features, vocabulary, procedures, and syntax.

1.   Which of the following layers of the OSI model do not map to TCP/IP?

   A. Application Layer

   B. Physical Layer

   C. Transport Layer

   D. Data Link Layer

2.   How many ICMP packets does your computer send to a destination computer after you run the PING command?

   A. 6

   B. 4

   C. 1

   D. 2

3.   What type of transmission does ARP use?

   A. Multicast

   B. Router

   C. Broadcast

   D. TTL

4.   Which layers of the OSI model correspond to the TCP/IP Application layer?

   A. Internet Layer

   B. Session Layer

   C. Application Layer

   D. Presentation Layer

5. What is the name of the mathematical calculation that performs error-checking and adds a number to the data packet trailer?

    A. DNS

    B. Nbstat

    C. Route

    D. CRC

6. How many addresses does the IPv4 version of IP allow?

    A. 4.3 billion

    B. 2128

    C. 6.022x1023

    D. 3.4x1038

7. What is a software object that connects two applications?

    A. Port

    B. Socket

    C. MAC

    D. NIC

8. What criteria does Windows 2000 use to automatically create NetBIOS names?

    A. Random number generation

    B. First 15 characters of the hostname

    C. Octets

    D. Binary conversion

9. Which two of the following tools resolve hostnames and IP addresses?

    A. Hosts File
    B. DNS
    C. Lmhosts
    D. WINS

10. Which two of the following tools resolve NetBIOS names and IP addresses?

    A. Hosts File
    B. DNS
    C. Lmhosts
    D. WINS

Answers to Lesson 4 Quiz

1. Answers B and D are correct. The Physical and Data Link layers of the OSI model doesn't map to TCP/IP.

    Answers A and C are incorrect. TCP/IP does link to the Application and Transport Layers of the OSI.

2. Answer B is correct. Your computer sends four ICMP packets asking for a reply from the destination computer after you run the PING command.

    Therefore answers A, C, and D are incorrect.

3. Answer C is correct. ARP uses broadcast transmissions to resolve the IP address to a MAC address.

    Answer A is incorrect. IGMP uses multicasting, the process of sending one copy of data to multiple computers at the same time.

    Answer B is incorrect. Neither router nor TTL define data transmission types. Time To Live, the header field for a packet that indicates the length of time it should be kept, defines how many hops to make, (or how many routers a packet may travel through), before it is no longer valid. Routers segment networks and pass on data transmissions that have destination addresses.

4. Answers B, C, and D are correct. The Application, Presentation, and Session layers of the OSI model correspond to the TCP/IP Application layer.

    Answer A is incorrect. The Internet Layer is a layer in the TCP/IP model. The Internet Layer in the TCP/IP model corresponds to the Network Layer in the OSI model.

5. Answer D is correct. The Cyclical Redundancy Check is a mathematical calculation of the data, which is used to add a number to a data packet trailer for error-checking purposes.

    Answer A is incorrect. DNS is a Transport Layer protocol that resolves IP addresses to hostnames.

    Answer B is incorrect. NBstat is the TCP/IP diagnostic utility that displays currently active NetBIOS over TCP/IP sessions.

    Answer C is incorrect. Route is TCP/IP diagnostic utility that displays the local routing table, and not a mathematical calculation formula.

6. Answer A is correct. The IPv4 version of IP supports 32-bit addresses, and allows about 4.3 billion IP addresses.

    Answers B, C and D are incorrect. The next release of IP (IPv6) will support 128-bit addressing, for a maximum of 2128, or about 3.4x1038 IP addresses.

7. Answer B is correct. A socket is a software object that connects an application to an application on a destination computer. Just like a network cable ends in a physical socket, a TCP/IP transmission ends in a software socket.

    Answer A is incorrect. A port identifies individual applications within a computer. Each port is assigned a number from 0 to 65,535 and may contain multiple sockets. There are both TCP ports and UDP ports.

    Answers C and D are incorrect. MAC is a Media Access Control address number, and is burned into the NIC, the Network Interface Card, at the factory.

8. Answer B is correct. Windows 2000 uses the first 15 characters of the hostname to automatically create NetBIOS names, and you cannot alter them.

    Answers A, C, and D are incorrect. Windows uses hostnames to generate NetBIOS names, and not numbers. In Windows 2000 you can only assign a hostname to a computer.

9. Answer A is correct. Computers refer to a static table called a Hosts file to resolve hostnames and IP addresses.

    Answer B is correct. Hostnames and IP addresses are resolved by DNS. DNS converts IP addresses into hostnames and also converts the names back into IP addresses as necessary.

    Answer C and D are incorrect. Lmhosts and WINS resolve NetBIOS names.

10. Answer C is correct. The Lmhosts file that must be manually updated. On NetBEUI networks, you can use it to map NetBIOS names to IP addresses on another network segment.

    Answer D is correct. WINS provides a dynamic way to map IP addresses to NetBIOS names. A WINS server provides a client computer with the appropriate IP address to use, based on the requested NetBIOS name.

    Answer A and B are incorrect. The Hosts file and DNS resolve hostnames and IP addresses, not NetBIOS names.

Lesson 5: IP Addresses and Subnets

TCP/IP is a routable protocol that carries data from one network segment to another through hardware devices known as routers. In order to route data, there must be a mechanism in place to determine the location of every host (object) on the network. The Internet Protocol (IP) is responsible for addressing and routing TCP/IP packets. Every host has a unique IP address, and every address has a subnet mask.

In a small network, all computers are located on the same network segment. However, much of the network traffic that generates is in the form of broadcast messages that require the attention of every computer. As the number of computers on a network increases, so does the number of broadcasts, and this increased traffic results in a less efficient network. One way to reduce traffic is to break the network into smaller segments (or subnets). Each segment connects to another through a router. Routers forward directed data, but do not allow broadcast messages to reach other segments.

The subnet mask specifies the segment (or subnet) on which a host resides. Using the combination of a host's IP address and subnet mask, a sending computer determines if the destination is local (on the same subnet) or remote (on another subnet), and sends the message accordingly. If the host is local, the message transmits directly to the destination. If remote, the message transmits to a router.

This lesson covers how IP addresses and subnet masks are determined for each host. You will also learn how computers use IP addresses and subnet masks to route data from its source to destination. After completing this lesson, you should have a better understanding of the following topics:

- IP Addressing

- Network Segmentation

- IP Classes

- Classless Inter-Domain Routing (CIDR)

IP Addressing

IP works at the Network Layer of the Open System Interconnection (OSI) model. Network Layer protocols are responsible for addressing and routing data packets. In a network, this is accomplished using IP addresses and subnet masks. Both the IP address and subnet mask are 32-bit numbers. Before exploring how IP addresses work, you must spend some time learning about binary numbers.

 Note: The current version of TCP/IP is called IPv4 or IP Version 4. The next generation of TCP/IP, IPv6, is will be released in the next couple of years. Upon its release, IPv4 and IPv6 will be used concurrently for several years. For more information, visit www.ipv6.com on the Internet.

Using Binary

A bit is a single binary digit (a 0 or 1). Binary is a numbering system that only uses 1s and 0s to represent all numbers, while decimal notation (the numbering system we use daily) uses the digits 0 through 9 to represent values. Computers and networks only work in binary—a circuit is either on (represented by 1) or off (represented by a 0). Because binary deals with only two values, it is known as Base 2 format, and all numbers are powers of 2. Decimal is known as Base 10 numbering.

When working in binary bits, we generally work with 8 bits (1 byte) at a time:

11011010

Ignore the 1s and 0s and just look at the 8-bit positions. In binary, you always read numbers from right to left. Starting from the right, each bit position represents a power of 2 (Table 5.1). The right-most bit represents 2^0, and the left-most bit represents 2^7, and the bits in the middle follow a regular progression (2^1, 2^2, 2^3, 2^4, 2^5, and 2^6).

Table 5.1 Powers of 2 in a Byte

Bit Position	8	7	6	5	4	3	2	1
Binary Value	2^7	2^6	2^5	2^4	2^3	2^2	2^1	2^0
Decimal Value (per bit)	128	64	32	16	8	4	2	1

Conversion of binary numbers to decimal numbers or decimal numbers to binary is very important when working with TCP/IP networks. There are two ways to determine the decimal number from a binary number and vice versa. The easier of the two ways involves using the Calculator program included with Windows 2000. However, you need to understand the process and theory behind the automatic conversion and be able to do the conversions manually before using a calculator. Without this prior knowledge, the calculation could confuse or mislead you.

Manual Binary Conversion

To determine the value of a byte, you add up the decimal values for each on bit (a bit represented by 1, as opposed to an off bit, represented by 0).

For example, the binary number 11011010 has an on bit in the second, fourth, fifth, seventh, and eighth positions (remember, in binary you count from right to left). Begin by placing these values in a conversion table (Table 5.2).

Table 5.2 Binary Conversion Table

Bit	1	1	0	1	1	0	1	0
Decimal	128	64	32	16	8	4	2	1
Value	?	?	?	?	?	?	?	?

For every on bit, carry the decimal value of that bit position down to the third row. For every off bit (0), write a 0 in the third row (Table 5.3).

Tip: When filling in the third row, multiply the first row by the second row. The third row will always have a 0 or the number from the second row.

Table 5.3 Manual Binary Conversion

Bit	1	1	0	1	1	0	1	0	
Decimal	128	64	32	16	8	4	2	1	Sum
Value	128	64	0	16	8	0	2	0	218

Note that only the decimal values that correspond with on bits (the 1s) carry down to the value row. Finally, add up all of the values in the third row (128+64+16+8+2) to determine the decimal value of the binary number. In this example, the binary number 11011010 equals 218.

Note: Using 8 bits of data, you can create 2^8 (256) possible numbers, from 0 to 255.

As another exercise, convert the following 8-bit number to decimal:

00101011

Using the conversion table, enter the binary digits, fill in the third row, and then sum the values in the third row (Table 5.4).

Table 5.4 Conversion Example

Bit	0	0	1	0	1	0	1	1	Sum
Decimal	128	64	32	16	8	4	2	1	
Value	0	0	32	0	8	0	2	1	43

The binary number 00101011 equals 43 in decimal notation.

Converting Decimal to Binary

As a final exercise, convert the decimal number 179 to binary. In this case, you use a different table (Table 5.5).

Table 5.5 Decimal-to-Binary Conversion 1

Decimal Value	Binary Digit	Binary Value
	128	
	64	
	32	
	16	
	8	
	4	
	2	
	1	

Begin by entering the decimal value in the first column, first row. If you can subtract 128 from the decimal value (and keep a positive remainder), place a 1 in the binary value column, and write the remainder in the second row of the first column (Table 5.6).

Table 5.6 Decimal-to-Binary Conversion 2

Decimal Value	Binary Digit	Binary Value
179	128	1
51	64	
	32	
	16	
	8	
	4	
	2	
	1	

If you can subtract the binary digit from the decimal value, enter a 1 in the third column. If you cannot, enter a 0 and write the decimal value in the new row. In this example, the remainder from the first step is 51. You cannot subtract 64 from 51, so you enter a 0 in the binary value column, and move the 51 down to the next row (Table 5.7).

Table 5.7 Decimal-to-Binary Conversion 3

Decimal Value	Binary Digit	Binary Value
176	128	1
51	64	0
51	32	
	16	
	8	
	4	
	2	
	1	

Continue this same process down through the column until you have reached the bottom. If you did it correctly, you always end up with no remainder, and the third column will have the binary number (Table 5.8).

Table 5.8 Decimal-to-Binary Conversion 4

Decimal Value	Binary Digit	Binary Value
176	128	1
51	64	0
51	32	1
19	16	1
3	8	0
3	4	0
3	2	1
1	1	1

Through this conversion method, you determine that the decimal number 179 is represented in binary as `10110011`.

Using the Calculator

The Windows 2000 Calculator program allows you to convert binary numbers to decimal, and, conversely, decimal numbers to binary. To open Calculator, from the Start Menu, choose Programs, Accessories, and then select Calculator. By default, Calculator opens in Standard mode. To do binary conversion, use Scientific mode. From the menu bar, choose View, and then select Scientific (Figure 5.1).

Figure 5.1 Calculator Scientific Mode

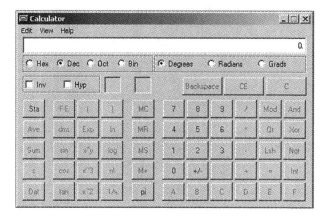

To convert from binary to decimal, follow these steps:

1.   Choose Bin.

2.   Enter the binary number.

Tip: The Windows 2000 Calculator program does not accept leading 0s. When you enter the binary number, begin with the first 1 on the left (for example, for the binary number 00100011, enter 100011).

---

3.   Choose Dec.

The display changes to show the decimal equivalent (Figure 5.2)

Figure 5.2 Binary-to-Decimal Conversion in Calculator

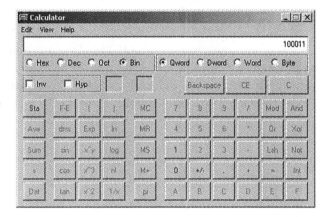

To convert a decimal number to binary, follow the steps for converting from binary to decimal in reverse. Choose Dec, enter the number, and then select Bin. The resulting number is the binary equivalent of the decimal number.

 Warning: If the binary number is not eight digits long, Calculator leaves off preceding 0s. When using the number for IP addresses, be sure to include the 0s at the beginning (left side) of the number, not on the right side.

Using IP Addresses

The following is an example of a 32-bit-long IP address:

```
11000000101010000011100000000001
```

IP addresses that are 32 bits long, and which may soon be 128 bits long, pose great difficulty for recall. In addition, the likelihood mistyping a digit greatly increases with these lengths. To alleviate this problem, IP addresses are written in decimal format with each group of 8 bits written as a number separated by a decimal point. The following is an example of an IP address:

```
11000000101010000011100000000001
```

The same address as an IP address is written in groups of 8 bits like the following example:

```
11000000.10101000.00111000.00000001
```

And then written as:

```
192.168.56.1
```

The 32-bit IP address lies at the heart of TCP/IP data transmissions. Each host on the network must have a unique IP address.

The Role of InterNIC

If the Internet is a TCP/IP-based network, and every host on a TCP/IP network must have a unique IP address, then every computer connected to the Internet must have a unique IP address.

IP addresses are assigned to requesting companies and individuals through InterNIC, a semi-private agency. InterNIC ensures that no two computers are granted the same IP address.

Note: Almost all of the existing IP addresses have already been used. If you want to connect a computer to the Internet, you must rent an IP address from an Internet Service Provider (ISP). ISPs own a group of IP addresses, and will let you use one or more for a monthly fee. When IPv6 is released, many more IP addresses will become available.

Network Segmentation

When your network grows too large, you can segment the network to reduce broadcast traffic and increase overall network performance. When you segment a network, you create two or more subnets (Figure 5.3) that are joined together using routers. A router can be a stand-alone device used specifically for routing, or may be a computer with two or more Network Interface Cards (NICs) installed.

Figure 5.3 Network with Three Subnets

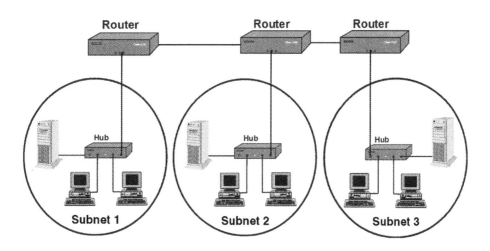

Creating Subnets

When creating subnets, it is important to consider the flow of network traffic. For example, if you have a group of users who frequently share information with one another, place them together on the same subnet. The goal of creating subnets is to reduce the amount of traffic crossing the routers.

Tip: You determine when to segment the network based on your user needs and budget.

Routers and Multihomed Computers

When segmenting, you can purchase a router to connect each subnet, or you can add a second NIC to a computer and use that computer as a router. A computer with more than one NIC is considered multihomed—it is at home on more than one subnet.

Whether you use a multihomed computer or a router on a Windows network to segment, computers on the network see the device as the default gateway. Although the term makes sense—data must pass through this gateway (the router) to and from the subnet—it should not be confused with gateways, network devices that connect two different network types. Routers are not gateways because they connect two of the same network types (Figure 5.4).

Figure 5.4 A Router and a Gateway

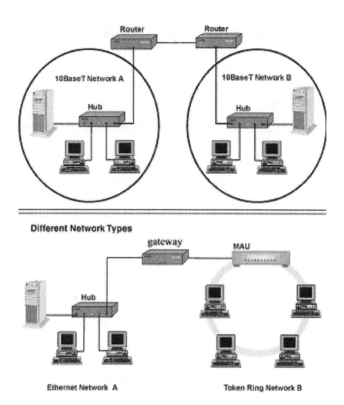

Using Subnet Masks

Every IP address has two components, a host ID and a network ID. The host ID is specific to the computer, while the network ID identifies the subnet on which the computer resides. IP addresses are like postal addresses. The numerical or postal address describes the exact location of your residence, while the city name, for example, describes the specific geographical area in which you live. Many people live in the same city, just like many hosts populate a single subnet. Therefore, just as many people share the same city name in their postal address, many hosts use the same network ID for part of their IP address.

 Note: Two devices can have the same host ID as long as they have different network IDs (they are on different subnets).

Subnet masks are also 32-bit numbers, and distinguish the network ID and host ID in an IP address. This lesson reviews the general concepts of subnets with examples and then covers the more specific aspects of subnet masks.

Like an IP address, a subnet mask is written as four octets separated by decimal points. The following rules apply to standard subnet masks:

- Each octet is either 0 or 255. In binary, this means that each octet contains either eight 1s or eight 0s.

- Once a 0 is used for one octet, the octets to the right must also be 0. For example, 255.255.255.0 and 255.0.0.0 are valid subnet masks, while 255.0.255.0 and 0.255.255.255 are not valid subnet masks.

Computers use subnet masks to determine whether the destination computer is local (on the same subnet) or remote (on a different subnet). This determination is possible from comparing the subnet mask and the IP address of the destination computer. In the subnet mask, the maximum values (the 255s) mark the position of the network ID, and the minimum values (the 0s) mark the host ID. For example, suppose a host has an IP address of 192.168.55.33 and a subnet mask of 255.255.0.0. The network ID is 192.168, and the host ID is 55.33 (Figure 5.5).

Figure 5.5 Subnet Mask and IP Addresses

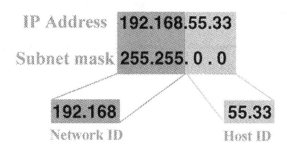

Table 5.9 lists other examples of IP address and subnet mask combinations with the corresponding network and host Ids. The last three examples use the same IP address with different subnet masks. Notice how changing the subnet mask also changes the host ID, even if though the IP address remains the same.

Table 5.9 IP Address Examples

IP Address	Subnet Mask	Network ID	Host ID
10.3.250.1	255.0.0.0	10	3.250.1
36.35.34.33	255.255.0.0	36.35	34.33
192.45.45.45	255.255.255.0	192.45.45	45
101.202.76.4	255.255.255.0	101.202.76	4
101.202.76.4	255.255.0.0	101.202	76.4
101.202.76.4	255.0.0.0	101	202.76.4

Tip: All hosts on the same subnet must use the same subnet mask.

Determining the Number of Hosts

Subnet masks determine the maximum number of hosts on any given network. For example, if you use the subnet mask 255.255.255.0, the network ID uses the first three octets, which means only the last octet is used to assign host IDs. The last octet has 8 bits, so the maximum number of different host addresses is limited to   8 bits (2^8), or 256 hosts. Likewise, the number of different subnets you are able to use with that mask is limited to 24 bits (2^{24}), or 16,777,216 subnets. In most cases, this is not very useful. Most networks have more than 256 computers on one segment, and very few networks divide into millions of subnets.

Tip: 8 bits means eight 1s and 0s. If you include every possible combination of 1s and 0s for eight digits, your result is exactly 256 possible combinations.

If you use the subnet mask 255.0.0.0, your network can support no more than 256 subnets (the network ID only uses the first octet), but each segment may contain over 16 million hosts.

The subnet mask 255.255.0.0 uses two octets for both the network ID and the host ID. This subnet mask allows you to support up to 2^{16} (65,536) subnets, and up to 2^{16} (65,536) hosts.

Note: Although there are 256 possible combinations in an octet, you cannot use the numbers 0 and 255 for host IDs, leaving only 254 valid host IDs for each octet used.

Determining Local and Remote Hosts

Using the subnet mask to determine the network ID and host ID, a computer can determine whether another host is local or remote (a local host has the same network ID, whereas a remote host has a different network ID). If the destination computer is local, the message transmits directly to the destination. If the destination computer is remote, the message must be sent to the router, and the router must then forward the message to the appropriate subnet.

For example, suppose you have two computers named Computer1 and Computer2 (Figure 5.6). Computer1 has an IP address of 192.168.34.56 and Computer2 has an IP address of 192.168.34.250. Both computers have the same subnet mask, 255.255.255.0.

Figure 5.6 Local and Remote Example

Computer 1

IP Address:
192.168.34.56

Subnet Mask:
255.255.255.0

Computer 2

IP Address:
192.168.34.250

Subnet Mask:
255.255.255.0

Computer1 wants to send a message to Computer2 but must first determine whether Computer2 is local or remote. Computer1 matches Computer2's subnet mask and IP address. The subnet mask indicates that the first three octets of the IP address define the network ID (the first three octets of the subnet mask are 255.255.255), and only the last octet defines the host ID. Computer1 now knows that Computer2 is on the subnet with a network ID of 192.168.34. Computer1 analyzes its IP address and subnet mask and sees it is also on a subnet with a network ID of 192.168.34. Since computers are on the same subnet, Computer2 is a local host (Figure 5.7).

Figure 5.7 Comparing Subnet Masks

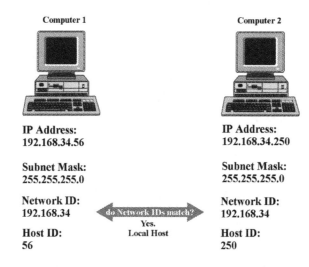

Again, this process is similar to postal addresses. Suppose you want to send a package to a company. If the company is in the same city, you use a local delivery agency. If the company is outside of your city, you must use a different agency. Naturally, your first concern is determining whether the company is in the same city. You compare their city address to your city address. If the city names match, you are in the same city. Of course, we don't need to think about where we live, but computers must constantly make this comparison.

As a second example, suppose a user on Computer1 needs to send information to the user on Computer2. Both computers use the same subnet mask (255.255.0.0). Computer1 has an IP address of 10.10.23.77 and Computer2 has an IP address of 10.11.23.77. Using the subnet mask, Computer1 determines the network ID for Computer2 is 10.11 (The network ID uses only the first two octets). Computer1 then calculates its network ID as 10.10. In this case, the two computers have different network IDs and are on different subnets. Since computers are on different subnets, Computer2 is a remote host.

 Note: When determining subnets, it is irrelevant whether two computers have the same host IDs. The network ID is of primary importance when identifying subnets.

Table 5.10 lists other examples of subnet determination. For practice, cover the right-hand column with a piece of paper, and see if you can determine whether the destination host is local or remote with respect to the sending computer.

Table 5.10 Subnet Determination

Source IP Address	Destination IP Address	Subnet Mask	Local or Remote
12.34.56.78	123.45.6.78	255.0.0.0	Remote (The network IDs are 12 and 123.)
200.32.195.5	200.32.195.6	255.255.0.0	Local (The network ID is 200.32 for both.)
200.32.195.5	200.32.195.6	255.0.0.0	Local (The network ID is 200 for both.)
192.168.55.5	192.167.5.5	255.255.0.0	Remote (Network IDs are 192.168 and 192.167.)
99.2.1.14	99.2.2.14	255.255.255.0	Remote (The network IDs are 99.2.1 and 99.2.2.)
99.2.1.14	99.2.2.14	255.255.0.0	Local (The network ID is 99.2 for both.)

IP Classes

IP addresses categorize into five address classes. InterNIC was responsible for forming these classes during the process of assigning IP addresses to requesting companies. Although the classes are no longer in use, the terminology remains, and it is not uncommon to see test questions that include the term IP classes.

Using Default IP Classes

There are five default IP classes from A through E. IP addresses are classified according to the value of the first octet. If you write an IP address in the form w.x.y.z, where w, x, y, and z are octets, classes are based on the value of w Table 5.11).

Table 5.11 IP Classes

IP Address Class	Valid Range for w	Examples
A	1 to 126	22.45.200.1 and 126.2.1.1
B	128 to 191	129.192.55.3 and 160.2.34.88
C	192 to 223	192.168.1.1 and 220.5.3.72
D*	224 to 239	Not used for host assignment
E*	240 to 254	Not used for host assignment

Note: Only Classes A, B, and C addresses are used to assign IP addresses to hosts. Class D and E addresses are reserved for special TCP/IP functions, like multicast transmissions.

Default Subnet Masks

Each IP address class has a default subnet mask (Table 5.12). The default subnet mask determines the number of networks and hosts each class supports. Remember that subnet masks separate the host ID and network ID in an IP address.

Table 5.12 Default Subnet Masks

Class	Default Subnet Mask
A	255.0.0.0
B	255.255.0.0
C	255.255.255.0

The following are the characteristics of address classes that use the default subnet masks:

Class A—There are only 126 Class A network IDs available, and each network can have up to 16,777,214 hosts.

Class B—There are 16,384 Class B networks IDs available, and each network can have a maximum of 65,534 hosts.

Class C—There are over 2 million Class C network IDs (2,097,152). Each Class C network can have a maximum of 254 hosts.

Classless Inter-Domain Routing (CIDR)

Categorizing IP addresses into classes has been an inefficient and ineffective use of the remaining available IP addresses. If this system had been continued, all IP addresses would have been depleted. At the present time, millions of addresses in Classes A and B are not being used. For example, a very large company that purchased the Class A address 24.x.x.x has the right to use all 16+ million IP addresses that begin with 24. However, very few, if any, companies have more than 16 million computers in their entire organization. Consequently, many companies holding excess Class A addresses are selling or renting some of these unused addresses.

A newer addressing scheme called Classless Inter-Domain Routing (CIDR) splits IP addresses at the bit level rather than the byte level. Previously, IP addresses classes were divided between octets; now addresses are divided within an octet. Splitting an address at the bit level requires using more complicated subnet masks. The subnet masks used with traditional classes (with values of 0 and 255) only work when an entire octet (or octets) defines the network ID. If you are using part of an octet to define a network ID, you must use a subnet mask that masks only part of the octet.

Creating Binary Subnet Masks

Table 5.13 shows the three subnet masks, written in octet and binary form, used with IP address classes.

Table 5.13 Decimal and Binary Subnet Masks

Decimal Subnet Mask	Binary Subnet Mask		
255.0.0.0	11111111	00000000.00000000.00000000	
	Network ID	Host ID	
255.255.0.0	11111111.11111111	00000000.00000000	
	Network ID	Host ID	
255.255.255.0	11111111.11111111.11111111	00000000	
	Network ID	Host ID	

You already know that a subnet mask works so that the octets with maximum values (the 255s) represent the network ID, and the octets with minimum values (the 0s) represent the host ID. Table 5.13, shows you how the network ID is determined by the location of the 1s in the subnet mask, and the host ID begins where the 0s begin in the subnet mask.

Table 5.13 also shows why subnet masks are either 255 or 0. If you convert the binary number 11111111 to decimal, you get (128+64+32+16+8+4+2+1 = 255). Of course, converting the binary number 00000000 to decimal yields 0.

All subnet masks up to this point in the lesson have used 8, 16, or 32 bits   (1, 2, or 3 octets). But suppose you want to define your subnet using 18 bits of data. This allows you to use the remaining 14 bits for host IDs. You write the subnet mask in binary that looks like this:

11111111.11111111.11000000.00000000

You can now convert each of the octets to decimal to form the following subnet mask:

255.255.192.0

Using this method, you can create your own subnet masks that fit the needs of your network more closely than the standard IP addresses classes. Table 5.14 lists several examples of classless subnet masks. For practice, cover the right-hand column and calculate the decimal value for each binary subnet mask.

Table 5.14 Classless Subnet Masks

Binary Subnet Mask	Decimal Conversion
11111100.00000000.00000000.00000000	252.0.0.0
11111111.11111000.00000000.00000000	255.248.0.0
11111111.11111111.11111110.00000000	255.255.254.0
11111111.10000000.00000000.00000000	255.128.0.0

Table 5.15 provides a good cross-reference that allows you to quickly convert a partially used octet to its decimal value, and vice versa. All allowable subnet mask values are included in this table. For example, 255.255.200.0 and 255.125.0.0 are not valid subnet masks.

Table 5.15 Binary-to-Decimal Reference

Binary	Decimal
11111111	255
11111110	254
11111100	252
11111000	248
11110000	240
11100000	224
11000000	192
10000000	128
00000000	0

CIDR Notation

Using the new subnet masks, you can write an IP address with the subnet mask in a shorthand method called CIDR notation. CIDR notation uses the IP address appended with the number of bits used for the network ID.

For example, suppose you use the IP address 192.168.5.25, and you use a subnet mask of 255.255.240.0. The subnet mask uses exactly 20 bits for the network ID (255 uses 8, 255 uses another 8, and 240 uses 4; refer to Table 5.15). Using CIDR notation, this IP address is written as 192.168.5.25/20. The IP address 14.32.200.1 with a subnet mask of 255.128.0.0 is written as 14.32.200.1/9 (the subnet mask uses 9 bits).

Determining Local and Remote Hosts with CIDR

The process of determining local and remote hosts using CIDR is similar to the process already described. The theory remains the same: you use the subnet mask to determine the network ID for both computers, and then see if both computers are on the same subnet. In the case of CIDR, determining the network ID is a bit more complicated. Figures 5.8 and 5.9 provide two different examples of how to determine whether computers are local or remote with respect to one computer.

Figure 5.8 Local/Remote Host Determination: Example 1

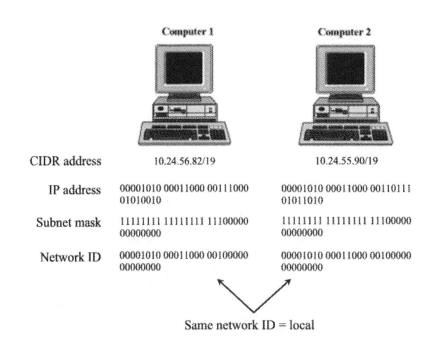

	Computer 1	Computer 2
CIDR address	10.24.56.82/19	10.24.55.90/19
IP address	00001010 00011000 00111000 01010010	00001010 00011000 00110111 01011010
Subnet mask	11111111 11111111 11100000 00000000	11111111 11111111 11100000 00000000
Network ID	00001010 00011000 00100000 00000000	00001010 00011000 00100000 00000000

Same network ID = local

Figure 5.9 Local/Remote Host Determination: Example 2

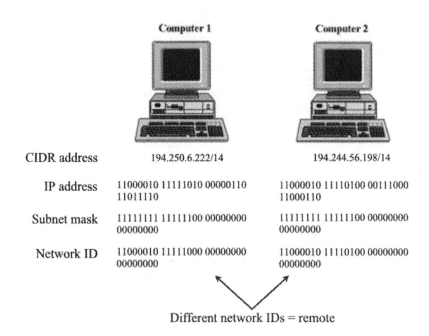

	Computer 1	Computer 2
CIDR address	194.250.6.222/14	194.244.56.198/14
IP address	11000010 11111010 00000110 11011110	11000010 11110100 00111000 11000110
Subnet mask	11111111 11111100 00000000 00000000	11111111 11111100 00000000 00000000
Network ID	11000010 11111000 00000000 00000000	11000010 11110100 00000000 00000000

Different network IDs = remote

Vocabulary

Review the following terms in preparation for the certification exam.

Term	Description
binary	A numbering system that only uses 1s and 0s to represent all numbers. It is also known as Base 2 because all the numbers are powers of 2.
bit	A single binary digit, represented by either 1 or 0.
broadcast	A broadcast transmission simultaneously sends data to all computers on the network segment.
byte	Eight bits equal a byte.
CIDR	Classless Inter-Domain Routing is a new addressing scheme in which IP addresses split at bit level, not byte level, and classes divide within an octet.
CIDR notation	A Classless Inter-Domain Routing notation is a shorthand method for writing the IP address with a subnet mask. The number of bits used for the network ID appends the IP address.
decimal notation	The numbering system, also known as Base 10, that uses the digits 0–9 to represent values.
default gateway	A Microsoft term given to Windows devices such as multihomed computers or routers because data passes through them to and from a subnet. However, routers are not actually gateways since they connect two of the same network types.

Term	Description
default subnet mask	Determines the number of networks and hosts each IP class supports. Subnet masks separate the host ID and the network ID in an IP address.
gateway	Network devices that connect two different network types.
host	Any object (computer, printer, and so forth) on a TCP/IP network.
InterNIC	A collaboration among AT&T, Network Solutions, Inc. (NSI), and the National Science Foundation that ensures no two computers have the same IP address assignment.
IP	The Internet Protocol is one part of the TCP/IP protocol suite responsible for addressing and routing TCP/IP packets to individual computers.
IP	Five categories, A-E, of IP addresses were once assigned to requesting companies by InterNIC. Categories are classified by the value of the first octet.
IP address	A 32-bit number that identifies hosts (objects) on a TCP/IP network, in the form of aaa.bbb.ccc.ddd, Every host has a unique IP address, and for every IP address there is a subnet mask.
IPv4	The current version of the TCP/IP protocol is also known as IP Version 4. IPv4 and the next-generation protocol, IPv6, will be used concurrently for several years.
IPv6	The next generation of the TCP/IP protocol after Ipv4, known as IP Version 6, is in draft review and will operate concurrently with IPv4 for several years.
ISP	An Internet Service Provider is a company that provides IP addresses and Internet access to users.

Term	Description
multicast transmissions	Multicast transmissions simultaneously send one copy of data to multiple requesting computers, and use Class D and E addresses.
multihomed	A computer with more than one NIC resides, or is at home, on more than one subnet is considered multihomed.
NIC	The Network Interface Card, also called network adapter, is a hardware device inside a computer that allows a computer to access a network, and is manufactured with a MAC address.
octets	Each number in an IP address is called an octet because it represents exactly 8 bits of data.
OSI	The Open Systems Interconnection network model is a seven-layer model that provides a foundation for all network communication. Each layer is responsible for and addresses one part of network communication.
packet	Data divided into smaller pieces sent across a TCP/IP network.
router	Devices that segment and connect a network and pass on data transmissions with destination addresses.
segment	One section of a TCP/IP network separated from other segments by a router.
subnet mask	A 32-bit number that specifies the segment (subnet) where a host resides, and separates the host ID and the network ID in an IP address.
subnets	A method of reducing traffic on a small network is to break it into smaller segments (subnets) that connect to each other through a router.
TCP/IP	Transmission Control Protocol/Internet Protocol is the routable protocol of the Internet and many smaller networks.

In Brief

If you want to...	Then do this...
Reduce traffic on a larger network to increase network efficiency	Use routers to break the network into smaller segments or subnets.
Understand IP addressing and subnet masks in TCP/IP networks	First learn about the binary numbering system that uses 1s and 0s to represent all numbers.
Convert binary numbers to decimal numbers and decimal to binary when working with TCP/IP networks	Use the Windows 2000 Calculator program to convert binary numbers to decimal numbers, and vice versa.
Distinguish the network ID and host ID in an IP address	Compare the subnet mask and the IP address of the destination computer. In the subnet mask, the maximum values (255) mark the position of the network ID, and the minimum values (0s) mark the host ID.
Determine the number of possible hosts on a network	Determine the number of bits used for the host ID and then calculate the number of hosts represented by those bits (e.g., 2^8)
Determine the number of networks supported by each IP address class	Look at the default subnet mask scheme for Classes A, B, and C.
Use a more efficient addressing scheme that fits the needs of your network more closely than the standard IP addresses classes	Use the CIDR addressing scheme, which splits IP address at the bit level, not the byte level; use a subnet mask for only part of the octet.
Write the CIDR IP address with a subnet mask in a shortened version	Write the IP address with the number of bits used for the network ID appended (with a slash) to the IP address. For example, the IP address 14.32.200.1 with a subnet mask of 255.128.0.0 is written as 14.32.200.1/9 (the subnet mask uses 9 bits).

Lesson 5 Activities

Complete the following activities to better prepare you for the certification exam.

1. Draw a conversion table and convert the binary number 11101010 to a decimal value, and explain the steps to convert the binary number 11101010 to a decimal value.

2. Draw a conversion table and convert the decimal number 125 to binary, and explain the steps to convert the decimal number 125 to binary.

3. Describe how to start the Windows Calculator program, and list the steps to convert a binary number to a decimal number.

4. Explain why it is important to change 32-bit-long IP addresses to a more usable format.

5. Give the main reason for creating subnets, and explain two methods for data transmission among subnets.

6. Give two basic rules that apply to subnet masks.

7. Explain how a computer determines whether or not a host is local or remote, and use examples.

8. Name the five IP address classes and give the value range of their first octet.

9. Give three subnet masks used with IP address classes, written in octet form and binary form.

10. Explain CIDR notation and show an example CIDR notation for the IP address 14.32.200.1, with a subnet mask of 255.128.0.0 (Refer to Table 5.15.).

Answers to Lesson 5 Activities

1.

bit	1	1	1	0	1	0	1	0	
Decimal	128	64	32	16	8	4	2	1	Sum
Value	128	64	32	0	8	0	2	0	234

To determine the value of a byte, you add up the decimal values for each on bit (a bit represented by a 1, as opposed to an off bit, which is represented by a 0).

For example, the binary number 11101010 has an on bit in the second, fourth, sixth, seventh, and eight positions (in binary you count from right to left). Begin by placing these values in a conversion table.

For every on bit, carry the decimal value of that bit position down to the third row. For every off bit (0), write a 0 in the third row. The third row will always have a 0 or the number from the second row. Finally, add up all of the values in the third row (128+64+32+8+2) to determine the decimal value of the binary number. In this example, the binary number 11101010 equals 234.

2.

Decimal Value	Binary Digit	Binary Value
125	128	0
125	64	1
61	32	1
29	16	1
13	8	1
5	4	1
1	2	0
1	1	1

To convert the decimal number 125 to binary, use the table above.

Begin by entering the decimal value in the first column, first row. If you can subtract 128 from the decimal value (and keep a positive remainder), place a 1 in the binary value column, and write the remainder in the second row of the first column. Continue this same process down through the column until you have reached the bottom. If you did it correctly, you will always end up with no remainder, and the third column will have the binary number.

Using this conversion method, you have determined that the decimal number 125 can be represented in binary as 01111101.

3. With the Windows 2000 Calculator program, you can convert binary numbers to decimal, and decimal to binary. To open Calculator, from the Start Menu, choose Programs, Accessories, and then select Calculator. By default, Calculator opens in Standard mode. To do binary conversion, you must use Scientific mode. From the menu bar, choose View, and then select Scientific.

    To convert from binary to decimal, follow these steps:

    1. Choose Bin.

    2. Enter the binary number.

    Calculator will not accept leading 0s. When you enter the binary number, begin with the first 1 on the left (for example, for the binary number `00100011`, enter `100011`).

    3. Choose Dec.

    The display changes to show the decimal equivalent.

4. IP addresses are 32 bits long, like this:

    `11000000101010000011100000000001`

    If all IP addresses are 32-bits long (and are soon to be 128 bits long), we as humans would have a great difficulty in remembering IP addresses, and the likelihood of typing in a wrong digit is greatly increased. For our sake, IP addresses are written in decimal format, with each group of 8 bits written as a number separated by a decimal point. For example, the IP address:

    `11000000101010000011100000000001`

    can be divided into four groups of 8 bits each like this:

    `11000000.10101000.00111000.00000001`

    and then written as:

    `192.168.56.1`

    The 32-bit IP address lies at the heart of TCP/IP data transmissions. Each host on the network must have a unique IP address.

5.   The goal of creating subnets is to reduce the amount of traffic crossing the routers.

When segmenting, you can purchase a router to connect each subnet, or you can add a second NIC to a computer and use that computer as a router. A computer with more than one NIC is said to be multihomed—it is at home on more than one subnet.

Whether you use a multihomed computer or a router on a Windows network, computers on the network see the device as the Default Gateway. Although the term makes sense—data must pass through this gateway (the router) to get to and from the subnet—it is easily confused with gateways, network devices that connect two different network types. Routers are not gateways, because they connect two of the same network type.

6.   Subnet masks are 32-bit numbers, and are used to distinguish the network ID and host ID in an IP address. Like an IP address, a subnet mask is written as four octets separated by decimal points.

The following rules apply to standard subnet masks:

- Each octet is either 0 or 255. In binary, this means that each octet contains either eight 1s or eight 0s.

- Once a 0 is used for one octet, the octets to the right must also be 0. For example, 255.255.255.0 and 255.0.0.0 are valid subnet masks, while 255.0.255.0 and 0.255.255.255 are not.

7.   Using the subnet mask to determine the network ID and host ID, a computer can determine whether another host is local or remote (a local host will have the same network ID, whereas a remote host will have a different network ID). If the destination computer is local, the message is sent directly to the destination. If the destination is remote, the message must be sent to the router, and the router must then forward the message to the appropriate subnet.

For example, suppose you have two computers, named Computer1 and Computer2. Computer1 has an IP address of 19.18.200.56 and Computer2 has an IP address of 19.18.200.250. Both computers have the same subnet mask, 255.255.255.0.

Computer1 wants to send a message to Computer2, so it must first determine whether Computer2 is local or remote. Computer1 matches Computer2's subnet mask and IP address. The subnet mask indicates that the first three octets of the IP address define the network ID (the first three octets of the subnet mask are 255.255.255), and only the last octet defines the host ID. Computer1 now knows that Comnputer2 is on the subnet with a network ID of 19.18.200. Computer1 analyzes its own IP address and subnet mask, and sees that it, too, is on a subnet with a network ID of 19.18.200. Both computers are on the same subnet, so Computer2 is a local host.

8.   The five IP address classes and the value range of their first octet are as follows:

IP Address Class
Valid Range

A
1 to 126

B
128 to 191

C
192 to 223

D
224 to 239

E
240 to 254

9. Class A addresses use the default subnet mask 255.0.0.0. Class B addresses use 255.255.0.0, and class C addresses use 255.255.255.0. In binary, these masks are written as follows:

    ```
    255.0.0.0              11111111.00000000.00000000.00000000


    255.255.0.0            11111111.11111111.00000000.00000000


    255.255.255.0          11111111.11111111.11111111.00000000
    ```

10. Using the new subnet masks, you can write an IP address with the subnet mask in a shorthand method called CIDR notation. CIDR notation uses the IP address, appended with the number of bits used for the network ID.

    For example, suppose you use the IP address 192.168.5.25, and you use a subnet mask of 255.255.240.0. The subnet mask uses exactly 20 bits for the network ID (255 uses 8, 255 uses another 8, and 240 uses 4). Using CIDR notation, this IP address is written as 192.168.5.25/20. The IP address 14.32.200.1 with a subnet mask of 255.128.0.0 is written as 14.32.200.1/9 (the subnet mask uses 9 bits).

Lesson 5 Quiz

These questions test your knowledge of features, vocabulary, procedures, and syntax.

1. Which of the following are reasons to segment a network?

   A. Increase overall performance of the network

   B. Reduce the amount of traffic received by a computer

   C. Complicate administration

   D. Block e-mail messages

2. Which of the following do computers use to determine whether the destination computer is local or remote?

   A. Subnet mask

   B. Cider

   C. IP address

   D. TCP/UDP

3. What is another name for the binary numbering system?

   A. 10Base2

   B. Base 10

   C. Base 2

   D. 2 Power

4. Which of the following bits in the binary number 11011010 are on?

   A. All

   B. Second, fourth, fifth, seventh, and eighth

   C. First, second, fourth, fifth, and seventh

   D. First, third, and sixth

5.   What is the decimal value of the binary number 11001010?

A. 253

B. 202

C. 125

D. 43

6.   Which of the following are used to segment a network?

A. Router

B. Gateway

C. Any computer

D. Computer with two NICs

7.   How many host IDs for each octet are valid to use?

A. 256

B. 0

C. 255

D. 254

8.   If the default subnet mask for a Class A IP address is 255.0.0.0, how many network IDs are available, and how many hosts can each network have?

A. 126 network IDs available, with up to 16,777,214 hosts

B. 16,384 network IDs available, with a maximum of 65,534 hosts

C. 2 million network IDs, with a maximum of 254 hosts

D. 1.2 million network IDs, with a maximum of 254 hosts

9. What is the name of a new classless addressing scheme that splits IP addresses at the bit level and not the byte level? (Choose all that apply.)

    A. CIRD

    B. InterNIC

    C. DIRC

    D. CIDR

10. Which is the correct decimal conversion for the classless subnet mask 11111111.11111111.11111110.00000000 ?

    A. 252.0.0.0

    B. 255.248.0.0

    C. 255.255.254.0

    D. 255.128.0.0

Answers to Lesson 5 Quiz

1. Answers A ad B are correct. Segmenting a network reduces the traffic received by each computer and increases the overall network performance.

    Answers C and D are incorrect. Network segmentation does not block e-mail messages, and it should never be your goal to complicate network administration.

2. Answers A and C are correct. Computers use subnet masks and IP addresses to determine whether the destination computer is local or remote.

    Answers B and D are incorrect. These are fictitious terms.

3. Answer C is correct. Base 2 is another name for the binary numbering system.

    Answer A is incorrect. 10Base2 is a thinnet cable type.

    Answer B is incorrect. Base 10 is the decimal system.

    Answer D is incorrect. 2 Power is fictitious.

4. Answer B is correct. The second, fourth, fifth, seventh, and eighth bits in the binary number 11011010 are on. Binary numbers are read from the right to the left, and the 1s indicate a positive or on state.

    Answer A is incorrect. 0s are not on, but off.

    Answer C is incorrect. The first, second, fourth, fifth, and seventh bits would be on, if binary numbers were read from left to right, but they are not.

    Answer D is incorrect. The first, third, and sixth bits are 0s, and therefore off.

5. Answer B is correct. The decimal value of the binary number 11001010 is 202.

    Answers A, C, and D are incorrect.

6. Answers A and D are correct. Routers and computers with two NICs can be used to divide a network into segments or subnets.

    Answer B is incorrect. A gateway connects two different network types.

    Answer C is incorrect. A computer must have at least two NICs to serve as a router.

7.   Answer D is correct. Although there are 256 possible combinations in an octet, the numbers 0 and 255 cannot be used for host IDs. Therefore there are only 254 valid host IDs for each octet.

Answers A, B, and C are incorrect.

8.   Answer A is correct. If the default subnet mask for a Class A IP address is 255.0.0.0, 126 network IDs are available, and each subnet can have up to 16,777,214 hosts.

Answer B is incorrect. The Class B default subnet mask is 255.255.0.0, and 16,384 network IDs are available, with a maximum of 65,534 hosts.

Answer C is incorrect. The Class C default subnet mask is 255.255.255.0, and 2 million network IDs are available, with a maximum of 254 hosts.

Answer D is incorrect. 1.2 million network IDs, with a maximum of 254 hosts is fictitious.

9.   Answer D is correct. CIDR is the name of a new classless addressing scheme that splits IP addresses at the bit level and not the byte level. Where IP address classes are divided between octets, addresses are now divided within an octet.

Answers A, B, and C are incorrect. CIRD and DIRC are fictitious terms, and InterNIC is an Internet agency.

10. Answer C is correct. 255.255.254.0 is the correct decimal conversion for the classless subnet mask 11111111.11111111.11111110.00000000.

Answers A, B, and D are incorrect.

Lesson 6:
Planning and Implementing TCP/IP

The Transmission Control Protocol/Internet Protocol (TCP/IP) suite is the default protocol of Windows 2000 and is the sole protocol used on the Internet. It is relatively simple to implement, very scalable, flexible (it works on every size network), and is stable.

Central to the TCP/IP protocol suite is the Internet Protocol (IP). IP works at the Network Layer of the Open Systems Interconnection (OSI) model and is responsible for identifying every object (computers, printers, routers, and so forth) on the network and ensuring data is delivered properly among these objects.

Management of IP addresses is complicated. You must ensure each object has a unique IP address, and all objects share a common subnet mask. IP addresses and subnet masks are discussed fully in a separate lesson in this book. Thorough planning of a TCP/IP network before implementation reduces the need for future network administration.

This lesson addresses how to plan for, install and configure the TCP/IP protocol on computers running Windows 2000. The remainder of the lesson deals with automatic and manual assignment of IP addresses.

After completing this lesson, you should have a better understanding of the following topics:

*   IP Address Overview and Planning

*   TCP/IP Installation and Configuration

*   DHCP Installation and Configuration

*   TCP/IP Troubleshooting

IP Address Overview and Planning

One of the strengths of the TCP/IP protocol is its ability to work on any size network. If your network grows too large, and the increase of network traffic slows production, you can divide your network into smaller pieces called subnets. Subnets are divided by routers, computers that direct network traffic to its intended destination. TCP/IP is a routable protocol, which means that it works with routers on segmented networks.

The TCP/IP network protocol uses IP addresses to identify each computer (host) on the network. IP addresses are 32-bit numbers (32 1s and 0s), written as four octets separated by decimal points (for example, 192.168.200.1). The subnet mask is also a 32-bit number. The subnet mask is used to break the IP address into its two components, the network ID and host ID. The network ID identifies the subnet on which the host is connected, and the host ID identifies the host.

IP addresses are classified according to the value of the first octet. Table 6.1 lists the three common IP classes and their default subnet masks.

Table 6.1 Three Common IP Classes

Class	IP Range	Default Subnet Mask
A	1.x.y.z to 126.x.y.z	255.0.0.0
B	128.x.y.z to 191.x.y.z	255.255.0.0
C	192.x.y.z to 223.x.y.z	255.255.255.0

Using IP classes, the subnet mask only contains the values 0 and 255, and always includes one, two, or three whole octets. In other words, the subnet mask always uses 8, 16, or 24 bits to define the network ID. This makes inefficient use of IP addresses.

Many networks still use IP classes, but the Classless Inter-Domain Routing (CIDR) system is also available. With CIDR, the network ID is defined by only the bits you specify.

Planning the Network

The first step in implementing a TCP/IP-based network is network planning. When planning the network, consider the following guidelines:

Subnet mask—First determine the number of subnets you need on your network, and the number of hosts connected to each subnet. These variables determine what subnet mask to use.

Grouping—Place computers that frequently share information on the same subnet.

IP Reserved Addresses—Unless you have obtained IP addresses from InterNIC or an ISP, use one of the three reserved IP addresses for your intranet.

IP Classes—Although you can use CIDR notation, it may be simpler for both you and the users to adhere to one of the three common IP classes, depending on your network size.

Drawing the Network Layout

Before you configure any host on the network to use TCP/IP, draw out the network plan. The plan may be a simple sketch, or it may be complex enough to include every host. Some software programs (for example, Microsoft's Visio 2000) are specifically designed to aid developing network layout and design. Regardless of the level of detail or the software program you use, be sure to include every subnet and every server on each subnet in the layout design (Figure 6.1).

Tip: You and other network administrators will frequently have need to refer to the network layout drawings. Therefore, update them with each network change. The time that updating requires is miniscule compared to the benefits that result when a network problem or change arises.

Figure 6.1 Sample Network Layout

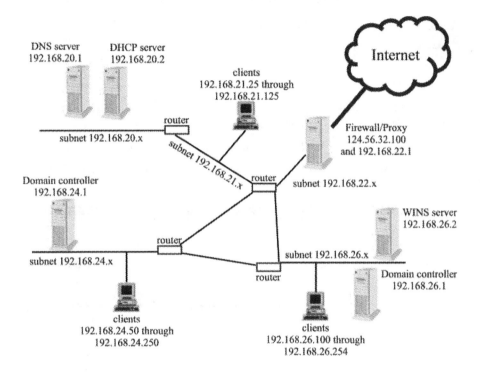

Following Addressing Guidelines

When you are ready to assign IP addresses to hosts, you must follow certain guidelines. TCP/IP has certain restrictions regarding the uses of IP addresses and subnet masks.

Subnet mask consistency—All computers on the same segment must use the same subnet mask.

Reserved IP addresses—One range of addresses for each IP address class is reserved for your Intranet use. These addresses are not valid IP addresses on the Internet, avoiding any conflicts. The allowable addresses ranges you can use for your network are as follows:

- Class A: 10.x.y.z (for example 10.200.131.4)

- Class B: 172.16.y.z to 172.31.y.z (for example 172.18.5.25)

- Class C: 192.168.0.z to 192.168.255.z (for example 192.168.33.1)

Special IP Addresses—Certain addresses are reserved for specific use and cannot be assigned to hosts. Follow these rules to avoid these special addresses:

- The Network ID cannot be 127. If your subnet mask is 255.0.0.0, do not begin an IP address with 127.x.y.z. Likewise, if your subnet mask is 255.255.0.0, you cannot use 127.0.x.y

Note: A Network ID of 127 is called the loopback address that is used to test a Network Interface Card (NIC).

- The host ID cannot be all 0s

- The Host ID cannot end in 255. Addresses that end in 255 are exclusively reserved for broadcast messages (data that simultaneously transmits to all computers on the subnet)

- The host ID must be unique on the subnet

Using Automatic IP Assignment

Every host on a network must have a unique IP address. No matter how well you plan and map your network, IP address assignment can become difficult, especially on larger networks. Windows 2000 includes two utilities to ease the administrative burden of IP address assignment—Dynamic Host Configuration Protocol (DHCP) and Automatic Private IP Addressing (APIPA).

Dynamic Host Configuration Protocol (DHCP)

DHCP is a service that runs on Windows 2000 servers. You configure a DHCP server to assign IP addresses, subnet masks, and other TCP/IP configuration information to other hosts on the network. Computers that receive the information are called clients. During the boot process, a DHCP client sends out a broadcast message over the network requesting an IP address from a DHCP server. If a DHCP server receives the broadcast message, it sends back the TCP/IP configuration information to the client, and the client can then participate in network activity.

Automatic Private IP Addressing (APIPA)

Windows 2000 supports a system that allows a client computer to assign itself an IP address when a DHCP server is unavailable. This system is called Automatic Private IP Addressing (APIPA). The IP address that a client issues to itself always writes in the format 169.254.x.y, where x and y are values between 0 and 254. The subnet mask is set to 255.255.0.0. APIPA allows you to run a Windows 2000-based network with automatic assignment of IP addresses and without a DHCP server. After the client computer assigns itself an address, it sends out a broadcast to make sure no other computers on the network have the same IP address. The client computer uses this address until a DHCP server provides updated IP information.

 Note: The range of IP addresses from 169.254.0.1 through 169.254.255.254 is reserved; any IP address that falls within this range cannot be used on the Internet.

The APIPA feature enables by default and is disabled only through editing the Registry. Instructions on disabling APIPA are found in the Windows 2000 Help file.

TCP/IP Installation and Configuration

TCP/IP installs automatically when you install Windows 2000. However, you may need to reinstall the TCP/IP protocol if it has been uninstalled. Once installed, you configure a TCP/IP host by assigning an IP address, subnet mask, default gateway, and other optional settings.

Installing TCP/IP in Windows 2000

To install TCP/IP on a Windows 2000 computer, follow these steps:

1. From the Desktop, right-click My Network Places and choose Properties.

2. From the Network and Dial-up Connections window, right-click Local Area Connection and choose Properties.

   The Local Area Connection Properties window opens (Figure 6.2).

Figure 6.2 Local Area Connection Properties

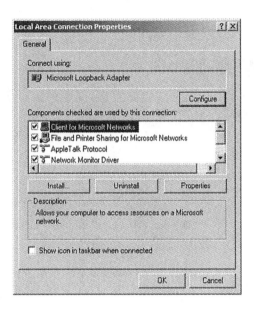

3. To add TCP/IP, choose Install.

4. From the Choose Network Component Type window, select Protocol, and then select Add.

   From the list of protocols, choose Internet Protocol (TCP/IP), and then select OK (Figure 6.3).

   Internet Protocol (TCP/IP) appears in the list of network components.

Figure 6.3 Protocol Selection

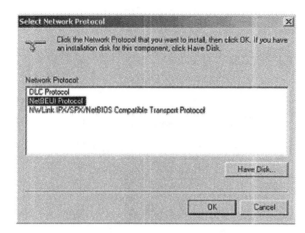

5.   Choose Close to save the changes and close the Local Area Connection Properties window.

Tip: From the Local Area Connection Properties window, you add, remove, and configure all of the network components.

Configuring TCP/IP

You configure TCP/IP on each host to match your network plan. The following are two ways to configure a TCP/IP workstation:

Static configuration—You type in an IP address, subnet mask, and other TCP/IP settings that do
not change.

Automatic configuration—The host looks for a DHCP server on the network. If a DHCP server is available, the DHCP server provides all of the TCP/IP configuration information for the workstation. The host is called a DHCP client.

The steps for configuring TCP/IP on a Windows 2000 server are the same as those for configuring the protocol on a workstation. However, follow certain unique guidelines when configuring TCP/IP on a server.

Static Configuration of TCP/IP on a Client

To manually configure TCP/IP on a Windows 2000 computer, follow these steps:

1.   From the desktop, right-click My Network Places and choose Properties.

2.   From the Network and Dial-up Connections window, right-click Local Area Connection, and then choose Properties.

3.   From the list of installed components, double-click Internet Protocol (TCP/IP).

     The Internet Protocol (TCP/IP) Properties window displays (Figure 6.4).

Figure 6.4 Internet Protocol (TCP/IP) Properties

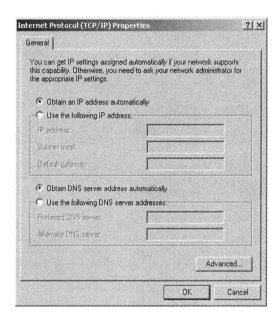

4. To manually assign IP information, choose Use the following IP address.

5. Type the IP address, subnet mask, and default gateway values (Figure 6.5). The default gateway is the IP address of the router through which remote messages travel.

Figure 6.5 IP Configuration

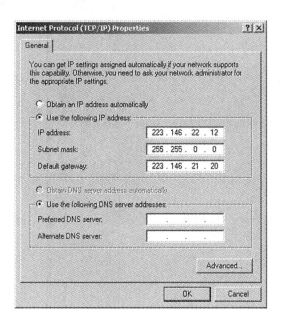

 Note: The default gateway must be on the same subnet as the host. Both addresses must have the same network ID.

6. Optionally, type the IP address for the primary and secondary Domain Name System (DNS) servers. DNS provides conversion from host names to IP addresses.

7. Choose OK to save your changes, and then select OK to close the Local Area Connection Properties window.

Creating a DHCP Client

By default, every new Windows 2000 host configures as a DHCP client. If you have a Windows 2000 that is configured statically and you wish to make it a DHCP client, follow these steps:

1. From the desktop, right-click My Network Places and choose Properties.

2. From the Network and Dial-up Connections window, right-click Local Area Connection, and then choose Properties.

3. From the list of installed components, double-click Internet Protocol (TCP/IP).

4. Choose Obtain an IP address automatically.

5. If you have configured a DHCP server to issue DNS information, choose Obtain DNS server address automatically.

6. Choose OK to save your changes, and then select OK to close the Local Area Connection Properties window.

Configuring TCP/IP on a Server

You configure TCP/IP on a server exactly as you do on a client (through the Local Area Connection Properties window). However, follow these guidelines when configuring TCP/IP on a network server:

- Make sure every DHCP server has a static IP address

- Make sure every DNS server has a static IP address

- Generally assign static IP addresses to all servers so that resources are always found at the same address

- Make sure Routers (and servers that act as routers) use the lowest host IDs on the subnet. On a subnet with a network ID of 192.168.5, assign the routers 192.168.5.1, 192.168.192.2, 192, and so forth

- Assign servers similar addresses. You may reserve the address range 192.168.192.10 to 192.168.192.25 for your servers. This does not affect network performance, it makes troubleshooting and administration easier

Using IPCONFIG

You can view TCP/IP settings by opening the Local Connection Properties window (as described in the steps for configuring TCP/IP), or you can view detailed information from a command prompt using the **IPCONFIG.EXE** command. IPCONFIG (short for Windows 2000 IP Configuration) displays current TCP/IP settings that administer a DHCP client computer.

To run IPCONFIG, from the Start Menu, choose Programs, Accessories, and then select Command Prompt. From the Command Prompt, type **IPCONFIG** and then press **ENTER**.

Tip: Here's a faster way to access the Command Prompt: from the Start Menu, choose Run, type **CMD** and press **ENTER**. Or, if you have a keyboard with the Windows Key, simultaneously press the Windows Key and R to open the Run window, and then type **CMD** and press **ENTER**.

IPCONFIG displays some basic TCP/IP configuration information (Figure 6.6). The initial listing includes the following four items:

- Connection-specific DNS suffix (the common DNS domain name, if one is used).

- IP address

- Subnet mask

- Default gateway

Figure 6.6 IPCONFIG Display

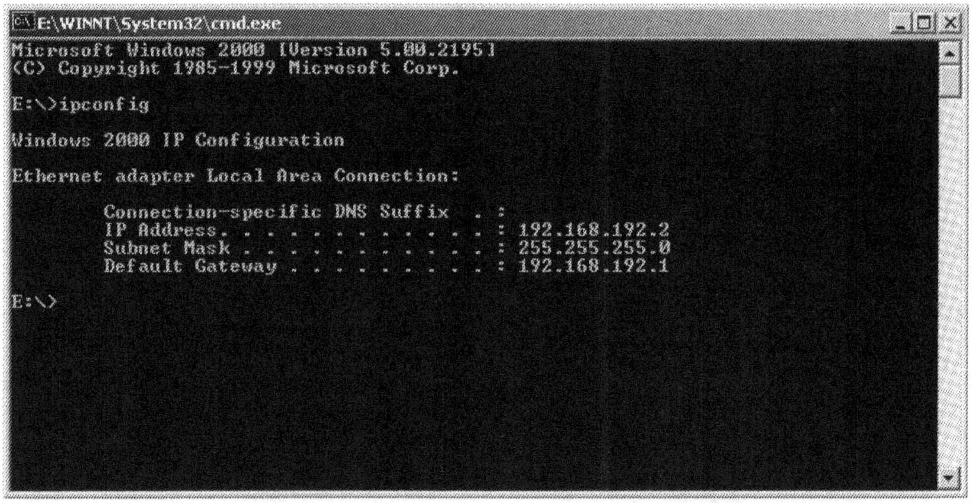

If the computer is a DHCP client, use IPCONFIG to ensure the computer is receiving an IP address and subnet mask.

To obtain more detailed information, type **IPCONFIG/ALL** and then press **ENTER**.

This displays all of the TCP/IP configuration information (Figure 6.7).

Figure 6.7 IPCONFIG/ALL Display

```
E:\WINNT\System32\cmd.exe                                    _ □ ×

E:\>ipconfig /all

Windows 2000 IP Configuration

        Host Name . . . . . . . . . . . : HERMIT
        Primary DNS Suffix  . . . . . . :
        Node Type . . . . . . . . . . . : Broadcast
        IP Routing Enabled. . . . . . . : No
        WINS Proxy Enabled. . . . . . . : No

Ethernet adapter Local Area Connection:

        Connection-specific DNS Suffix  . :
        Description . . . . . . . . . . : Intel EtherExpress PRO/100 Mobile PC
    Card 16 Adapter
        Physical Address. . . . . . . . : 00-A0-C9-7A-E2-1D
        DHCP Enabled. . . . . . . . . . : No
        IP Address. . . . . . . . . . . : 192.168.192.2
        Subnet Mask . . . . . . . . . . : 255.255.255.0
        Default Gateway . . . . . . . . : 192.168.192.1
        DNS Servers . . . . . . . . . . :

E:\>
```

Included in this listing are settings concerning DNS, Windows Internet Naming Service (WINS), and information about the NIC. NIC information includes the make and model of the card and the Media Access Control (MAC) address.

 Note: The MAC address is a permanent number assigned to every Ethernet network card. Ultimately, all TCP/IP communication uses MAC addresses to identify the source and destination computers. The Address Resolution Protocol (ARP) associates IP addresses with MAC addresses.

If you are running IPCONFIG on a DHCP client, you can force the client to release its IP address by running **IPCONFIG/RELEASE**. You can also force the client to release its IP address and then request a new one from a DHCP server by using the **IPCONFIG/RENEW** command.

Tip: IPCONFIG includes several other switches that are beyond the scope of this book. To learn more about IPCONFIG, from a command prompt type **IPCONFIG/?** and then press **ENTER**.

DHCP Installation and Configuration

DHCP is a service that assigns IP addresses to client computers when the computers become active on a network. In addition to assigning an IP address, you can configure DHCP to issue other TCP/IP-related settings, such as the default gateway (the default router on the subnet). The use of DHCP greatly simplifies network administration in TCP/IP-based networks. Without DHCP, you must manually assign an IP address to each host on the network, and keep track of which IP addresses have been used. Manual configuration can lead to accidentally assigning duplicate IP addresses in the network. A duplicate IP address causes conflicts on the network and prevents hosts with identical IP addresses from participating in network activity.

When you configure a DHCP server, you define a range of IP addresses the server gives out to requesting clients. You define this range (also called a scope) of addresses during your network planning. You are able to easily update and modify this if your network requires a change.

Installing a DHCP Server

It is possible to install DHCP on any computer running Windows 2000 Server. You can install DHCP during Windows 2000 Setup, or later using the Add/Remove Windows Components section of the Add/Remove Programs Control Panel. To install DHCP after installation of Windows 2000, follow these steps:

1.   From the Start Menu, choose Settings, and then select Control Panel.

2.   Double-click Add/Remove Programs.

3.   From the Add/Remove Programs window, choose Add/Remove Windows Components (Figure 6.8).

Figure 6.8 Add/Remove Programs

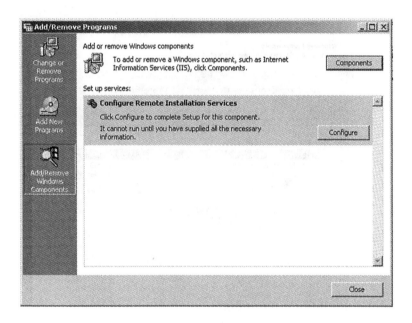

4. From the Windows Components Wizard window, choose Networking Services, and then click Details (Figure 6.9).

5. From the Networking Services window, in the Subcomponents of Networking Services list, choose the box next to Dynamic Host Configuration Protocol (DHCP), and then click OK (Figure 6.10).

Figure 6.9 Windows Components Window

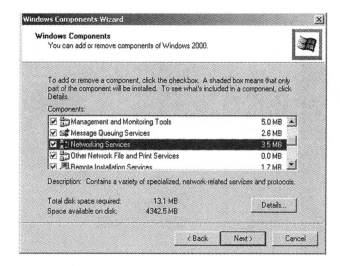

6. Click Next to begin the installation process.

7. When Windows 2000 is finished installing the software, click Finish.

8. Close the Add/Remove Programs Control Panel.

Figure 6.10 Networking Services Window

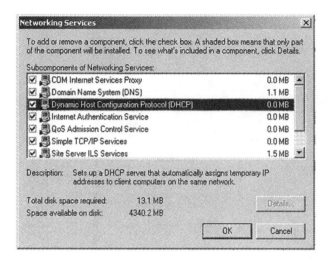

Installation of the DHCP service does not require a reboot of the server.

Creating a Scope

To configure a scope in DHCP, follow these steps:

1. From the Start menu, choose Programs, Administrative Tools, and then select DHCP.

 Note: Windows 2000 management tools are in the form of consoles and snap-ins that run within a common interface called the Microsoft Management Console (MMC). All consoles have similar interfaces, making it easier to learn new tools. Configuring a scope in DHCP requires you to open the DHCP Console.

---

2.   From the left pane of the DHCP console, choose the name of the server on which DHCP is installed. After a moment, the right pane will display help text (Figure 6.11).

Figure 6.11 DHCP Console

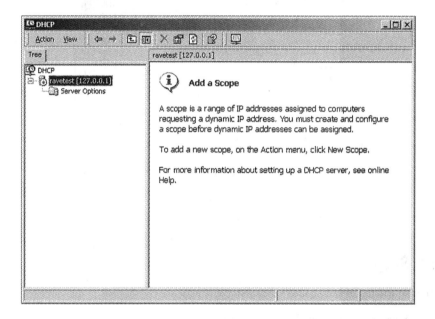

3.   From the left pane of the DHCP console, right-click the server, and then choose New Scope (Figure 6.12).

Figure 6.12 New DHCP Scope Creation

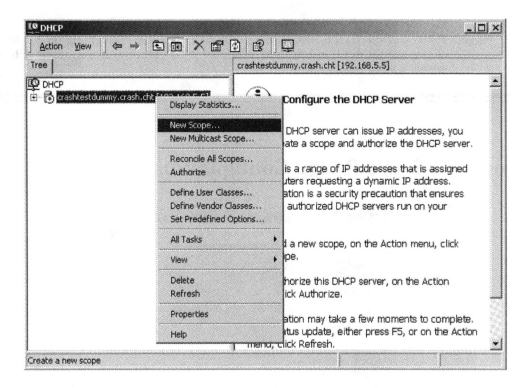

4. Click Next to begin the New Scope Wizard.

5. Enter a name and description for the scope, and then click Next.

6. Enter the Start and End IP addresses for the range of addresses in the scope, enter a subnet mask (or a length, in bits), and then click Next (Figure 6.13).

Note: When configuring the subnet mask, you can use CIDR notation. Enter the length
of the subnet mask in bits, and Windows 2000 automatically converts it to the
proper subnet mask.

Figure 6.13 Scope Range Configuration

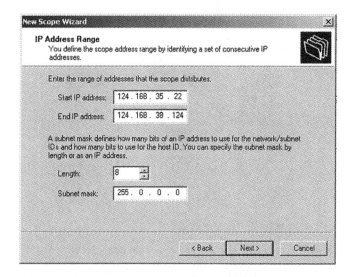

7.   To exclude any IP addresses from the range you created, enter the Start and End IP addresses
of the excluded range, click Add, and then click Next. For example, if you want to use some
of the addresses in the scope to statically assign to servers, include the range of addresses you
want to use (Figure 6.14).

Figure 6.14 Add Exclusions Window

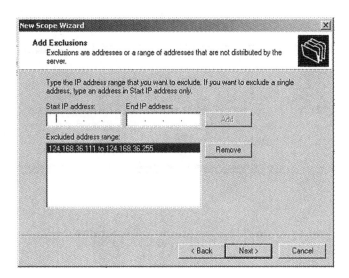

 Note: Lease duration defines the length of time a client keeps the same IP addresses before the address expires and the client has to again request an address. The default lease duration is eight days. However, every time a client boots, the system requests an IP address.

8. Enter the lease duration and then click Next.

9. To configure additional DHCP settings, click Yes, I want to configure these options now, and then click Next. If you do not wish to, click No, I will configure these options later, and then click Next.

10. If you chose to configure advanced settings, enter the IP address for the default gateway (router) DHCP clients will use, click Add, and then click Next.

11.   Enter the name of the parent domain for the clients, enter the IP address for the DNS servers the clients will use, click Add, and then click Next (Figure 6.15).

 Note: If you do not know the IP address for a DNS server, enter the server name and click Resolve. The DNS service resolves the IP address for you, and automatically puts it in the IP address box.

Figure 6.15 DNS Settings in the DHCP Scope

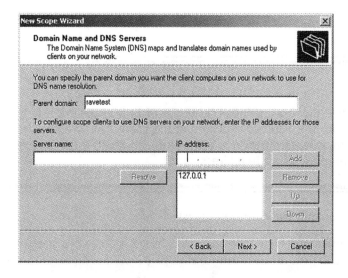

12.   Enter the name or IP address of any WINS servers on the network. If you enter the name, click Resolve to have DNS determine the IP address for you. Click Add, and then click Next.

13. To activate the scope immediately, click Yes, I want to activate the scope now, and then click Next. Otherwise, click No, I will activate this scope later, and then click Next.

14. Click Finish to save changes and close the wizard.

The DHCP scope is active, and each DHCP client on the network receives an IP address.

Creating a Superscope

From within DHCP, you can also create a superscope. A superscope is a collection of two or more scopes. For example, suppose your network consists of one physical subnet. You use three different IP address ranges (logically separating computers), to create three logical subnets on the same physical subnet. You are able to administer all three logical subnets on one DHCP server by creating a superscope.

To configure a superscope, follow these steps:

1. From the Start menu, choose Programs, Administrative Tools, and then select DHCP.

2. From the left pane of the DHCP console, right-click the server, and then choose New Superscope.

3. Click Next.

4. Enter a name for the superscope, and then click Next.

5. Choose one or more scopes from the list, and then click Next.

6. Click Finish.

Tip: You can choose more than one scope by pressing and holding down the Control key while selecting Scopes.

TCP/IP Troubleshooting

The utilities included with the TCP/IP protocol that test the network and diagnose TCP/IP problems include IPCONFIG, PING, NETSTAT, and TRACERT.

Testing the Local Computer

If only one computer on the network is unable to connect to other computers, the problem is almost certainly with that computer. Your job is to determine the problem. Begin by checking the physical connections for the computer.

Physical Problems

Make sure the network cable is still attached to the computer at one end and a hub at the other (or another computer, as the case may be) and that the cable is in good condition. Look for obvious breaks or sharp bends in the cable. If the physical connection looks good, begin testing the TCP/IP configuration.

Logical Problems

To test the TCP/IP connection, follow the steps outlined in Table 6.2. Following the steps in the given order narrows down the problem.

 Note: Many of the procedures outlined in Table 6.2 require you to run commands from a command prompt. Open a command prompt from the Start Menu, choose Programs, Accessories, and then select Command Prompt.

Table 6.2 TCP/IP Diagnosis

Procedure	Result	Remedy
From a command prompt, type **IPCONFIG**, and then press **ENTER**. Check the IP address, subnet mask, and default gateway.	The computer has the wrong IP address or subnet mask.	If the computer was configured manually, reconfigure TCP/IP with the correct IP address and subnet mask. If the computer is a DHCP client, make sure the DHCP scope is configured properly. If the address begins with 169.254.y.z, the computer cannot find the DHCP server. Make sure the DHCP server is online.
	The computer has no IP address or subnet mask (they appear as 0.0.0.0).	The computer is manually configured with the same IP address as another computer. Change the IP address to be unique on the network.
	No default gateway address is listed (in this case, the computer should be able to communicate with other computers on the subnet, but cannot get beyond the local subnet).	If the computer is manually configured, add the IP address for the default gateway. If the computer is a DHCP client, ensure that you entered a subnet mask in the DHCP scope.

Procedure	Result	Remedy
Use the PING command to contact the loopback address (type **PING 127.255.255.0**, and then press **ENTER**).	The loopback responds with four successful replies.	The NIC is OK.
	The loopback address fails to respond.	There is a problem with the NIC. Use the device Manager to verify that the proper drivers were used for the NIC and that there are no resource conflicts.
	The loopback address responds successfully, but not every time.	The NIC is faulty and should be replaced.
Use the PING command to contact the local computer IP address (for example, **PING 192.168.2.45**).	The computer returns four successful replies.	TCP/IP is configured properly on this computer.
	The computer fails to respond.	There is still a problem with the TCP/IP configuration. Re-run **IPCONFIG** and verify the settings.
Use the PING command to contact the default gateway IP address (the router).	The gateway returns four successful replies.	The connection to the gateway is good. The computer should not have any problem reaching any computer on the local subnet.
	The gateway fails to respond.	Check all physical connections. Ensure that other computers on the same subnet can ping the router. Make certain the router is operational.

Procedure	Result	Remedy
Use TRACERT to find the bad link. Type **TRACERT w.x.y.z**, where w.x.y.z is the IP address of a remote computer to which you cannot connect.	TRACERT reports every router through which the data passes, and lists the destination computer's IP address as the final hop.	The network is working properly, and this computer can access remote computers. The network problem is probably not related to TCP/IP.
	TRACERT reports one or more routers, and then reports Request timed out repeatedly.	The router last listed may be malfunctioning. Check it.

Tip: The Windows 2000 CD-ROM includes the **NETDIAG** utility in the \Support\Tools directory. **NETDIAG** simultaneously runs several of the TCP/IP diagnostics.

Vocabulary

Review the following terms in preparation for the certification exam.

Term	Description
APIPA	Automatic Private IP Addressing is a Windows 2000-supported system that allows client computers to self-assign an IP address if a DHCP server is unavailable.
ARP	Address Resolution Protocol associates IP addresses with MAC addresses.
broadcast messages	Data that simultaneously transmits to all computers on the subnet.
CIDR	Classless Inter-Domain Routing is a new addressing scheme in which IP addresses split at bit level, not byte level, and classes divide within an octet.
CIDR notation	A Classless Inter-Domain Routing notation is a shorthand method for writing the IP address with a subnet mask. The number of bits used for the network ID appends the IP address.
client	Any computer on a network that accesses resources on a server.
console	A module that is designed to work in the Windows 2000 MMC to provide a central location for management.

Term	Description
default gateway	A Microsoft term given to Windows devices such as multihomed computers or routers because data passes through them to and from a subnet. However, routers are not actually gateways since they connect two of the same network types.
default subnet mask	A number that contains the values 0 and 255 and includes one, two, or three octets that determines the number of networks and hosts each IP class supports. Subnet masks separate the host ID and the network ID in an IP address.
DHCP	Dynamic Host Configuration Protocol is a service that runs on Windows 2000 servers and automatically assigns IP addresses and other TCP/IP settings.
DNS	Domain Name System is a service that resolves IP addresses to hostnames, or hostnames to IP addresses.
host	Any object such as a computer or printer on a TCP/IP network.
host ID	The portion of an IP address that identifies the host.
InterNIC	A joint effort among AT&T, Network Solutions, Inc. (NSI), and the National Science Foundation to ensure no two computers have the same IP address assignment.
IP	The Internet Protocol is one part of the TCP/IP protocol suite that identifies every object on a network and ensures proper data delivery among all objects on the network.

Term	Description
IP address	An Internet Protocol address is a 32-bit number, written in four octets separated by decimal points, that identifies a computer on a TCP/IP-based network.
IP classes	Internet Protocol categories of IP addresses assigned to requesting companies, and classified by the value of the first octet in the address.
IPCONFIG	Internet Protocol Configuration is a Windows 2000 utility that displays TCP/IP settings and administers DHCP client computers.
ISP	An Internet Service Provider is a company that provides IP addresses and Internet access to users.
lease duration	The length of time a client keeps the same IP address before the address expires and the client must request an address again.
loopback address	A network ID of 127 that is used to test the NIC.
MAC address	Media Access Control addresses are permanent numbers assigned to Ethernet NICs for use with TCP/IP communication among source and destination computers.
MMC	Microsoft Management Console is a Windows 2000 tool that centralizes administrative tools, such as consoles and snap-ins that run within this common interface.
NetBIOS name	A name assigned to a computer on a NetBIOS-based network to identify it. Also called a WINS name.
NETSTAT	A utility that displays network statistics about the currently active TCP/IP connections.

Term	Description
network ID	The portion of an IP address that identifies the subnet on which the host is connected.
NIC	The Network Interface Card, also called network adapter, is a hardware device inside a computer that allows a computer to access a network, and is manufactured with a MAC address .
octet	Each number in an IP address that represents exactly 8 bits of data.
OSI	The Open Systems Interconnection network model is a seven-layer model that provides a foundation f or all network communication. Each layer is responsible for and addresses one part of network communication.
PING	A utility used to test the network to verify good connections, and diagnose TCP/IP problems.
routable protocol	Protocols that work with routers on segmented networks, such as TCP/IP.
routers	Computers or devices that direct network traffic to its destination.
scope	In Windows 2000, a range of IP address numbers from which the DHCP server assigns IP addresses to clients.
server	Any computer that shares resources over the network.
snap-ins	Modules that run within the MMC, each snap-in handles a different aspect of Windows 2000 management.

Term	Description
subnet mask	A 32-bit number that specifies the location of the local or remote segment (or subnet) on which a host is located. It separates the host ID and the network ID in an IP address.
subnets	Network segments that are divided by routers.
superscope	A DHCP scope that contains a collection o f two or more scopes used to create logical subnets on the same physical subnet.
TCP/IP	Transmission Control Protocol/Internet Protocol is the default protocol suite of Windows 2000 and is the sole routable protocol of the Internet.
TRACERT	A TCP/IP diagnostic utility that traces data and reports the routers that data passes through to reach a destination computer.
WINS	Windows Internet Naming Service tracks NetBIOS names on a network.

In Brief

If you want to...	Then do this...
Reduce future network administration	Thoroughly plan the implementation and management of your network, make a drawing of the network and update it when necessary.
Make your network traffic flow more efficiently	Segment your network into smaller pieces called subnets using routers and the TCP/IP protocol.
Subnet your network and assign IP addresses	First determine the number of subnets you need, group computers by shared information, and then assign IP addresses and subnet masks.
Automatically assign IP addresses to Windows 2000 computers	Install and configure the DHCP service on a server, or use APIPA.
Test and diagnose problems on the network	Use the IPCONFIG, PING, NETSTAT, AND TRACERT tools included with the TCP/IP protocol to troubleshoot physical and logical network problems.

Lesson 6 Activities

Complete the following activities to better prepare you for the certification exam.

1. Explain why it is important to understand IP addressing in the TCP/IP network, and the differences between IP classes and the CIDR system.

2. List and explain the three restrictions on how to use IP addresses and subnet masks.

3. Name two Windows 2000 utilities that automatically assign IP addresses and discuss some differences.

4. Discuss two types of TCP/IP configurations for a client workstation.

5. Explain why you would configure a DHCP client and how to do it.

6. Give some methods for viewing current TCP/IP settings.

7. Explain how to configure a subnet mask with CIDR notation in Windows 2000.

8. Discuss the best way to administer three different IP ranges on one subnet.

9. Discuss the sequence of steps to take when troubleshooting physical problems on your network.

10. Describe the diagnostic utility and procedure to use to check the connection of a NIC on your network.

Answers to Lesson 6 Activities

1. IP addressing is the heart of TCP/IP data transmissions. Each host on the network must have a unique IP address to which TCP/IP sends and receives data transmissions. In addition to individual addresses for each host, networks are logically divided into subnets using subnet masks-special numbers that break an IP address into the network ID and the host ID. All objects on a subnet must share a common subnet mask. It is important to understand how IP addresses and subnet masks are formulated, created, and used, so you can properly configure servers, hosts and subnets with addresses that will efficiently operate with TCP/IP.

    The IP addressing classes provide a numbering scheme for 32-bit IP addresses and their corresponding 32-bit subnet masks. TCP/IP uses the IP Class subnet masks for routing information among networks. The CIDR system defines the network ID by only the bits you specify.

2. Three restrictions on how to use IP addresses and subnet masks are:

    1) You must use the same subnet mask for all computers on a subnet.

    2) For internal IP addresses, you must use one of the reserved address ranges to avoid conflicts with Internet IP addresses. The reserved addresses are as follows:

    Class A: 10.x.y.z (for example 10.200.131.4)

    Class B: 172.16.y.z to 172.31.y.z (for example 172.18.5.25)

    Class C: 192.168.0.z to 192.168.255.z (for example 192.168.33.1)

    3) You must not assign certain special addresses that are used for specific purposes to hosts. Follow these rules to avoid the special addresses:

    *   Do not use 127 for the network ID

    *   Do not use all zeros for the host ID

    *   Do not end the host ID in 255. Addresses that end in 255 are exclusively for broadcast messages

    *   Do not use the host ID more than once on the same subnet. The host ID must be unique on the subnet

3. Two Windows 2000 utilities that automatically assign IP addresses are the Dynamic Host Configuration Protocol (DHCP), and Automatic Private IP Addressing (APIPA). Broadcast

messages are sent out during DHCP client boot process. The DHCP server receives the client request for an IP address, and sends the DHCP client TCP/IP configuration information, including IP address. The client can then participate in network activity. The APIPA client assigns itself an IP address with no aid from a DHCP server. Unless a DHCP server sends updated IP information to an APIPA client, the APIPA client continues to the self-assigned IP address.

4.   Two types of TCP/IP configurations for a client workstation are the static configuration and the automatic configuration.

You manually enter the IP address, subnet mask, and other TCP/IP information into the system. The settings never change unless you manually change them.

The automatic configuration for a client workstation begins when the DHCP client looks for a DHCP server on the network. If the DHCP server detects the client, it provides all of the TCP/IP configuration information. If no DHCP server is found, the client uses APIPA to assign itself an address.

5.   Because Windows 2000 configures a DHCP client by default, you may never need to configure a DHCP client. However, if a DHCP client has been statically configured, you may want to change it back to the automatic DHCP client configuration.

To change a DHCP static configuration of a client back to automatic, from the desktop, right-click My Network Places and choose Properties. Then right-click Local Area Connection and choose Properties. From the list of installed components, open the Internet Protocol (TCP/IP).

Choose Obtain an IP address automatically. If you have configured a DHCP server to issue DNS information, select Obtain DNS server address automatically. Choose OK to save your changes, and then click OK to close the Local Area Connection Properties window.

6.   There are several methods for viewing TCP/IP settings. From My Network Places, Properties, choose the Network and Dial-up Connection window. To see the TCP/IP settings, open the Local Connections Properties window.

Another method to view TCP/IP current settings is to run the **IPCONFIG.EXE** command. There are three ways to run this command. To use the more conventional method, from the Start Menu, choose Programs, Accessories, and then choose Command Prompt. From the Command Prompt, type **IPCONFIG** and press **ENTER**. A second and faster way to run the **IPCONFIG** command is to access the Command Prompt from the Start Menu, choose Run, type **IPCON-FIG**, and press **ENTER**. The third, and fastest way, to run **IPCONFIG** is to press the

Windows Key on your keyboard simultaneously with the R key to open the Run Window, and type IPCONFIG and press **ENTER**.

To view more in-depth details of the TCP/IP configurations on DHCP clients, at the Command Prompt type **IPCONFIG /all** and press **ENTER**.

7. As you configure a scope in DHCP, you can configure the subnet mask with CIDR notation. From within the New Scope Wizard,, enter the length of the subnet mask in bits. Windows 2000 will automatically convert it to the proper subnet mask.

8. If you use three different IP address ranges to logically separate some computers from others, you have created three logical subnets on the same physical subnet. The best way to administer all three logical subnets on one DHCP server is to create a superscope from within DHCP.

9. If you have a physical problem on your network, first determine the scope of the problem-is only one computer failing, or is the entire network inoperable? After narrowing the location of the problem, troubleshoot physical problems on your network beginning with the network cable. Inspect the network cable connection on the computer at one end and then at the computer or hub at the other end. Make sure the problem is not caused by frays, breaks, or sharp bends in the network cable. If all the connections are secure and in good condition, inspect the network cards, hubs, and other hardware devices. You then use the TCP/IP utilities to narrow down your search for the problem.

10. To check a NIC on a network, use the PING utility command. Ping the loopback address of 127.255.255.0. If four successful answers are returned, then the NIC may not be the problem. If the loopback address doesn't return answers, then there is a problem with the NIC. Use the device Manager to verify the proper drivers were used for the NIC, and that there are no resource conflicts. If the loopback address intermittently returns answers, the NIC may be the problem.

Lesson 6 Quiz

These questions test your knowledge of features, vocabulary, procedures, and syntax.

1. Which of the following are default subnet masks for the IP classes?

    A. 255.0.0.0

    B. 255.255.0.0

    C. 255.254.0.0

    D. 255.255.255.0

2. Which variables determine which subnet mask you will use for your network?

    A. Number of hosts on each subnet

    B. Number of subnets

    C. Number of NICs

    D. Number of routers

3. Why is the Network ID 127 a special address number?

    A. It is exclusive for broadcast messages

    B. It is the address of the Pentagon router.

    C. It is the loopback address

    D. It is a host number

4. With the APIPA system, clients issue IP addresses to themselves. What is the IP address form the number always takes?

    A. 255.255.0.0

    B. 169.254.x.y where x and y are between 0 to 254

    C. 10.169.x.y where x and y are between 0 to 254

    D. 192.168.x.y where x and y are between 0 to 254

5.   How is APIPA disabled?

A. With uninstall

B. Editing the Registry

C. Reinstalling TCP/IP

D. Reinstall Windows 2000

6.   Although TCP/IP is configured in the same way on servers and clients, which of the following apply only to servers?

A. Assign servers addresses using DHCP.

B. Assign static IP addresses to all servers.

C. Do not assign the DNS server an IP address.

D. Use APIPA to assign an IP address to the DHCP server.

7.   What basic TCP/IP configuration information does the IPCONFIG command display?

A. Default gateway

B. Connection-specific DNS suffix

C. Subnet mask

D. IP address

8.   What does TCP/IP ultimately use to identify the source and destination computers?

A. ARF

B. MAC addresses

C. WINS names

D. NIC

9. From which MMC console do you create scopes and superscopes?

    A. The snap-in console

    B. The New Scope console

    C. The Active Directory console

    D. The DHCP console

10. Which of the following diagnostic commands lists the destination computer's IP address as the final hop?

    A. PING

    B. NetSTAT

    C. TRACERT

    D. IPCONFIG

Answers to Lesson 6 Quiz

1. Answers A, B, and C are correct. The default subnet masks for the IP classes are 255.0.0.0 (for Class A), 255.255.0.0 (for Class B), and 255.255.255.0 (for Class C).

    Answer D is incorrect. You can only use this subnet mask with CIDR notation.

2. Answers A and B are correct. The number of hosts on each subnet and the number of desired subnets determine which subnet mask you will use for your network.

    Answers C and D are incorrect. The number of NICs and number of routers don't determine which subnet mask you will use for your network.

3. Answer C is correct. The Network ID 127 a special address number used for the loopback address. The loopback address is used to test the NIC.

    Answer A is incorrect. Broadcast messages use a host ID of 255.

    Answers B and D are incorrect.

4. Answer B is correct. With the APIPA system, clients issue IP addresses to themselves always in the IP address form number form of 169.254.x.y where x and y are between 0 and 254

    Answers A, C, and D are incorrect.

5. Answer B is correct. APIPA is enabled by default and can only be disabled by editing the Registry.

    Answers A, C, and D are incorrect. Because only editing the Registry can disable APIPA, no other methods apply.

6. Answer B is correct. Although you do not need to, it is a good idea to assign servers static IP addresses so that they do not change.

    Answer A is incorrect. Although you can use DHCP to assign IP addresses to servers, it is not the best choice.

    Answer C is incorrect. All computers-including a DNS server-must have a valid IP address.

    Answer D is incorrect. The DHCP server must have a statically-assigned IP address.

7.   Answers A, B, C, and D are correct. IPCONFIG displays the connection-specific DNS suffix, IP address, subnet mask, and default gateway.

8.   Answer B is correct. TCP/IP ultimately uses the MAC address to identify the source and destination computers. The ARP protocol resolves IP addresses to MAC addresses.

Answer A is incorrect. ARF is fictitious.

Answer C is incorrect. WINS is the Windows Internet Naming Service used to resolve NetBIOS names to IP addresses.

Answer D is incorrect. A NIC is a Network Interface Card.

9.   Answer D is correct. Scopes and superscopes are created from the DHCP console in the MMC.

Answers A, B, and C are incorrect. Snap-ins are a generic name for modules that run in the MMC, the New Scope console is fictitious, and the Active Directory Console is not the console for scope and superscope creation.

10.   Answer C is correct. The diagnostic command TRACERT lists the destination computer's IP address as the final hop.

Therefore answers A, B, and D are incorrect. PING, NetSTAT, and IPCONFIG do not list the destination computer's IP address as the final hop.

Lesson 7:
Network Administration

As a Windows 2000 network administrator, you must be familiar with the tools available to perform some of the more common administrative tasks. This lesson covers several common administrative chores as well as the resources available to help you accomplish those tasks.

Windows 2000 includes an extensive Help database where you can search for topics of interest. The Help file has an interactive and easy-to-use interface similar to a Web page that allows you jump from one topic to another and return quickly to the previous topic.

Many utilities are available in Windows 2000 for both computer and network administration. This lesson introduces several of these utilities to give you a good foundation to start administering Windows 2000 servers and workstations.

After completing this lesson, you should have a better understanding of the following topics:

*   Administrative Tasks

*   Administrative Tools

*   Windows 2000 Help

Administrative Tasks

As administrator, you can perform administrative tasks on a regular basis. Depending on the size of your organization and your position within the organization, you can perform all administrative tasks on the network.

Understanding Common Administrative Tasks

Administrative tasks on Windows 2000 computers are classified into the following three categories: Security, Data Management, and Network and System Integrity.

Security Tasks

Computer and network security is of paramount concern. You secure a Windows 2000 network two ways: creating user accounts and limiting access to resources. Resources include files, folders, and printers.

User Account Creation—Central to Windows 2000 security is the single-user, single-logon method. Every user who accesses your Windows 2000 network needs a user account and password. Only one user account and password is needed per user, and only one user should use any given account.

Note: Access to individual Windows 2000 computers is restricted to those who have valid user accounts. Any user can access the files on a Windows 95 or Windows 98 computer, but files on Windows 2000 computers are secure.

Securing Resources—Once a user has access to a computer or network, you must ensure that the user only accesses the necessary resources. You make resources available over the network by sharing them, and you secure resources by assigning permissions. In Windows 2000, you can assign the following two types of permissions:

- NTFS permissions control who can access files locally and over the network, and the kind of user access

- Share permissions control who can access folders and printers over the network and the kind of user access

Note: To simplify administration, user accounts are put into groups, and groups are assigned permissions to shared resources.

Data Management Tasks

Proper management of data—the files created by users—ensures that the data is always available when users need it. Windows 2000 Server supports several levels of fault-tolerance and includes an efficient tape backup utility.

Fault-tolerance is the ability of a system to recover from failure. In the case of data, a fault-tolerant system uses more than one physical hard drive to store the same data. If one hard drive fails, the other(s) still contain the data. Normally, a hard drive failure means a loss of data. With fault-tolerance, the data remains intact.

More important than implementing fault-tolerance is the implementation of a regular backup schedule using the backup utility. Windows 2000 Backup allows you to copy data to various media. If the computer fails, or more than one hard drive crashes, you can restore data from the backup copy. No level of fault-tolerance can handle a major disaster, but a regular backup schedule keeps your users working with minimal interruption.

 Note: No network management scheme is complete without a well-planned backup strategy.

Network and System Integrity Tasks

Maintaining a well-running network means that all users have access to the resources they need without significant delays. When users connect to resources on the server, both network performance and server performance affect connection speeds. Using tools included with Windows 2000, you can monitor and optimize network and system performance. As an administrator, you should look for bottlenecks (slow points) in the network and strive to eliminate them.

Note: Every system has a bottleneck, which represents the slowest component in a system.

Scheduling Tasks

You may wish to automate those administrative tasks you execute on a regular basis (like running the Backup utility or archiving system log files). Using the Task Scheduler, you can arrange to have administrative tasks run automatically, even if you are not logged in to the system.

To open Task Scheduler, follow these steps:

1.   From the Start Menu, choose Settings, and then Control Panel. From the Control Panel, double-click Scheduled Tasks (Figure 7.1).

Figure 7.1 Scheduled Tasks Control Panel

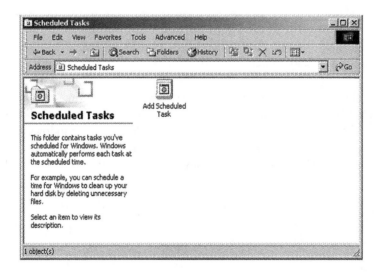

2.   Double-click Add Scheduled Task to begin the Scheduled Task Wizard (Figure 7.2).

Figure 7.2 Scheduled Task Wizard

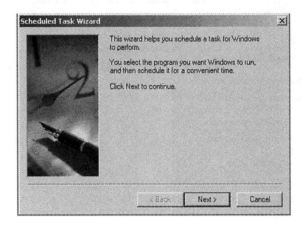

The wizard steps through the process of selecting an application to schedule and determines the schedule interval. You can employ the following timeframe options for scheduling a task:

•   Daily

•   Weekly

•   Monthly

•   One time only

•   When my computer starts

•   When I log on

Once you create a scheduled task, it appears in the Scheduled Tasks folder in the Control Panel (Figure 7.3).

Figure 7.3 Scheduled Tasks Folder

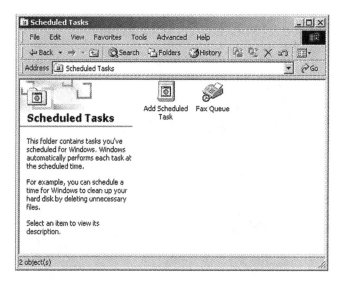

Tip: You can force a task to run immediately by right-clicking the task and choosing Run.

Administrative Tools

Many of the tools you use to administer a Windows 2000 environment run within a common interface called the Microsoft Management Console (MMC). The MMC itself does not provide any management tools, but allows tools to share a common interface. Once you learn the MMC interface, individual Windows 2000 tools are much easier to use.

Many other administrative tasks are accomplished through the Control Panel. The Control Panel is a collection of applets, each addressing a specific Windows 2000 setting or feature. Changes made with Control Panel applets write to the Registry.

Using the Microsoft Management Console (MMC)

When you open the MMC, you are opening a console. A console contains management utilities. Each utility is called snap-in, and a single console can contain multiple snap-ins. In this way, the MMC provides a common interface for most management tools.

By providing a common interface for the management tools in Windows 2000, the MMC centralizes control of the computer and of the entire network. Rather than run every system management tool as its own unique program, the MMC allows multiple tools to run together.

An example of this is the Computer Management console. To open the Computer Management console from the desktop, right-click My Computer, and then choose Manage (Figure 7.4).

Figure 7.4 Computer Management Console

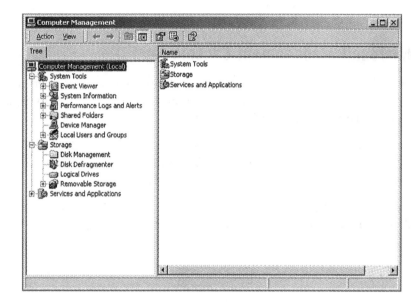

The Computer Management console contains several snap-ins that manage the computer. You will learn to use many of these snap-ins in the sections that follow.

Working with Snap-Ins

Each snap-in in the MMC performs a different task, ensuring differences among the tools. However, since all snap-ins must conform to the MMC, they all share some common features.

The general form of a console includes two panes. The left pane is called the Tree pane, and contains a list of snap-ins included in the console (Figure 7.5).

Figure 7.5 Computer Management Console Tree Pane

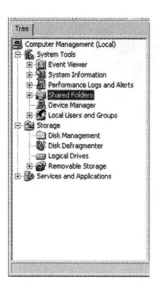

The Tree pane displays folders as well as snap-ins. Folders are MMC objects that contain other snap-ins. Folders have a small plus sign (+) next to them. Clicking the plus sign (+) or double-clicking the folder name expands the folder, revealing its contents. Some snap-ins also expand, revealing items within the snap-in. It is this branching, hierarchical structure that gives the name Tree to this left-hand pane (Figure 7.6).

Figure 7.6 Expanded Tree Pane

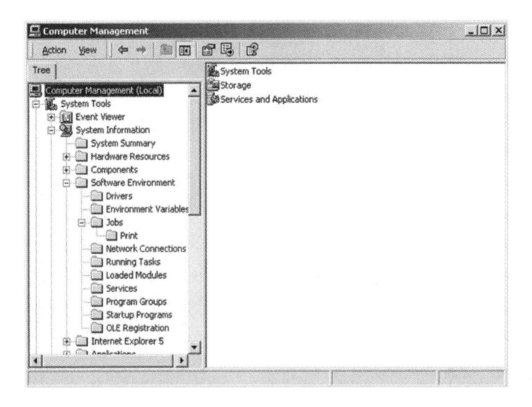

The right-hand side of the console contains the Details pane. If you choose a folder in the Tree pane, the Details pane displays the contents of the folder. If you select a snap-in in the Tree pane, the Details pane displays the snap-in-specific information and features. The Details pane displays a variety of information, including Web pages, graphics (charts, tables, and pictures), and columns.

For example, in the Tree pane of the Computer Management console, expand System Tools, expand Event Viewer, and then select System. The Details pane displays the System Log for the Event Viewer, with the information listed in columns (Figure 7.7).

Figure 7.7 System Event Log

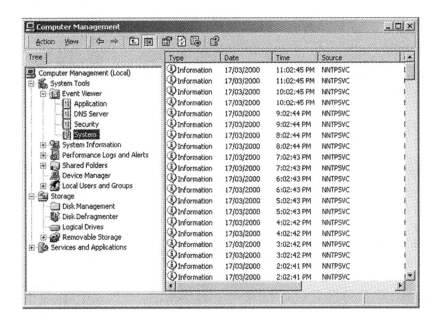

You can rearrange and resize the columns in the Details pane, and order the data by column type. As another exercise, expand Storage in the Tree pane, and then choose Disk Management. The Details pane displays graphical information about the computer's hard disk drives (Figure 7.8).

Figure 7.8 Disk Management Console

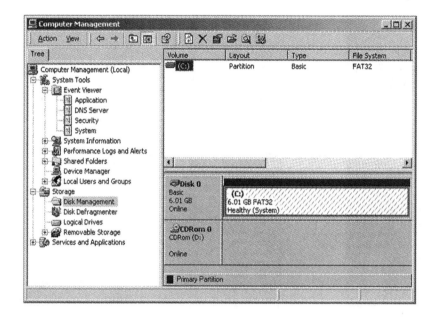

In this instance, the Details pane splits horizontally. The upper portion of the Details pane contains data that lists in columns, and the lower portion contains a graphical representation of the physical and logical drives in the computer.

Using the Computer Management Console

Of all the consoles for the MMC, the single-most encompassing is the Computer Management console. The Computer Management console includes the snap-ins you need to manage user and group accounts, view and change hardware settings, and view error logs.

To open the Computer Management console, from the desktop, right-click My Computer and choose Manage.

Tip: You can also open the Computer Management console from the Start Menu. From the Start Menu, choose Programs, Administrative Tools, and then select Computer Management.

The following sections describe some of the snap-ins found in the Computer Management console.

Event Viewer Snap-In

In the Tree pane of the Computer Management console, expand System Tools and then expand Event Viewer (Figure 7.9).

Figure 7.9 Event Viewer

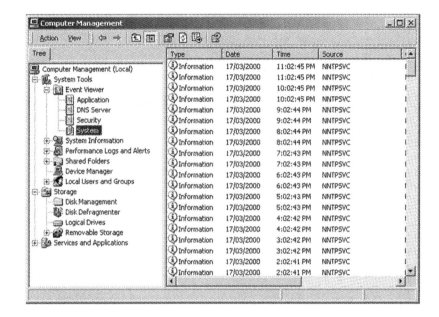

Event Viewer contains the following three log files:

Application log—Records errors applications generate.

Security log—Records audited events. that you choose to monitor for security reasons.

System log—Records errors that Windows 2000 generates.

 Note: As you load new services on a Windows 2000 server, other log files may be included in the Event Viewer.

The Application and System log files contain the following three different event types:

Information—Indicates a successful operation. Some drivers, services, and applications record a successful operation in the Event log. Information events require no action on your part.

Warning—Indicates a possible problem, or a future error of an unresolved problem. Review Warning events and correct any problem as soon as possible.

Error—Indicates a driver, service, or application has failed. You must correct the problem immediately to restore full system functionality.

You use the Event Viewer to check on overall system health. If problems are occurring, first check the System log. Even if everything appears to be running normally, you should check the Event Viewer on a regular basis for Warnings.

 Tip: You can open Event Viewer in its own MMC console. From the Start Menu, choose Programs, Administrative Tools, and then select Event Viewer.

System Information Snap-In

In the Tree pane of the Computer Management console, expand System Tools, and then expand System Information (Figure 7.10).

Figure 7.10 System Information

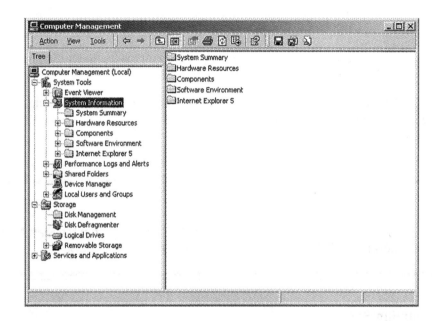

System information contains at least four folders that includes the following:

System Summary—Lists information about Windows 2000 and the computer, including the amount of memory installed, the computer name and type, and the version of Windows 2000 (Figure 7.11).

Figure 7.11 System Summary

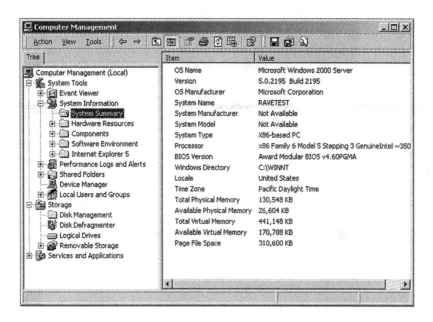

Hardware Resources—Contains folders that display information about several hardware resources and detected resource conflicts.

Components—Contains folders that list hardware device settings. Folders include displays for video, printer, and Universal Serial Bus (USB) settings (Figure 7.12).

Software Environment—Contains folders that display information about the currently active programs, system tasks, and drivers, and network connections.

Note: As you load new programs onto a Windows 2000 computer, other folders may add under the System information snap-in. For example, Internet Explorer Version 5.01 (which installs automatically with Windows 2000) creates its own folder, as does Microsoft Office 2000.

Figure 7.12 Components

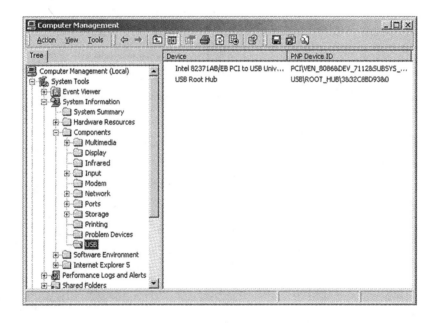

Performance Logs and Alerts Snap-In

From the Tree pane of Computer Management, expand System Tools, and then expand Performance Logs and Alerts. Performance Logs and Alerts allow you to create logs and alerts of real-time system performance data.

A log records the state of selected objects at a specified interval. For example, you may wish to monitor the Central Processing Unit (CPU) to see its rate of use. You can create a log that looks at the percentage of CPU usage every 15 minutes.

An Alert watches the selected objects and notifies you when usage exceeds the limit you specify. For example, suppose you want to know when CPU usage exceeds 80%. You can create an alert that notifies you every time this occurs.

Tip: You can view the Performance log data graphically using the System Monitor snap-in (from the Start Menu, choose Programs, Administrative Tools, and then select Performance).

Shared Folders Snap-In

From the Tree pane of the Computer Management console, expand System Tools, and then expand Shared Folders. The Shared Folders snap-in contains information about the open connections to your computer (people accessing shared folders on your computer).

Note: A shared folder is a folder on your computer that you have made available on the network to other users.

The following three folders are included in the Shared Folders snap-in:

Shares—Lists all shared folders on your computer (Figure 7.13).

Figure 7.13 Shares

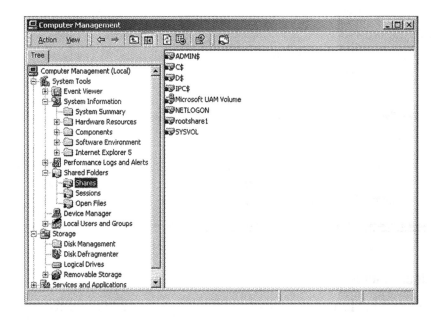

Tip: Share names that end with a dollar sign ($) are hidden shares. They do not appear when people browse the network.

Sessions—Lists all users who are currently connected to your computer and are accessing shares.

Open Files—Displays the files and folders that users are currently accessing.

Device Manager Snap-In

From the Tree pane of the Computer Management console, expand System Tools, and then choose Device Manager. Device Manager displays every hardware device in the computer in a branching, tree-like manner (Figure 7.14).

Figure 7.14 Device Manager

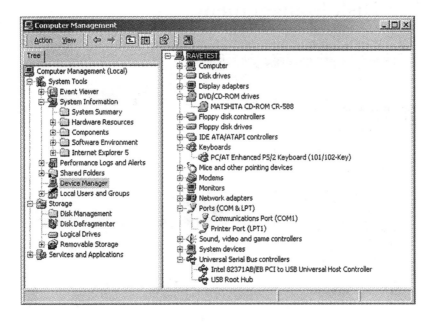

Using Device Manager, you can view devices, change the resources used by devices, resolve hardware conflicts, and remove devices.

Local Users and Groups Snap-In

From the Tree pane of the Computer Management console, expand System Tools, and then expand Local Users and Groups. Local Users and Groups allows you to create new user and group accounts, delete accounts, and change account information.

Disk Management Snap-In

From the Tree pane of the Computer Management console, expand Storage, and then choose Disk Management. Disk Management provides a graphical representation of the hard disk drives in your computer and the partitions created on these drives (Figure 7.15).

Figure 7.15 Disk Management

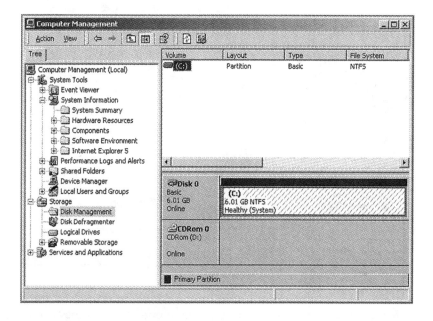

From the Disk Management console, you create and delete partitions, access drive properties, and perform other management tasks. To access a partition's properties page, in the Details (right) pane, right-click any drive letter and choose Properties (Figure 7.16).

Figure 7.16 Drive Properties

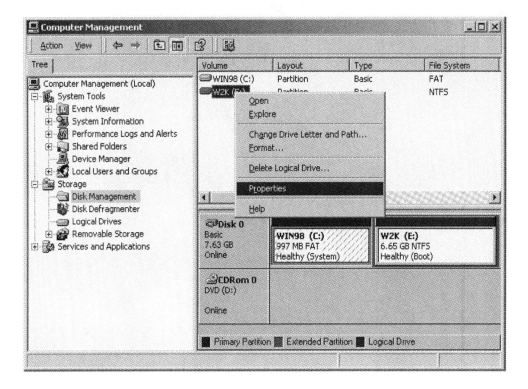

From the Drive Properties window, choose the General property page (Figure 7.17). This page shows the amount of disk space used and allows you to use the Disk Cleanup utility. Disk Cleanup searches your drive for temporary files and unneeded Internet cache files and allows you to safely delete them.

Figure 7.17 Hard Drive General Property Page

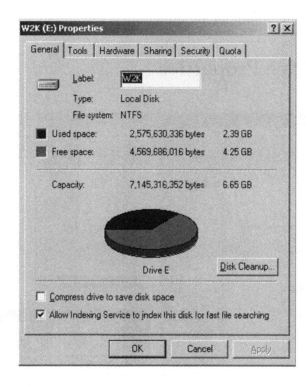

From the Drive Properties window, choose the Tools property page (Figure 7.18).

Figure 7.18 Tools Property Page

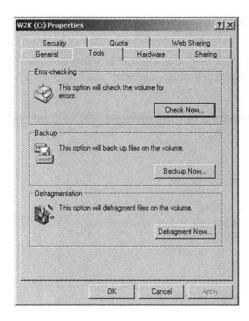

From this page, you can run the following three drive-related utilities:

Error-checking—Checks the drive for logical and physical problems and corrects them before data is lost.

Backup—Runs the Backup utility that backs up data to a removable storage device, like a tape drive.

Tip: To open the Backup utility, from the Start Menu, choose Programs, Accessories, select System Tools, and then select Backup.

Defragmentation—Runs the Disk Defragmenter that rearranges the data on a disk to make it more quickly accessible.

Tip: You can run the Disk Defragmenter from the Computer Management console. In the Tree pane of the console, expand Storage, and then choose Disk Defragmenter.

Using Control Panel

The Control Panel provides a central location for several small applications (applets) that customize Windows 2000. To open the Control Panel, from the Start Menu, choose Settings, and then select Control Panel (Figure 7.19).

Figure 7.19 Control Panel

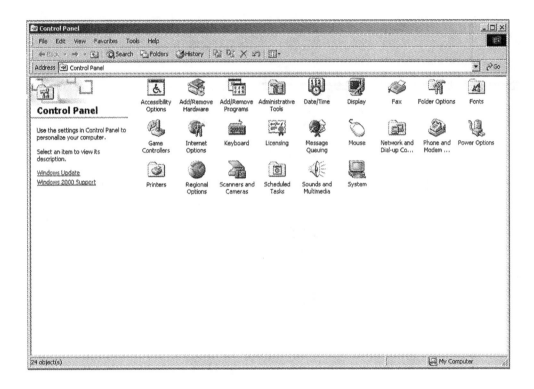

It will be necessary for you to use the Control Panel frequently to manage a Windows 2000 computer. You will also find it necessary to use the Control Panel applets frequently, especially the System Properties applet.

System Properties

The System Control Panel applet (or System Properties) allows you to view and change settings for many aspects of the computer. To access System Properties, from the Control Panel, double-click System.

Tip: From the desktop, you can open System Properties by right-clicking My Computer and choosing Properties.

From the System Properties windows, choose the General property page (Figure 7.20).

Figure 7.20 System Properties General Property Page

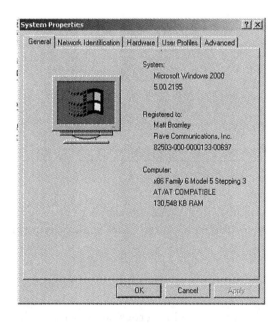

The General property page displays general information about the computer, the Windows 2000 version, and the registered owner of the Windows 2000 license. Choose the Network Identification property page (Figure 7.21).

Figure 7.21 Network Identification Property Page

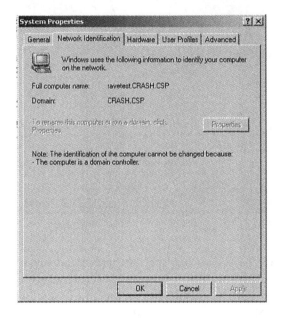

Change the name of the computer and domain or workgroup to which the computer belongs from the Network identification property page. Next, choose the Hardware property page (Figure 7.22).

Figure 7.22 Hardware Property Page

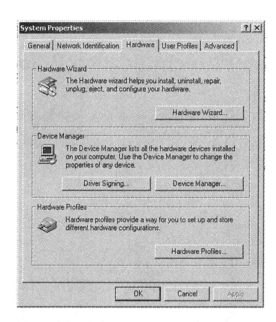

From the Hardware property page, you manage the hardware devices in the computer, add and remove devices using the Hardware Wizard, access the Device Manager, and configure hardware profiles. Hardware profiles allow you to have multiple configurations for your computer, most commonly used on portable computers. Now choose the User Profiles property page (Figure 7.23).

Figure 7.23 User Profiles Property Page

The User Profiles property page allows you to manage user profiles. A user's profile contains information about the user's customized settings. Each user owns a profile, ensuring that every user has a unique desktop.

For example, if a user changes the desktop color to bright green and places a shortcut icon on the desktop, these settings store in the profile. When that user logs in again, the desktop retains the previous settings. However, other users who log on receive their own desktop settings.

Finally, choose the Advanced property page (Figure 7.24).

Figure 7.24 Advanced Property Page

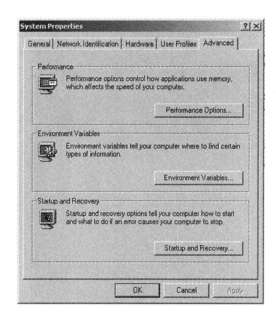

The Advanced property page allows you to adjust advanced settings for the computer. Your three options are as follows:

Performance Options—Allows you to change memory usage settings and the size of the page file.

Environment Variables—Allows you to define where system files are located.

Startup and Recovery—Sets variables regarding the startup menu and how to handle major system failures (Blue Screens) during the boot process.

Using the Backup Utility

You use the Backup utility to make a backup copy of data to a removable storage device, copy data to a tape, a floppy disk, a recordable CD (CD-R), or any other removable media, and also backup data to another hard drive.

A data backup is the single most important method of preserving data. Data stores on hard disks, and hard disks fail. When a hard disk fails, the data stored on that disk is usually lost. The only way to recover the data is to restore it from a backed up copy.

You can use the Windows 2000 Backup utility to perform the following tasks:

*   Back up data to tape

*   Archive data to a hard disk or CD-R

*   Create an Emergency Repair Disk (ERD) that restores the system state in case of a failure

*   Back up the system state, a collection of files, and the Registry that define crucial Windows 2000 settings

*   Schedule data back ups at regular intervals

Using the Configure Your Server Utility

On computers running Windows 2000, you can run the Configure Your Server utility to perform the following tasks:

Upgrade the server to a domain controller—Allows you to upgrade any Windows 2000 server to a domain controller. Domain controllers are computers that store the Active Directory database on a Windows 2000 domain.

Register Windows 2000—Allows you to receive information on product updates when you register Windows 2000 with Microsoft.

Install additional services—Allows you to install the Domain Name System (DNS), Dynamic Host Configuration Protocol (DHCP), Remote Access, and Routing services on the server.

Install and configure Internet Information Service (IIS)—Allows you to host Internet sites on your server.

Configure a File, Printer, or Application Server—Allows you to share folders, printers, and applications.

Windows 2000 Help

The primary resource for administrators of Windows 2000 computers is the Windows 2000 Help program. Help is a database that contains information about many of the common administrative tasks and problems encountered while operating Windows 2000. Using Help, you can learn the steps to configure the computer, view detailed information about most of the Windows 2000 tools, and troubleshoot many of the common problems you encounter with Windows 2000.

 Note: The Help program for Windows 2000 Server differs from the Help program included with Windows 2000 Professional. Although the interfaces are similar, the Server version includes additional material.

Using Windows 2000 Help

This section covers the steps for running Windows 2000 Professional Help. To run Windows 2000 Help, from the Start Menu, choose Help (Figure 7.25).

Figure 7.25 Windows 2000 Help

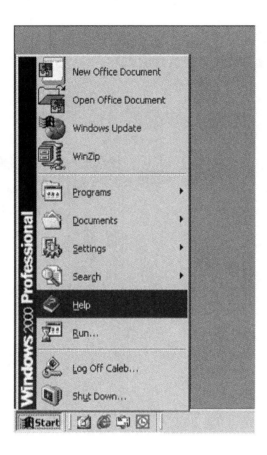

Once open, there are three different ways you can use Windows 2000 Help. Each method has its benefits, and all three are described here.

Browsing the Help Contents

Browse the contents of the Windows 2000 Help database by category, narrowing your search until you find the specific topic of interest. For example, if you want more information on how to make a Windows 2000 computer easier to use for a visually impaired user.

To browse the Windows 2000 Help database, follow these steps:

1.   From the Windows 2000 Help screen, choose the Contents property page (Figure 7.26).

Figure 7.26 Contents Property Page

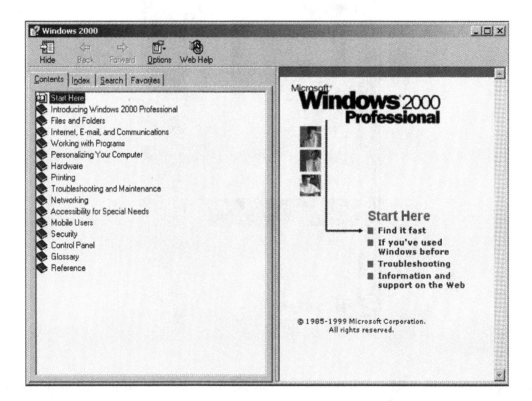

2.　In the left pane of the Contents property page, choose the general category that applies to your needs. In this case, select Accessibility for Special Needs.

The subcategories display below the main topic (Figure 7.27).

Figure 7.27 Expanding a Help Topic

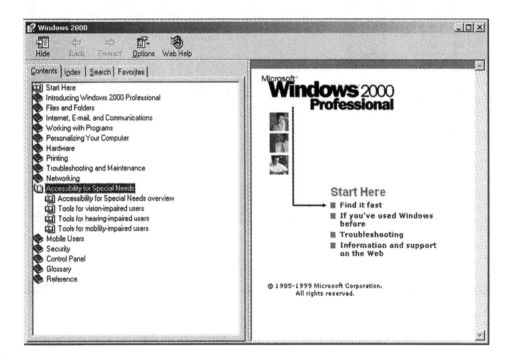

3.　From the left pane, choose Tools for vision-impaired users.

The right pane contains the Help file information on the selected topic (Figure 7.28).

Figure 7.28 Help File Information

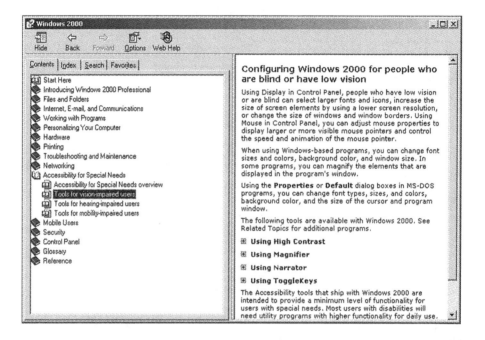

Tip: If either Help Topic pane is not wide enough to fully display the contents, move the mouse curser over the vertical line that divides the panes. When the curser changes to a double-arrow icon, click and drag the divider bar to the right or left to expand the desired pane.

4.   From within the right pane, you have the option to choose various links to more detailed information. For example, if you wish to learn more about using the Magnifier tool, select Using Magnifier.

The display expands to show detailed information (Figure 7.29).

Figure 7.29 Detailed Help Information

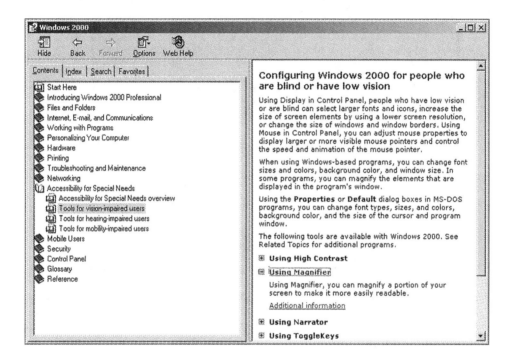

5.   Some links in the right pane replace the text with new text. For example, under the newly expanded Using Magnifier topic, choose Additional information.

New information displays in the right pane, with text entitled Magnifier overview (Figure 7.30).

Figure 7.30 New Text in Right Pane

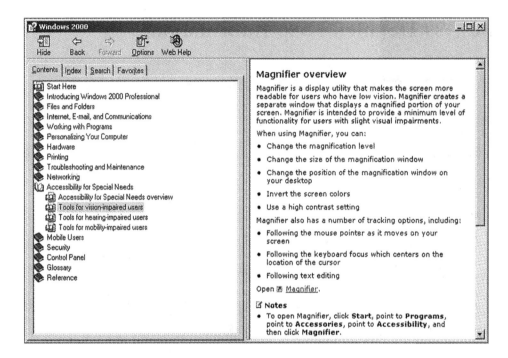

6.   To return to the previous topic, from the Toolbar at the top, choose the left-pointing arrow labeled Back.

Using the Help Index

For some users, browsing the Help file is not the most efficient way to find information. You can also find a topic by viewing an alphabetical listing of all Help topics. From the Help window, choose the Index property page (Figure 7.31).

Figure 7.31 Index Property Page

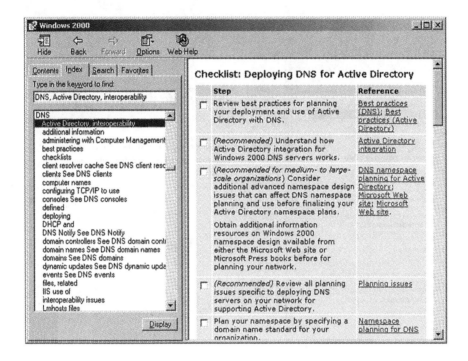

Using the sliding bar in the left pane, find the topic of interest to you. You also have the option to type the first few letters of the topic, and Help highlights the first topic that matches those letters (Figure 7.32).

Figure 7.32 Navigating the Index

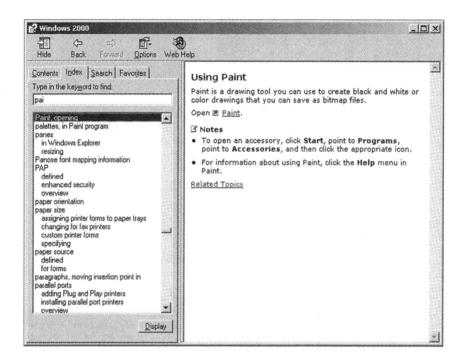

Searching for Keywords

You may wish to search for a keyword within a topic. For example, you may want to learn how to change a user's password. You can do this from the Search property page of Windows 2000 Help. From the Help window, choose the Search property page (Figure 7.33).

Figure 7.33 Search Property Page

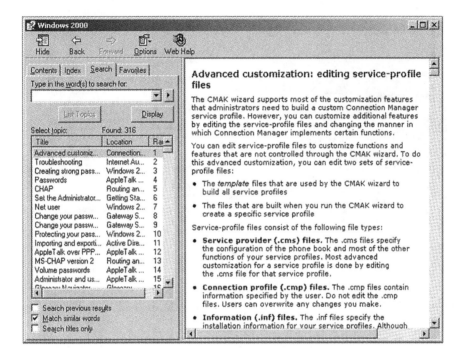

In the Type in the keyword to find box, type your search query. In this case, type **CHANGE USER PASSWORD**, and then press **ENTER** or choose List Topics (Figure 7.34).

Figure 7.34 Search Query

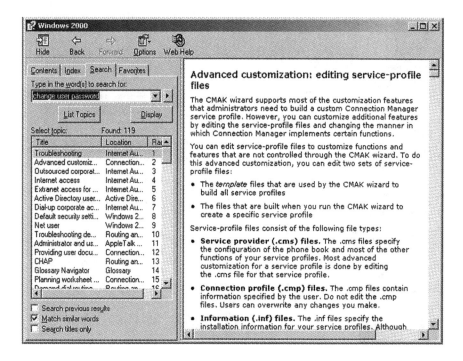

Help searches for topics that contain the text or close matches thereof, and displays the results. In this case, notice that the second search result in the list is Change a user's password. Select this topic and then select Display (or double-click the topic), and the topic displays in the right pane (Figure 7.35).

Figure 7.35 Search Results

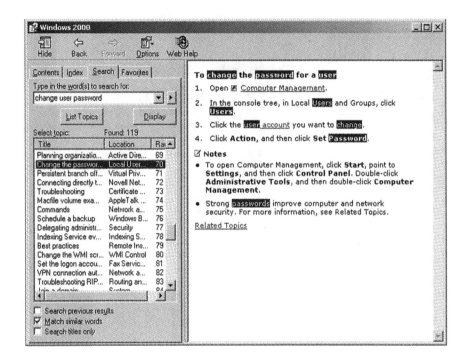

Customizing Help

You can customize Windows 2000 Help by adding favorites. Favorites are Help topics you frequently view and, therefore, need quick access, or Help pages you wish to bookmark as Favorites to access them later.

Adding Favorites

To add bookmarks to your list of Favorites, follow these steps:

1. From the Help utility, browse for (or search for) a particular topic. Find the page you wish to bookmark.

2. From Help, choose the Favorites property page (Figure 7.36).

Figure 7.36 Favorites Property Page

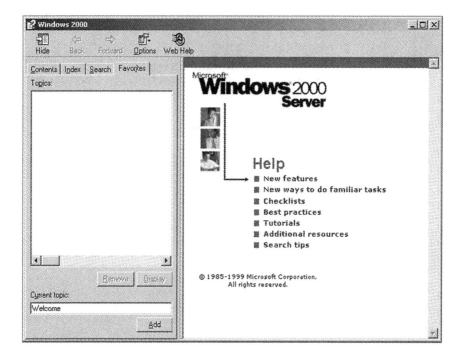

3.   Ensure that the Help topic you wish to add is listed in the Current Topic field (Figure 7.37).

Figure 7.37 Current Topic Selection

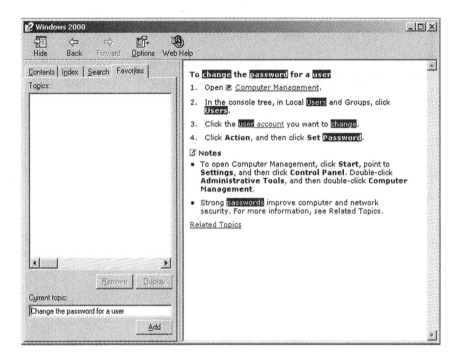

4. Choose Add to add the page to the list.

Tip: You can change the name of a topic once it has been added to the Favorites list by right-clicking the topic and choosing Rename. Type a new name for the topic and press **ENTER**.

Viewing Favorites

To view a previously saved Favorites, follow these steps:

1. From the Help window, choose the Favorites property page.

2. Choose the topic you wish to view, and then select Display. You can display a topic by right-clicking the topic and choosing Display or by double-clicking the topic.

3. The topic displays in the right pane of the Help window.

Using Help to Troubleshoot

Windows 2000 includes a series of help topics called the Troubleshooters. The Troubleshooters step you through many of the common problems users and administrators encounter.

Running Troubleshooters

On a computer running Windows 2000 Professional, follow these steps:

1. From the Start Menu, choose Help.

2. From the Windows 2000 Help window, choose the Contents page.

3. Choose Troubleshooting and Maintenance, and then choose Windows 2000 Troubleshooters.

To find the troubleshooters on a computer running Windows 2000 Server, follow these steps:

1. From the Start Menu, choose Help.

2. From the Windows 2000 Help window, choose the Contents page.

3. Choose Troubleshooting and Additional Resources, choose Troubleshooting, and then select General Troubleshooting.

From the list of topics, choose the one that most closely matches the problem you are having. Help leads you through a series of steps to diagnose and solve the problem.

Tip: Windows 2000 Help is available on the Internet at the following addresses:

http://windows.microsoft.com/windows2000/en/professional/help/ (for Windows 2000 Professional).

http://windows.microsoft.com/windows2000/en/server/help/ (for Windows 2000 Server).

Vocabulary

Review the following terms in preparation for the certification exam.

Term	Description
Active Directory	Active Directory is the new service that defines and supports the organization of a network. In Windows 2000, domain controllers are servers providing the Active Directory service.
applets	Small application programs used to customize other programs or utilities.
bottleneck	The slowest component in a system.
Computer Management Console	The Computer Management console is a module that contains management utilities or snap-ins that work in the MMC to provide a central location for Windows 2000 management. The console has two panes: the Tree pane and the Details pane.
console	A module that contains management utilities or snap-ins, designed to work in the MMC to provide a central location for management. The general form of a console includes two panes.
Control Panel	The Control Panel is a collection of applets designed to work in the MMC to provide a central location for management. Each applet addresses a specific Windows 2000 setting or feature.
CPU	The Central Processing Unit is the brain of the computer that processes all actions.

Term	Description
Details pane	The right side of the MMC contains the Details pane that displays the contents of folders and information specific to the snap-ins.
domain controller	A computer that stores the Active Directory database on a Windows 2000 domain.
ERD	The Emergency Repair Disk is a floppy disk used to rebuild a corrupted installation of Windows 2000.
fault tolerance	The ability of a system to recover from failure. In the case of data, a fault-tolerant system uses more than one physical hard drive to store the same data.
Favorites	Sites that are bookmarked for quick and frequent access.
folders	Folders are MMC objects that contain other snap-ins. Folders display with a plus sign (+) next to them.
MMC	The Microsoft Management Console provides a centralized, common interface for management tools (consoles or snap-ins).
NTFS	NT File System works with Windows NT and Windows 2000 operating systems and supports advanced features from long filenames to object-oriented files with user and system-defined attributes.
profiles	Specifications for certain criteria that define an action, object, or configuration.
Registry	The Windows 2000 central database of system configuration information.
shared folder	A folder on a computer that is available on the network to others.

Term	Description
snap-ins	An administrative tool or utility in Windows 2000 that runs within the MMC.
system state	A collection of files and the Registry that define crucial Windows 2000 settings.
Tree pane	The left side of the MMC contains the Tree pane that contains a list of snap-ins included in the console, and also displays folders.
utility	An application or program that solves problems narrow in focus, also known as a snap-in.

In Brief

If you want to...	Then do this...
Secure a Windows 2000 network	Create user accounts and limit access to resources such as files, folders, and printers to secure a Windows 2000 network.
Make resources available over the network and secure them	Share resources and assign permissions.
Ensure data is always available	Implement fault-tolerance and schedule regular backups.
Automate routine administrative tasks	Use the Task Scheduler to automate routine tasks.
Administer the Windows 2000 environment with its many administrative tools	Learn the common interface called Microsoft Management Console (MMC) and the individual snap-ins for the MMC.
Manage user and group accounts, view and change hardware settings, and view error logs	Use the Computer Management console, which is the most encompassing of all the MMC consoles.
Perform various server tasks such as upgrades, registrations, service installations, or configure resources	Use the utility called Configure Your Server to perform administrative configuration tasks on and with your server.
Browse and search for Windows 2000 topics quickly and efficiently	Use the Windows 2000 Help file.
Reference solutions for some common network problems	Use the Troubleshooter utility in Help to step through common network problems.

Lesson 7 Activities

Complete the following activities to better prepare you for the certification exam.

1. List and describe the two types of permissions you can assign to secure resources.

2. Explain a data management fault-tolerant system, and how Windows 2000 provides for it.

3. Discuss why you would use Task Scheduler and describe how to access it.

4. Describe the most encompassing console for the MMC, and give some alternative methods to access it.

5. Describe the snap-in you would use to obtain information about open connections to your computer, and give the steps to access it.

6. Name the Control Panel applet that controls system settings, give the steps to access it, and list five Property Pages within it.

7. What is an ERD and how do you create one?

8. Explain how to access the backup utility.

9. Explain how to customize Windows 2000 Help.

10. Explain the difference between steps to access Troubleshooters in the Windows 2000 Professional and Windows 2000 Server.

Answers to Lesson 7 Activities

1. Two types of permissions you can assign to secure resources in Windows 2000 are NTFS permissions and Share permissions.

    The NTFS permissions features facilitate secure resources by controlling who can locally and remotely access files. Share permissions allow you to assign permissions that control who can access folders and printers over the network, as well as the kind of access for each user.

2. Fault-tolerance is the ability to recover from a failure. Data created by users should be available whenever they need it. A fault-tolerance system ensures that the data is available and ready and remains intact after a drive failure. This is possible through duplicate or redundant systems such as more than one physical hard drive that stores the same data.

    In addition to fault tolerance, the Windows 2000 Backup utility allows you to copy data onto various types of removable media for fast data restoration in case of a hard drive crash or fault-tolerance failure in a major disaster.

3. Task Scheduler is a utility that automates routine data management tasks such as backups or system log file archiving. Task Scheduler allows you to schedule tasks to run even when you are logged off from the system. The Task Scheduler is actually a wizard that helps you through the scheduling selection process.

    Open Task Scheduler from the Start Menu, choose settings, and select Control Panel. Select Scheduled Tasks, and then choose the Schedule Task Wizard to begin scheduling a task. You can choose the application to use and schedule the intervals when it should run. You can find the scheduled task in the Schedule Tasks folder in the Control Panel.

4. The most encompassing MMC console is the Computer Management console. It includes many snap-ins to manage user and group accounts, change hardware settings, and view error logs. Some snap-ins to use for system management include the Event View, System Information, Performance Logs and Alerts, Shared Folders, Device Manager, Local Users and Group, and Disk Management snap-ins.

    One way to access the Computer Management console from the desktop is by right-clicking My Computer and choosing Manage. Another way to access the Computer Management console is from the Start Menu. Choose Programs, Administrative Tools, and select Computer Management.

5.   Use the snap-in called Shared Folders and look at the Sessions and Open Files folders to find out information about who is accessing your computer through shared folders.

Shared folders are folders you have made available on the network for others to use. The Shared Folders snap-in includes three categories of information: Shares, Sessions, and Open Files. Shares lists all of the shared folders on your computer. Sessions lists everyone currently connected and accessing your computer shares, and Open Files lists the specific files and folders that share users are using.

To access Shared Folders, from the Tree pane of the Computer Management console, expand System Tools and expand Shared Folders. Then choose Sessions or Open Files to see who is accessing your computer and shared files.

6.   The System Properties control panel is used to modify system settings. You access it from the Control Panel by double-clicking System, or by right-clicking My Computer and choosing Properties. The five property pages in the System Properties window include the General, Network Identification, Hardware, User Profiles, and Advanced property pages.

7.   The Emergency Repair Disk (ERD) is used to help Windows 2000 Setup restore a corrupted version of Windows 2000. You create an ERD from within the Windows 2000 backup utility.

8.   You can run the Backup utility from the Disk Management Console or from the Start Menu.

To access Backup utility from the Disk Management Console, from the Details pane, right-click any drive letter and choose Properties. From the Drive Properties window, choose the Tools property page. The Tools Property Page allows you to run three drive-related utilities-the Error-checking utility, the Backup utility, and the Disk Defragmenter utility.

To run the Backup utility from the Start menu, choose Programs, Accessories, select System Tools, and then select Backup.

9. You can add Help bookmarks, called Favorites, to topics you visit frequently to customize Windows 2000 Help. You can bookmark favorite topics or favorite pages to quickly access them again.

    To customize Help with a favorite bookmark, from the Help utility, browse for your particular favorite topic. Find the page you want to bookmark. Then choose the Favorites property page. Make sure that the topic you want to add is in the Current Topic field list. Then select Add to add the page to the list.

10. In both Windows 2000 Professional and Windows 2000 Server, begin by opening Help, and then selecting the Contents property page. In Windows 2000 Professional, choose Troubleshooting and Maintenance, and then choose Windows 2000 Troubleshooters. In Windows 2000 Server, select Troubleshooting and Additional Resources, choose Troubleshooting, and then select General Troubleshooting. You choose a topic from a list and follow the steps to troubleshoot a problem.

Lesson 7 Quiz

These questions test your knowledge of features, vocabulary, procedures, and syntax.

1. Which of the following are ways to secure a Windows 2000 network?

    A. Create a single-user, single-logon method

    B. Assign NTFS permissions

    C. Assign Share permissions

    D. Assign Group permissions

2. Which of the following intervals can be scheduled through the Scheduled Task Wizard?

    A. When I logoff

    B. When I logon

    C. Once

    D. On computer start-up

3. Which of the following are characteristics of snap-ins?

    A. Designed to perform a specific task

    B. Must conform to the MMC

    C. Contain consoles

    D. Can run independently

4. How many panes does the general form of a console include?

    A. None, there is only one window

    B. Three

    C. Only one

    D. Two

5. The Details pane is a flexible tool. Which of the following can be displayed in a Details pane?

    A. Data ordered by column type

    B. Web pages

    C. Logs

    D. Graphical reports and charts

6. Which snap-in allows you to view a log of your system's performance?

    A. Shares

    B. Device Manager

    C. Performance Logs and Alerts

    D. Disk Management

7. Which one of the following symbols indicates that a folder is a hidden share name, and does not appear when people browse the network?

    A. #

    B. $

    C. @

    D. &

8. Which of the following options are located in the Advanced Property Page and allow you to adjust your computer's settings?

    A. Error-checking

    B. Performance options

    C. Environment variables

    D. Startup and recovery

9. On computers running Windows 2000 Server, which utility can you run to install and configure the Internet Information Service?

    A. Systems Properties

    B. MMC

    C. Configure Your Server utility

    D. Computer Management console

10. Other than browsing the Help file, which of the following are methods to search Help for information?

    A. Keywords

    B. Index

    C. Bookmarks

    D. Favorites

Answers to Lesson 7 Quiz

1.   Answer A is correct. Create a single-user, single-logon to secure a Windows 2000 network.

   Answer B is correct. To secure a Windows 2000 network, you can assign NTFS permissions to control access to local and remote files.

   Answer C is correct. You can secure the network with Share permissions that control folder and printer access.

   Answer D is correct. You can secure user accounts by putting them into groups and assigning permissions to shared resources.

2.   Answer B is correct. When I logon is an interval option in the Scheduled Task Wizard.

   Answer C is correct. One time only is an interval that can be scheduled through the Scheduled Task Wizard.

   Answer D is correct. On computer start-up can be scheduled through Scheduled Task Wizard.

   Answer A is incorrect. Although you can schedule an interval when you are not logged on, you cannot schedule anything to occur when you log off.

3.   Answers A and B are correct. Snap-ins must conform the MMC, and are designed to perform specific tasks.

   Answer C is incorrect. A console can contain several snap-ins, but a snap-in cannot contain consoles.

   Answer D is incorrect. All snap-ins require the MMC to run.

4.   Answer D is correct. The general form of a console includes two panes, the left pane is called the Tree pane, and the right pane is called the Details pane.

   Answers A, B, and C are incorrect.

5.   Answers A, B, C, and D are correct. The Details pane displays data ordered by column type, Web pages, logs, and graphical reports and charts, among others.

6.   Answer C is correct. The Performance Logs and Alerts snap-in allows you to view a log of your system's performance.

Answers A, B, and D are incorrect. Shares is fictitious. The Device Manager displays hardware, and the Disk Management shows partitions created on all of the hard drives in your computer.

7.   Answer B is correct. The dollar sign ($) at the end of a share name indicates that the file is a hidden share name, and does not appear when people browse networks.

Answers A, C, and D are incorrect.

8.   Answers B, C, and D are correct. The Performance options, Environment variables, and Startup and Recovery are all located in the Advanced Property Page and allow you to change system settings.

Answer A is incorrect. Error-checking is a setting in the Tools Property page of a hard drive.

9.   Answer C is correct. On computers running Windows 2000 Server, you can run the Configure Your Server utility to install and configure the Internet Information Service (IIS).

Answers A, B, and are incorrect. Systems Properties, MMC, and Computer Management console do not handle IIS installation.

10.   Answers A, B, and D are correct. Searching with keywords, using the index, and creating Favorites are all methods for accessing the Help file without browsing.

Answer C is incorrect. Bookmarks are called Favorites in the Help file.

Lesson 8: Network Security

Network resources must be protected from unauthorized access. With the ever-increasing number of corporate networks that connect to the Internet, the ability for hackers to access your private network only increases. The need to keep sensitive information confidential is paramount.

In Windows 2000 networks, access to all resources depends upon user accounts and passwords. Access to Windows 2000 computers and to the network is denied to everyone except those who know the password associated with a valid username. Through assignment of user accounts, you keep unwanted users out and also provide authorized users with access to specific resources.

You can combine user accounts into group accounts for administrative purposes, and then assign permissions for resources to these group accounts. For example, you may assign the Read permission for a file to the Temps group, and give all users in the Temps group the ability to read but not delete the file.

Every authorized user has certain rights on the network. These rights may include the right to log on to a workstation, the right to access a server over the network, or the right to create new user accounts. You assign rights to user accounts and group accounts to restrict or extend what an individual user can do on the network.

After completing this lesson, you should have a better understanding of the following topics:

- User Accounts
- Group Accounts
- Permissions
- User Rights

User Accounts

Each user on a Windows 2000 network has a user account. When logging on to the network, the user enters the username and password. The user account facilitates the network to do the following:

- Grant access to the network (log on)

- Grant or deny access to network resources (like opening a shared folder or printing to a network printer)

- Restore the user's personal files and customized desktop (in the user's profile) at logon

The two user accounts in Windows 2000 are as follows:

Local user account—Grants the user permission to log on to a specific computer (the local computer) and access certain files on that computer. A local user account does not grant permission to access the network.

Domain user account—Allows the user to log on to the network (called a domain in Windows 2000) using almost any computer and access network resources. The user also has access to certain files on the local computer.

Administrators create user accounts. The administrator of the local computer creates local user accounts, and a domain administrator creates domain user accounts. In addition to newly created accounts, Windows 2000 includes two built-in accounts.

Using Local User Accounts

A local user account allows a user to log on locally to gain access to the local computer and its resources. It does not grant a user access to the network or any resources beyond the local computer. Local user accounts are created for stand-alone computers not attached to a network, and computers on small workgroup networks.

 Note: You create local user accounts on computers running Windows 2000 Professional and on member servers. You cannot create local user accounts on domain controllers.

Using the Local Users and Groups Snap-in

You create and modify local user accounts in the Local Users and Groups snap-in in the Computer Management console. To open Local Users and Groups, follow these steps:

1. From the desktop, right-click My Computer and choose Manage.

   The Computer Management Console displays (Figure 8.1).

Figure 8.1 Computer Management Console

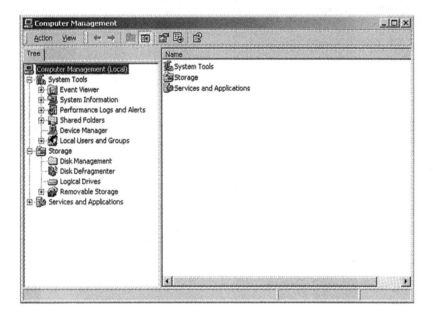

2. From the Tree (left) pane of the Computer Management console, choose the plus sign (+) next to System Tools to expand it, and then expand Local Users and Groups (Figure 8.2).

Figure 8.2 Local Users and Groups

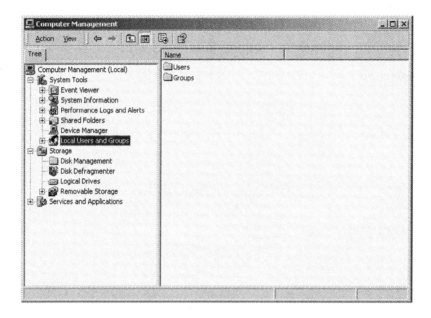

3.   Choose the Users folder. All local user accounts display in the right pane (Figure 8.3).

Figure 8.3 Local User Accounts

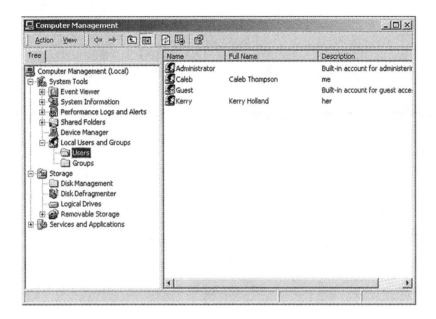

Built-in Local Accounts

Included in the list of local accounts are two accounts created when Windows 2000 installs. These two accounts serve very different purposes on your computer and are as follows:

Administrator account—When you install Windows 2000, you are asked to supply a password for the Administrator account. Use the Administrator account to log on to the local computer after installation. The Administrator account has the following features:

*   It cannot be deleted or disabled

*   It can never be locked out from the computer

*   It can be used to perform all administrative tasks on the computer

Tip: The Administrator account is very powerful and allows you to do things that may render the computer unbootable. Therefore, it is good practice to create a user account for your use during log on, and only use the Administrator account when absolutely necessary.

You cannot delete the Administrator account, but you may rename it.

Tip: For security, rename the Administrator account and assign it a password that would be very difficult for someone to guess.

Guest account—The Guest account can be used for temporary access to a computer. By default, the Guest account is disabled and has no password (the password is left blank). Like the Administrator account, the Guest account cannot be deleted but can be renamed.

Tip: Because the Guest account has no password by default, it is a good idea to leave it disabled unless absolutely necessary.

Using Domain User Accounts

A domain is a collection of computers on a Windows 2000 network. The core of a domain consists of domain controllers, Windows 2000 servers running the Active Directory service. Active Directory is a database that contains information about every object on the network, including user accounts, files, folders, and printers.

When you need to grant users access to the Windows 2000 network, create domain user accounts. You can create these accounts on any domain controller. A user logs on to a computer using the domain user account and password, and the first available domain controller verifies the credentials and authenticates the user.

 Note: All domain controllers on a domain share the same Active Directory database. When you create a domain user account, it replicates (copies) to all other domain controllers so that any domain controller can authenticate a user.

Using Active Directory Users and Computers

You create domain user accounts in the Active Directory on a domain controller. You use the Active Directory Users and Computers console to create, edit, and delete these accounts. To open Active Directory Users and Computers, follow these steps on a domain controller:

1. From the Start Menu, choose Programs, Administrative Tools, and then select Active Directory Users and Computers.

    The Active Directory Users and Computers console displays (Figure 8.4).

Figure 8.4 Active Directory Users and Computers

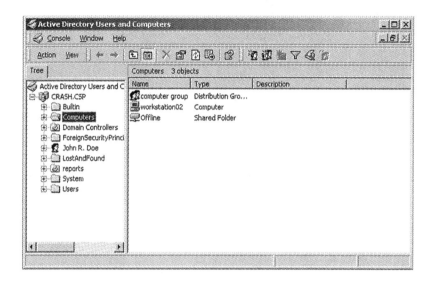

2. In the Tree (left) pane, choose the plus sign (+) next to the domain name to expand the domain, and then select Users.

    The user accounts stored in the Users folder are displayed in the right pane (Figure 8.5).

Built-in Domain Accounts

When you install Active Directory on a Windows 2000 server, the two built-in accounts, Administrator and Guest, add to the Active Directory and become domain user accounts. You cannot delete but can rename these accounts.

Figure 8.5 Domain User Accounts

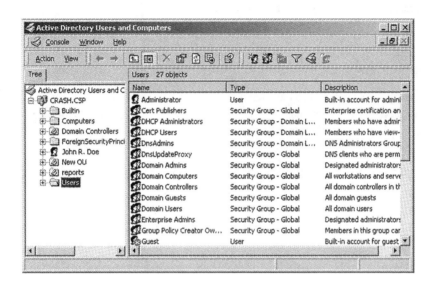

Group Accounts

Network organization simplifies administration. You use groups to organize users based on security needs and other administrative reasons. When working with user accounts, it makes sense to combine user accounts into groups of similar needs. For example, if you have 120 users on your network who need access to a printer, it makes sense to place them in a group and assign the group permission for the printer. The alternative is to assign permission to each individual user.

When you have thousands of users and thousands of resources on a network, groups are not only helpful but necessary. Suppose one user is assigned individual permissions to 25 different files, and that user is promoted from manager to vice president, requiring a higher level of access to files. This requires you as the network administrator to reassign all 25 permissions. However, if you had originally placed the user in the Managers group, you would simply have to remove the user from the old group and place the user in the VicePresidents group.

Understanding Group Types

Windows 2000 has the following two different group types:

Security groups—These groups grant or deny permission to network resources. User accounts and computer accounts may be added to a security group. Security groups can also be used for e-mail distribution.

Distribution groups—These groups are used specifically for sending e-mail messages to groups of users. E-mail-enabled applications, like Microsoft Exchange Server, use distribution groups. You cannot assign security permissions to distribution groups.

 Note: Security groups can also be used for e-mail distribution, but they cause more network traffic.

Understanding Group Scopes

Both security and distribution groups have a scope attribute. The scope determines membership within the group and where the group is used in the network. The scope also determines the domains from which users can be added, as well as from which domains the group can access resources.

 Note: You create domains for organizational purposes, and a single network can consist of multiple domains.

The three group scopes are as follows:

Domain local group—Contains members from any domain on the network, and has permissions only within the local domain.

Global group—Contains members only from the domain in which the global group has been created, and has permissions to resources in any domain.

Universal group—Contains members from any domain in the network, and has permissions to any resource in the network.

Group membership rules are summarized in Table 8.1.

Table 8.1 Group Membership

Group Scope	Group Membership	Network Membership	Permissions
Domain local	Any user account, global group, or universal group in the network Other domain local groups from the same domain	Domain local groups in the same domain	Resources in the same domain
Global	User accounts and global groups from the same domain	Any universal or domain local group in the network Global groups in the same domain	Resources in any domain in the network
Universal	Any user account, global group, or universal group in the network	Any domain local or universal group in the network	Resources in any domain in the network

Note: Although you can use universal groups for all of your network security needs, they generate more network traffic than other groups.

Using Built-in Groups

Windows 2000 includes several built-in groups. The built-in groups have pre-assigned user rights and permissions, so once a user account is added to the group, the user account obtains those permissions and rights.

Built-in Domain Local Groups

You create built-in domain local groups on domain controllers to allow users to perform tasks within the Active Directory. The following are the types of built-in domain local groups and permissions:

Account operators—Members mange user and group accounts.

Server operators—Members perform many administrative tasks on the server.

Print operators—Members manage printers and print jobs.

Administrators—Members have full control over the domain controller.

Backup operators—members have permission to perform data backups.

Users—Members have few rights on a domain controller.

Guests—By default, the Guest account is the only member and has temporary access.

Built-in Global Groups

Built-in global groups do not have permissions assigned by default. Their purpose is to group users, and then the global groups are put in domain local groups. The four built-in global groups are as follows:

- Domain Users

- Domain Admins

- Domain Guests

- Enterprise Admins

Built-in System Groups

Unlike built-in global and domain local groups, built-in system groups exist on all computers running Windows 2000. You cannot view or modify membership in built-in system groups, and membership changes dynamically. Windows 2000 uses built-in systems groups to allow certain users access at specified times. The five built-in system groups are as follows:

Everyone—Membership includes all current network users, including anyone using the Guest account. When you log on to the network, you are added to the Everyone group. When you log off, your account is removed from this group.

Authenticated Users—Membership includes all current network users except the Guest account.

Creator Owner—Membership depends on specific resources. When you create a new file, your account adds to the Creator Owner group for that file.

Network—Membership includes all user accounts that are currently accessing a resource over the network. For example, every user printing to your shared network printer adds to the printer's network group.

Interactive—Membership includes only those users logged on locally to the computer.

Using Local Groups

Local groups are used to assign permissions to resources only on the computer on which they are created. Generally, you use domain local groups for this purpose, but if the computer is not attached to a domain (for example, the computer is a member of a workgroup), you must use local groups.

 Note: Use local groups on any computer that is not a domain controller. However, if the computer is a member of a domain, you should use domain local groups.

Built-in Local Groups

The following are six built-in local groups:

- Administrators

- Backup operators

- Guests

- Power users

- Replicator

- Users

Permissions

Permissions determine the level of access a user, or more commonly a group of users, has to an object. An object is a shareable network resource that includes a file, folder, or printer. The permissions you assign to objects vary depending on the object type. For example, you can assign a user the Manage Printers permission to a printer, but not to a folder or file.

Permissions apply to both local users and network users. Locally, NTFS permissions apply to files and folders. Even if a user can log on to your computer locally, you can prevent the user from accessing certain files using NTFS permissions. For network access to resources, both NTFS permissions and Share permissions determine user access rights.

Using Share Permissions

Before a user is able to access a resource over the network, the object must be shared. Once shared, you assign Share permissions to grant or restrict access.

 Note: Share permissions only apply to access over the network.

You can share both folders and printers, but you cannot share individual files. If you have one file you wish to share over the network, you must place it in its own folder and share the folder.

The following are the three Share permissions you can assign to a folder:

Read—Allows a user to see the contents of the folder, open files, run applications stored in the folder, open subfolders, and view file attributes.

Change—Gives users Read permission as well as the ability to create new folders and files, modify the contents of files, change file attributes, and delete files and folders.

Full Control—Allows users to do everything granted with Read and Change permissions as well as change file and folder permissions, and take ownership of files.

The following rules apply when you share a folder:

*   Share permissions apply to the folder only, not to subfolders or files

*   The default permission when you share a folder is to grant the Everyone group Full Control

*   A user granted access to a shared folder receives the Read share permission by default

*   When you copy a shared folder, the copy is not shared, but the original remains shared

 Warning: The default share permission grants the Everyone group (that includes the Guest account) Full Control to the folder. This means a temporary guest on your network could delete the contents of your shared folder or change the permissions so that nobody else can access the files!

Viewing Share Permissions

As an administrator, you can view the Share permissions for a folder. To do so, follow these steps:

1.   From the desktop, right-click My Computer and choose Explore.

    Windows Explorer opens (Figure 8.6).

Figure 8.6 Windows Explorer

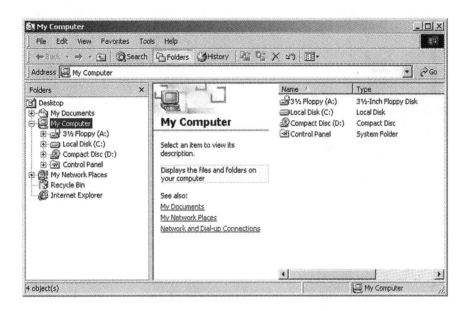

2.   From the left pane of Windows Explorer, expand the hard drive that contains the shared folder, and then expand folders as necessary to find the shared folder (Figure 8.7).

Note: A shared folder appears in Windows Explorer with a hand underneath it.

Figure 8.7 Shared Folder

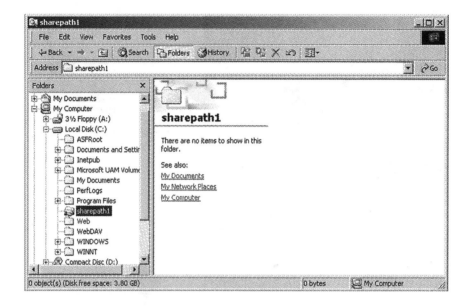

3. Right-click the shared folder and choose Sharing.

    The Folder Properties window opens with the Sharing property page selected (Figure 8.8).

Tip: If the folder is not yet shared, use the Sharing property page and choose Share
this folder to share it.

Figure 8.8 Sharing Property Page

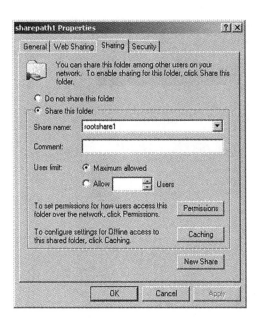

4. From the Sharing Property Page, choose Permissions.

    The Permissions window opens. All user and group accounts that have permissions to this folder are listed (Figure 8.9).

Figure 8.9 Share Permissions

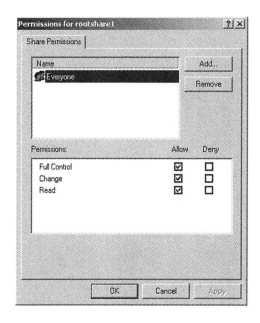

5.   To view the permissions assigned to a user or group account, choose that account from the list. The check marks below indicate the assigned permissions.

 Note: The three share permissions—Read, Change, Full—can be granted or denied to users and groups. Denied permissions override granted permissions.

Using NTFS Permissions

The Windows NT File System (NTFS) is a file system used to format hard drives. Both Windows NT 4.0 and Windows 2000 support NTFS. One of the major benefits of using NTFS over other file systems, like the File Allocation Table (FAT) file system, is that it supports NTFS permissions. You can assign NTFS permissions to individual files and folders, and apply local and network accesses.

When you use Share permissions to primarily make a resource available on the network, NTFS permissions fine-tune the access rights. There are only three Share permissions, but there are five NTFS permissions for both files and folders.

 Note: In order to assign NTFS permissions, the file or folder must reside on an NTFS-formatted partition. Files and folders on FAT and FAT32 (32-bit FAT) partitions can only be assigned Share permissions.

File Permissions

You can assign the following NTFS permissions to a file:

Read—Allows a user to read the contents of the file and view the file attributes, permissions, and ownership.

Write—Allows a user to overwrite the file and change file attributes, but not to modify the original file as well as view file permissions and ownership.

Read and Execute—Allows a user the permissions granted with Read, and to run the application (when this permission is assigned to an executable file).

Modify—Allows a user to change the file, delete the file, and the permissions granted by the Write and Read and Execute permissions.

Full Control—Allows a user to perform all tasks granted by the other NTFS permissions, and to change file permissions and take ownership of the file.

Folder Permissions

The following are the six NTFS permissions you can assign to folders:

Read—Allows a user to see the folder contents and view folder permissions, attributes, and ownership.

Write—Allows a user to create files and folders within the folder and change folder attributes. Also includes the Read permission rights.

List Folder Contents—Allows a user only to view the names of files and folders within the folder.

Read & Execute—Allows the user all the permissions granted by the Read and List Folder Contents permissions, and also allows a user to navigate through folders to reach subfolders.

Modify—Allows a user to perform all tasks granted by the Read & Execute and Write permissions, and also to delete the folder.

Full Control—Allows the user all other NTFS permissions but also allows the user to change folder permissions, take ownership of the folder, and delete all files and subfolders.

Viewing NTFS Permissions

You can view NTFS permissions for any file or folder on an NTFS volume. To do so, follow these steps:

1. From the desktop, right-click My Computer and choose Explore.

2. From the left pane of Windows Explorer, expand an NTFS-formatted volume.

3. Right-click the folder or file you want to view, and then choose Properties.

    The Folder (or File) Properties Windows opens (Figure 8.10).

Figure 8.10 Folder Properties Window

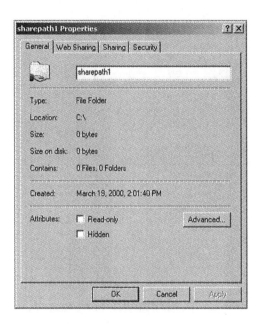

4.   From the Folder Properties window, choose the Security property page.

Each user or group that has permissions to the folder is listed. Select a user or group account to view the permissions (Figure 8.11).

 **Warning:**   Like the default Share permission, the default NTFS permission grants the Everyone group Full Control.

Figure 8.11 NTFS Permissions

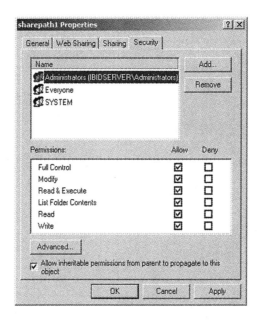

Using Printer Permissions

Printer permissions are assigned to printers, whether or not the printer is shared. They act like NTFS permissions, affecting users who access the printer locally and over the network.

The following are the three Printer permissions you can grant or deny to a user and groups:

Print—Allows the user to connect to a printer and print documents. This permission also allows a user to pause, resume, restart, and cancel queued printer documents.

Manage Documents—Allows the user all the rights granted by the Print permission but also includes the ability to pause, resume, restart, and cancel all print jobs and control the job settings.

Manage Printer—Allows the user all of the rights of Manage Documents but also includes permissions to share the printer, change printer properties, delete the printer, and change the printer permissions.

Viewing Printer Permissions

To view printer permissions, follow these steps:

1. From the Start Menu, choose Settings, and then select Printers.

2. From the Printers folder, right-click the printer you wish to view, and then choose Properties.

   The Printer Properties window opens (Figure 8.12).

Figure 8.12 Printer Properties

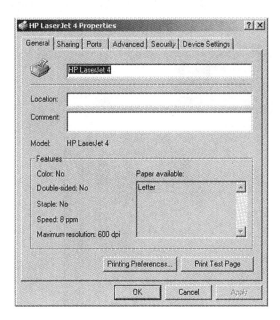

Note: A shared printer appears with a hand beneath the icon.
A printer does not need to be shared before you view the printer permissions.

3.   From the Printer Properties window, choose the security property page (Figure 8.13).

Figure 8.13 Printer Security Property Page

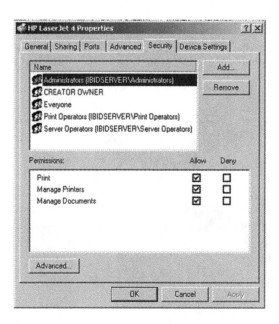

Each group and user account that has permissions for the printer lists. Choose any one account to view the assigned permissions.

User Rights

User rights determine what a user can do and cannot do on a network. Permissions apply to specific resources, while user rights apply to the entire computer or domain. Many of these rights may not be aware to the user—the right to log on to the network using a workstation, the right to change the system time, the right to shut down or restart the computer—but each of these rights, and many more, are granted when a user logs on.

You assign user rights to individual users, but like permissions, it is much easier to assign rights to groups, and then place users in the groups. Many of the built-in groups have pre-defined user rights to accommodate your needs.

Understanding Common User Rights

Some of the common user rights you can assign or deny users include the following:

Log On Locally—Allows the user to log on to the network from a specific computer. Most users have this right on most computers, but cannot log on locally to a domain controller.

Note: Only administrators and backup operators can log on locally to a domain controller.

Change System Time—Allows a user to change the system time on a computer. This right is normally available to users, except on domain controllers.

Shut Down the System—Allows a user to shut down and restart the computer. Users have the right to shut down computers running Windows 2000 Professional, but not servers and domain controllers where this right is reserved for administrators or backup operators.

Backup Files and Folders—Allows administrators and backup operators group members to store data on removable media using the Windows 2000 Backup utility.

Tip: This right overrides any NTFS permissions assigned to the files and folders, so an administrator can back up files she can't otherwise read or access.

Take Ownership—Allows the user who creates a file or folder to be the owner with the ability to adjust file attributes and permissions. A user with the Take Ownership right has the ability to become the owner of the file. By default, only administrators have the Take Ownership right.

Using Default User Rights

Built-in groups have pre-defined user rights. When you add user accounts to these groups, the users inherit these pre-defined user rights. The rights for four built-in groups are shown in Table 8.2.

Tip: Although you can change the default pre-defined user rights for built-in groups, it is generally better to create a new group with the rights you want. This allows you and other administrators to know what rights the built-in groups have.

Table 8.2 User Rights for Built-in Groups

User Right	Users	Power Users	Backup Operators	Administrators
Share resources		X	X	X
Log on to a workstation	X	X	X	X

User Right	Users	Power Users	Backup Operators	Administrators
Shut down a workstation	X	X	X	X
Log on to a server	X	X	X	X
Shut down a server		X	X	X
Create local groups	X	X	X	X
Create user accounts		X	X	X
Delete all user accounts				X
Modify all group memberships				X
Take ownership				X
Back up files			X	X
Manage security				X

Vocabulary

Review the following terms in preparation for the certification exam.

Term	Description
Active Directory	Active Directory is the new service that defines and supports the organization of a network. In Windows 2000, domain controllers are servers providing the Active Directory service.
built-in accounts	Accounts created upon Windows 2000 installation for administrators and guests that provide a way to access local and domain computers and resources.
built-in groups	Groups created by Windows 2000 with pre-assigned configurations for user rights and permissions.
console	The main interface of the MMC, the console contains snap-ins.
domain	A logical grouping of computers in network that a share a common directory database.
domain controllers	Windows 2000 servers running the Active Directory service.
domain user account	A network account that allows permission to access a network domain with most computers in addition to local computer access.
global group	A group scope that may contain users only from the same domain, and may be assigned permission to resources in any domain.

Term	Description
group type	Defines the purpose of the group. The group type is either security or distribution.
groups	A collection of accounts or objects categorized by common characteristics or needs used for organization purposes in Windows 2000 networks.
local user account	A network account that allows permission to access files on a specific computer without access to the network.
MMC	The Microsoft Management Console provides a centralized location for administrative tools called snap-ins.
NTFS	NT File System works with Windows NT and Windows 2000 operating systems and supports advanced features from long filenames to object-oriented files with user and system-defined attributes.
NTFS permissions	Rights that allow access to files and folders on an NTFS-formatted volume. NTFS permissions apply whether folder access is local or remote.
object	Every network component (for example, a computer, printer, or user) is represented in the Active Directory by an object.
permissions	Authorization settings that determine the level of user or group access to specific objects or resources on the network.
scope	In Windows 2000, the group attribute that defines group membership in domains.

Term	Description
Share permissions	Access rights assigned to a folder that affect what rights users have to the folder and its contents during remote access to the network.
snap-ins	Modules that run within the MMC, each snap-in handles a different aspect of Windows 2000 management.
universal group	A group scope that contains users from any domain and who have assigned permissions to resources in any domain.
user account	An established way for an individual to access a computer, a network, and or resources, with a username and password.
user rights	Settings that determine what a user can and cannot do on a computer or network domain.

In Brief

If you want to...	Then do this...
Keep unwanted users out of your network and provide authorized users with access to specific resources	Assign local and domain user accounts and passwords and combine them into group accounts for specific access permissions.
Logon to the local computer after the initial Windows 2000 installation	Use the built-in local Administrator account to access the local computer after an initial installation of Windows 2000, and then create a new user account for yourself.
Grant access to your Windows 2000 network	Create domain user accounts in the Active Directory on a domain controller.
Organize and efficiently administrate a large number of individual users or resources	Combine user accounts or resources with similar needs into Windows 2000 groups.
Automatically assign user accounts rights and permissions	Use the Windows 2000 built-in groups, so once a user account adds to the group, the user account obtains the built-in permissions and rights.
Assign permissions to resources only on the computer from which they are created	Use Local groups to assign permissions to resources if the computer is not attached to a domain, or use Domain Local groups if the computer is the member of a domain.
Assign access rights of a user for local files and folders, and network resources like printers	Use the NTFS permissions and Share permissions to assign the level of access a user or group of users have to an object.

Lesson 8 Activities

Complete the following activities to better prepare you for the certification exam.

1. Give two types of Windows 2000 user accounts and discuss where to apply them and how to create or modify them.

2. Explain why it is important to organize users into groups with similar security needs.

3. List two types of groups and their use.

4. Explain how the scope types relate to the group types.

5. Describe three types of built-in groups.

6. Discuss how to share files on the network, and name the three share permissions.

7. Explain the difference between share permissions and NTFS permissions, and list the five NTFS permissions for both files and folders.

8. Explain how permissions are assigned to printers.

9. Explain the difference between user rights and permissions, and give some examples of common rights that are assigned or denied to users.

10. Built-in groups have default user rights. Users inherit the rights of a built-in group when you add them to the group. List some of the user rights that are NOT available for a user who is a member of the Users built-in group.

Answers to Lesson 8 Activities

1. Two types of Windows 2000 user accounts are local and domain user accounts. You create local and domain accounts with Windows 2000 snap-in tools. The local user account allows basic functionality, such as logon, for a specific computer, called the local computer. No domain accesses are given with these account types. Administrators usually create local user accounts on stand-alone computers or small workgroup networks that run Windows 2000 Professional. To create a local user account, use the Local Users and Groups snap-in from the Computer Management console.

    Administrators create domain user accounts on the domain controller to grant access to the Windows 2000 network. You create these accounts in the Active Directory Users and Computers console on a domain controller. From the Start Menu, choose Programs, Administrative Tools, and then select Active Directory Users and Computers.

2. It is especially important to organize a large number of users in big organizations into groups with similar characteristics or needs to simplify administration. By organizing users into groups with similar security needs, you eliminate the redundancy of administering many rights and permissions to each individual account. You can move an individual user into pre-assigned groups with the appropriate permissions, rather than changing many different settings for one user.

3. Two types of Windows 2000 groups are Security Groups and Distribution Groups. Security groups grant or deny permissions to user accounts or computer accounts for network resources. Security groups can be used for e-mail distribution, although it's not recommended because it causes more network traffic. However, the Distribution groups are specifically designed to send e-mail messages. Although Security groups can be used for distribution, Distribution groups cannot be assigned security permissions.

4. The scope defines the attributes of a group. It allows membership in the group if certain criteria are met. Three scopes are available for security groups and distribution groups: domain local groups, global groups, and universal groups. The Domain local group scope allows the group to access only the resources in the local domain, and allows only group members from the local domain to join the group. The Global groups scope assigns permissions to resources in any domain, and allows members only from the domain where the Global group is created. The Universal groups scope assigns permissions to any resource in the network, and allows members from any domain in the network.

5. Three types of built-in groups are: built-in domain local groups, built-in global groups, and built-in local groups. Built-in domain local groups are created on domain controllers. Built-in global groups do not have permissions assigned by default, and are used to group users for placement into domain local groups. The built-in system groups are available and standard on all computers running Windows 2000. They are not viewable or modifiable, and the membership changes dynamically.

6. Share permissions are given after an object is created. Once an object such as a folder or printer is shared, you can assign the appropriate permissions. However, you can't share files. To share a file, you must create a folder (object) and place the file in it. Then you can share the folder with the file in it. You can assign Share permissions to grant or restrict access to the folder.

    Three Share permissions you can assign to shared folders are Read, Change, and Full Control. The Read permissions only allow folder and file opening and viewing. In addition to the Read permissions, the Change permission allows folder and file creation, attribute modification, and deletion. The Full Control share permission allows all of the Read and Change permissions along with the ability to change the file and folder permissions and to take ownership of them.

7. There are major differences in the way shared permissions and NTFS permissions work. Shared permissions make folders or resources available to others on the network, with only three types of Share permissions. The NTFS, however, allows assignment of permissions to both files and folders, and applies them to local and network access. NTFS gives additional flexibility to fine tune access rights with five permissions each for files and folders.

    Five NTFS permissions for files include: Read, Write, Read and Execute, Modify, and Full control.

    Five NTFS permissions for folders include: Read, Write, List Folder Contents, Read and Execute, Modify, and Full Control.

8. Although a printer can be shared, you do not assign Share permissions to printers. Printer permissions are similar to NTFS permissions in that they are applicable to users who access the printer both locally and remotely.

9.   User rights apply specifically to user accounts or groups, and apply to the entire computer or domain. Permissions, however, apply to specific resources. User rights are granted when a user logs on.

Some common user rights which can be assigned or denied include:Log On Locally, Change System Time, Shut Down the System, Backup Files and Folders, and Take Ownership.

10. A member of the Users built-in group cannot share resources, shutdown a server, create user accounts, delete all user accounts, modify all group memberships, take ownership, backup files, or manage security.

Lesson 8 Quiz

These questions test your knowledge of features, vocabulary, procedures, and syntax.

1. For which of the following activities does the network use the user account?

    A. Access to the network is granted

    B. Grant or deny network resource access

    C. Restore user's personal files at logon

    D. Restore user's customized desktop at logon

2. Where should you create local user accounts?

    A. All computers in a domain

    B. All computers in a workgroup

    C. Member servers

    D. Domain Controllers

3. Which of the following features does the local built-in Administrator account have?

    A. It can be deleted

    B. It can be locked out from the computer

    C. It can perform all administrative tasks on the computer

    D. It can be renamed

4. Which two built-in accounts are made domain user accounts when you install Active Directory on a Windows 2000 server?

    A. Power user

    B. Administrator

    C. Backup operator

    D. Guest

5. Which of the following Windows 2000 group types grant and deny permission to network resources?

    A. Distribution groups

    B. Domain local groups

    C. Security groups

    D. Global groups

6. Which of the following group scopes can contain members from any domain in the network and assign permissions to any resource in the network?

    A. Global groups

    B. Universal groups

    C. Domain local groups

    D. Built-in groups

7. Which of the following are built-in domain local groups?

    A. Everyone

    B. Account operators

    C. Users

    D. Authenticated users

8. Which of the following are built-in global groups?

    A. Domain Users

    B. Domain Guests

    C. Domain Ghosts

    D. Enterprise Admins

9. Which of the following rules apply when you share a folder with Share permissions?

    A. Share permissions apply to the folder and not to subfolders or files.

    B. The default permission when you share a folder is to grant the Everyone group Full Control.

    C. A user granted access to a shared folder receives the Read share permission by default.

    D. When you copy a shared folder, the copy is also shared.

10. Which of the following built-in groups always includes the Guest account?

    A. Everyone

    B. Network

    C. Interactive

    D. Enterprise

Answers to Lesson 8 Quiz

1. Answers A, B, C, and D are all correct. The user account and password are used to log on a user to the network, grant access to resources, and restore the user's profile, which includes files and desktop settings.

2. Answer B is correct. You create local user accounts on computers in a workgroup.

    Answer A is incorrect. You should use domain user accounts in a domain.

    Answer C is incorrect. Member servers are typically members of a domain, and so you should not need to create local user accounts.

    Answer D is incorrect. You cannot create local user accounts on a domain controller.

3. Answer C is correct. The local built-in Administrator account can perform all administrative tasks on the computer.

    Answer D is correct. The local built-in Administrator account can be renamed, but it can't be deleted.

    Answer A is incorrect. The local built-in Administrator account can be cannot be deleted.

    Answer B is incorrect. The local built-in Administrator account can never be locked out from the computer.

4. Answers B and D are correct. The built-in Administrator and Guest accounts are added to the Active Directory and made domain user accounts when you install Active Directory on a Windows 2000 server.

    Answer A and C are incorrect. Power User and Backup Operator are not built-in accounts that are added to the Active Directory and made domain user accounts when you install Active Directory on a Windows 2000 server.

5. Answer C is correct. Security groups grant and deny permissions to network resources. Computer and user accounts may be added to a security group.

    Answer A is incorrect. Although the Distribution groups are a Windows 2000 group type, they are used specifically for e-mail message distribution.

Answers B and D are incorrect. Domain Local and Global groups are Group Scope types, which are attributes of the security and distribution groups.

6.   Answer B is correct. The Universal Groups scope can contain members from any domain in the network and assign permissions to any resource in the network.

Answer A is incorrect. The Global groups scope assign permissions to resources in any domain, but members can only come from the domain in which the global group is created.

Answer C is incorrect. Domain local groups grant permissions to resources within the local domain and members can come from any domain in the network.

Answer D is incorrect. Built-in groups are not group scopes.

7.   Answers A, B, C, and D are all correct. Each of these is a built-in domain group.

8.   Answers A, B, and D are correct. These groups are built-in Global groups.

Answer C is incorrect. Domain Ghosts is a fictitious group.

9.   Answer A is correct. Share permissions apply to the folder and not to subfolders or files.

Answer B is correct. The default permission when you share a folder is to grant the Everyone group Full Control.

Answer C is correct. A user granted access to a shared folder receives the Read share permission by default.

Answer D is incorrect. When you copy a shared folder, the copy is NOT also shared. However, the original remains shared.

10.   Answer A is correct. The Everyone group always includes the Guest account.

Answers B, C, and D are incorrect. Each of these groups may contain the Guest account at any given time, but none will always contain the account.

Lesson 9: Windows 2000 and the Internet

The line between private networks and public networks is often not easily defined. Many corporations use the Internet and other public networks to transfer private information between their networks. With Virtual Private Networking (VPN) technologies, you can securely send information over lines shared by thousands of other users.

Although it may be difficult to distinguish private and public networks at first glance, it is absolutely vital as a network administrator to separate the two. Private networks—and the private data carried on them—must remain confidential.

The heart of this lesson is the interconnectivity of private Windows 2000 networks and the Internet. The Transmission Control Protocol/Internet Protocol (TCP/IP) is the protocol suite used on the Internet, and so all of the technologies discussed in this lesson are part of the TCP/IP protocol.

After completing this lesson, you should have a better understanding of the following topics:

- Internetworking

- Internet Connectivity

- TCP/IP Technologies

- Client Configuration

- Internet Information Services (IIS)

Internetworking

Most networked companies have some connection to the Internet. Whether it is a one-way connection that allows employees to access Web pages or a Web page providing customers with information, the connection between private networks and the Internet is strong.

Defining Intranets, Extranets, and Internets

The interconnection of private networks and the public Internet is of chief concern for many network administrators. Private data must remain private. Before learning how to securely interconnect networks, you need to understand how networks are classified.

Networks are classified into three categories—intranets, extranets, and Internets.

Intranet—An intranet is a TCP/IP-based network that belongs to a single organization. Access is restricted to authorized users. The intranet may be attached to the Internet and have Web pages, but the intranet is separated from the Internet by a firewall.

Extranet—An extranet is an intranet with an external component. An extranet is a private network, and only authorized users can access the network, but some access is permitted to remote authorized users. For example, you may allow a remote sales staff to connect to your network by building a Virtual Private Network (VPN). These users can log on to your intranet over the Internet.

Internet—An internet is a collection of two or more networks connected by routers. A router is a device that forwards and routes data from its source to the destination. Generally, the term internet refers to the Internet—the global collection of thousands of networks, all connected by routers. The Internet is public, and, therefore, data on the Internet is intended for public use and is not secure.

Using the Domain Name System (DNS)

DNS is a record-keeping service responsible for maintaining a database file of information about the computers on your network. The information in this file includes the names and addresses of the computers, and may contain information about the role of each computer on the network. The purpose of this database file, and of DNS in general, is to simplify network use. It also makes Web browsing and most other Internet-related activities possible.

To access the Internet, you enter a server name into the address section of a Web browser (like www.lightpointlearning.net), and a Web page appears. Most users take for granted that they can access another computer over the Internet by entering its name. However, the Internet is based entirely on the TCP/IP network protocol, which uses numbers not names to identify computers. DNS is the service responsible for converting these TCP/IP numbers (called IP addresses) into familiar names, and converting names to addresses.

Tip: The Internet Protocol (IP) and IP addressing is discussed thoroughly in Lesson 5 of this book. If you are unfamiliar or uncertain about IP addressing, refer to this lesson. IP addressing is a fundamental part of Windows 2000 networking and you will be tested on your knowledge of TCP/IP.

Understanding the Domain Namespace

More specifically, a name server (a computer running the DNS) translates IP addresses into Fully Qualified Domain Names (FQDNs). A FQDN is the name of a computer (also called the hostname), plus the full name of the domain in which the computer exists. The full domain name is defined by the domain namespace in which a computer is located.

The domain namespace is a hierarchical structure that organizes groups of computers on the Internet. The term domain defines a level within this hierarchical structure. There are three main levels in the domain name system: the root-level domain, top-level domains, and second-level domains (Figure 9.1).

Figure 9.1 Domain Namespace

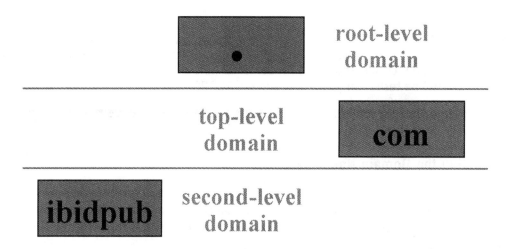

The root-level domain is at the top of the domain namespace hierarchy. It does not have a label, but is represented by a period (.). All domains on the Internet are members of the root domain. Below the root domain are a series of top-level domains. These domain names consist of two- or three-letter names that define the type of domain. Examples of top-level domains include the following:

- **.com** = Commercial organizations

- **.org** = Non-profit organizations

- **.edu** = Educational institutions

- **.gov** = Non-military American government organizations

- **.net** = Networks

- **.mil** = U.S. military

Some two-letter country abbreviations are as follows:

- **.ca** = Canada

- **.de** = Germany

Below the top-level domains are second-level domain names. These second-level domains contain hosts (host refers to any object on a TCP/IP network) and other domains, called subdomains. Second-level domains are typically company, agency, or university names. Let's look at an example.

Suppose you have a company named IBID Publishing, Inc., and you have an Internet domain name of ibidpub.com. The domain name officially ends with a . that represents the root domain. The period is often omitted, since all domains are members of the root domain. The .com is the top-level domain for corporations. Your company chose the name ibidpub because it represents the company's name.

Within your company, you have a Web server named www. The FQDN for your Web server is *www.ibidpub.com*. It includes the hostname (www), plus the full domain name (the root-, top-, and second-level domains).

 Note: The domain namespace is maintained by the non-profit organization InterNIC. To obtain a second-level domain name, you must register it with them at http://www.internic.net. When you register, they assign the IP address of your DNS server to the domain name.

Now, let's suppose that your company has several divisions. In an effort to organize the network structure, you gave each division a subdomain name, based on the division's role within your company. One of these subdivisions, Sales, wishes to have its own Web server. They have named the Web server webby. The FQDN for the computer may look something like webby.sales.ibidpub.com. Notice that .com and ibidpub have not changed because you added information below these levels on the hierarchy (Figure 9.2).

A name server resolves the FQDN to the IP address assigned to the computer. If the computer named webby.sales.ibidpub.com has an IP address of 169.254.30.3, a name server is responsible for recognizing this IP address and making the conversion to and from the name when required.

Figure 9.2 Domain Name Structure

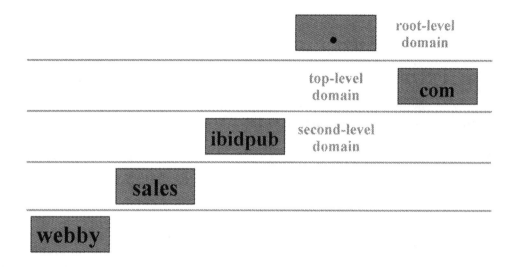

Understanding DNS Zones

A zone, or zone of authority, is the portion of the domain namespace for which a domain name server is responsible. This concept is important in understanding how DNS works. No DNS server can possibly know all of the 4.3 billion IP addresses as well as the FQDN that maps to each one. Most DNS servers have to be updated manually. If, as an administrator, you have to manually update a DNS server to know about all of the computers on the Internet, you have an impossible task on your hands.

Tip: Traditionally, a DNS server is manually configured and updated with every change in IP address or hostname for computers within its zone of authority. Windows 2000 eliminates this inconvenience by supporting dynamic updates.

The concept of zones limits a DNS server's responsibility. Responsibility shifts beyond the DNS zone of authority to a higher level name server. This process is called a forward lookup query.

A DNS server contains information in a lookup zone that maps FQDNs to IP addresses. A reverse lookup zone converts IP addresses to FQDNs.

Resolving DNS Names

When you ask for information from a DNS server (for example, when you browse the internet using FQDNs), your computer (the client) sends a request to the DNS server for your zone that is configured as the default name server.

 Note: The default name server can either be manually configured within the TCP/IP Properties sheet or dynamically assigned using DHCP.

This request is called a recursive request. The client computer is saying, give me an address or give me an error, but don't give me partial information. The default (also called local) name server needs to resolve a hostname to an IP address, so it first looks for the hostname in its own database file. If the hostname and IP addresses are found, the local name server sends this information back to your client. However, the request for an IP address is frequently beyond the zone of authority for the local name server. A local name server may only have information about computers on your local network. More often than not, the IP address you need is beyond your Local Area Network (LAN). If this is the case, your default DNS server must find the information for you (Figure 9.3).

Figure 9.3 Recursive Request to DNS Server

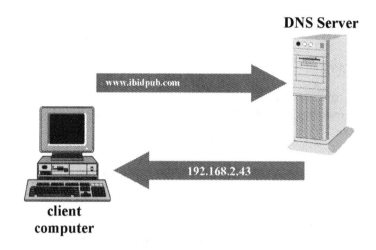

Let's go back to our scenario. You are working at a client computer in the ibidpub.com domain. Using a Web browser, you type in the Universal Resource Locator (URL) *http://www.cityu.edu*. The DNS server for your company (perhaps it is called dns_server.ibidpub.com) does not know the IP address for the computer

called www in the domain cityu.edu, so it performs a query to find the answer. Your local DNS server sends an iterative request to a root-level domain server. An iterative request simply asks for the best answer it can get, even if it contains only partial information. The iterative request process is as follows:

1.   The root name server receives a request from your local name server to resolve *www.cityu.edu*.

2.   The root name server does not know about a computer named www, or a domain named cityu, but it does have information about the first-level domain named edu. The root name server sends back the IP address of a top-level domain name server within the edu domain (Figure 9.4).

Figure 9.4 Iterative Request Response from Root

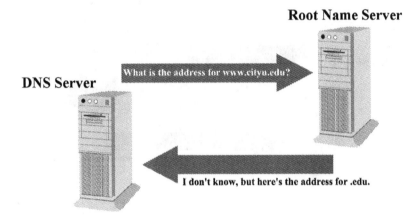

 Note: The client computer sends a recursive request for an IP address. It does not want the IP address for any other computer. Therefore, your local name server does not send the IP address it just received from the root-level name server. Instead, the name server uses it to find a better address.

3.   The local name server sends a request to the top-level domain name server for the edu domain.

4.   The top-level name server knows nothing of a computer named www, but it does know how to find the DNS server for cityu.edu. The top-level name server sends the IP address for a DNS server for cityu.edu back to your local DNS server (Figure 9.5).

5.   Your local DNS server sends a request to the cityu.edu DNS server.

Figure 9.5 Top-Level Iterative Request Response

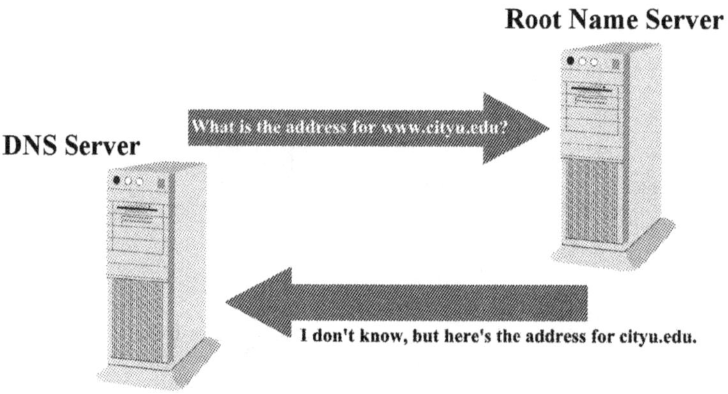

6. The name server for cityu.edu knows about a computer called www (it is within the name server's zone), and sends the IP address for www back to your local name server.

7. At this point, your local DNS server has an IP address for the computer you requested and it sends the information back to your computer (Figure 9.6).

Figure 9.6 IP Address Resolution

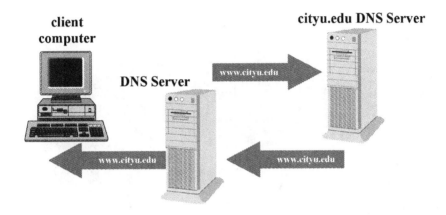

8. Your computer contacts www.cityu.edu using the IP address, and your Web browser displays the Web page (Figure 9.7).

Figure 9.7 Web Page Access

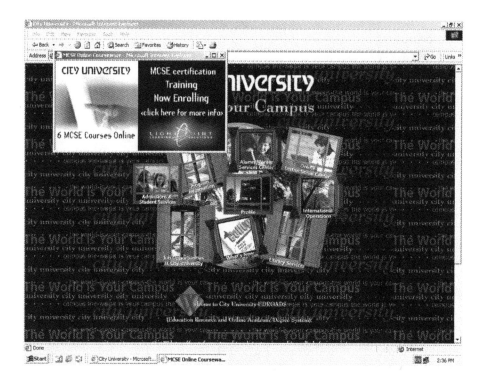

The following list reviews the 10 steps for resolving an IP address:

1.   The client contacts the local DNS server with a recursive request.

2.   The local DNS server contacts a root-level domain name server.

3.   The root-level DNS returns an IP address for a first-level name server.

4.   The local DNS sends a request to the first-level DNS.

5.   The first-level DNS send back the IP address for a second-level DNS.

6.   The local DNS sends a request to the second-level DNS.

7. The second-level DNS sends back the IP address of the computer.

8. The local DNS sends the IP address to the requesting client.

9. The requesting client sends a request for information directly to the target computer (in this case, it asks for a Web page from the computer www).

10. The target computer sends the requested information.

Internet Connectivity

When you connect an intranet to the Internet, you must deal with two issues. First, you must make sure that the network activities on the intranet are not visible to people on the Internet. Second, you must provide a way for users of your intranet to access the Internet.

Two of the more common ways to connect an intranet and the Internet are through using a firewall and using a proxy. The following sections describe each connection method.

Using a Firewall

A firewall is considered a first line of defense in protecting private information. It is a device that provides security by preventing unauthorized access to or from a private network. Firewalls are implemented in both hardware and software or a combination of both (Figure 9.8).

Figure 9.8 Intranet Firewall

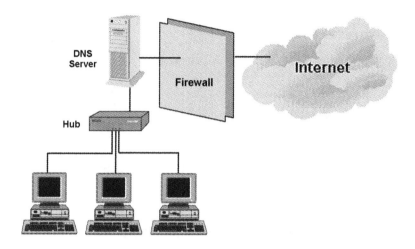

Firewalls prevent unauthorized Internet users from accessing private networks—especially intranets—connected to the Internet. Generally, an intranet is a network an organization uses exclusively for its members. Both the Internet and an intranet use the same protocols and technology, but information on the Internet is universally available while intranets limit information to authorized personnel within an organization.

Firewalls also prevent employees on a private network from accessing all or certain locations on the Internet. All messages entering or leaving the intranet pass through the firewall that examines each message and blocks those that do not meet the specified security criteria.

Firewall Disadvantages

Although firewalls provide a needed layer of security between an intranet and the Internet, they have drawbacks of which you should be aware. Consider the following two factors when deciding on the use of a firewall:

User privacy—The more rigorously the firewall checks the user's identity and activity, the more likely the user is to feel interrupted and frustrated with the process. Many employees may feel that monitoring activity is an infringement of privacy. Many companies argue that this activity occurs during the work day, on company time.

Internal security—Firewalls cannot solve problems with internal violations of security. Information can leak from your organization telephonically and through use of disks. Additionally, firewalls don't ensure your system against viruses. However, firewalls do prevent a great deal of potential data loss.

Using a Proxy Server

A proxy server allows many computers to share a single Internet connection. You may recall that every computer on the Internet must have a unique IP address. Unless your company purchases a valid IP address for every host (computer) on your network, the computers cannot connect directly to the Internet. However, you can install a proxy server, which acts as a gate through which data travels. The proxy server must have two IP addresses—a valid Internet IP address and an IP address that is part of your intranet scheme. The proxy server is the only computer that participates in Internet activity. All other computers must send and receive Internet data through the proxy.

How a Proxy Works

When you configure your network, you choose a range of IP addresses that are not valid on the Internet. These IP addresses are well defined and have been set aside specifically for building intranets. Routers on the Internet ignore these IP addresses, so computers throughout the world can use the same IP addresses and not worry about an IP address conflict. However, any computer with one of these reserved IP addresses cannot participate in Internet activity.

This is like the city giving you permission to build roads just like every other road, but they can't be connected to the city's roads. You can build a very extensive subdivision, but cars in your development can't get out to the city, and vice versa. You use these IP addresses to build roads that connect to one another and you give each road a name like 192.168.168.2 or 192.168.168.3. You also have one road that does connect to the city. This is the one valid IP address you have for the Internet (Figure 9.9). In this example, the city road has a name of 216.219.146.170.

Figure 9.9 Subdivision Analogy I

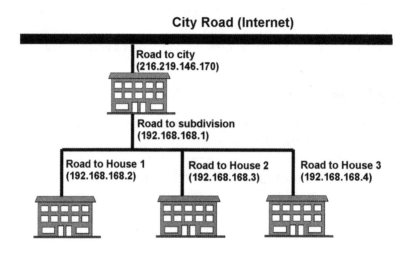

If you take the city road and give it a second name, one that fits the naming scheme of your subdivision (say, 192.168.168.1), it connects with the other roads you have built.

Carrying the analogy a bit further, people from the city will call the road 216.219.146.170, and people within your subdivision will call it 192.168.168.1. It is the same road, no matter the name. When data needs to get from one computer (one of the roads) to the Internet (the city), it travels from its IP address (192.168.168.4) to the internal IP address of the connecting road (192.168.168.1), and then goes off to the city on the same road (which is now called 216.219.146.170). You can see how this road with two names is like a gateway into and out of the subdivision. This road is the proxy server (Figure 9.10).

Figure 9.10 Subdivision Analogy II

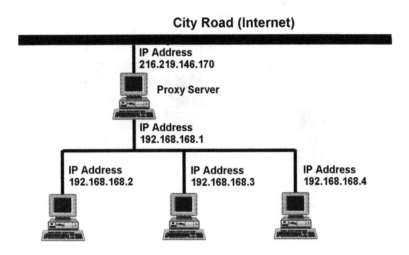

On a network, the proxy server receives all requests from client computers on its internal IP address, repackages them with its own external IP address, and then sends the request out on the Internet. When data arrives, the proxy server redirects the information to the original requesting computer (Figure 9.11).

Figure 9.11 Proxy Server

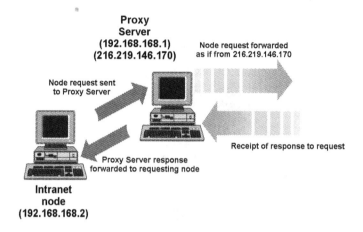

Proxy Features

You can use a proxy server as a cache server. Proxy servers store frequently accessed files. When a client computer requests a Web page that has been recently downloaded, the proxy server can send the data directly without sending information to the Web server. Client computers get considerably better response time when they access a Web page that is already in the proxy server's cache.

 Note: Install a large amount of Random Access Memory (RAM) in a proxy server and configure the server to cache large amounts of data. This allows many more users to share a single Internet connection without a noticeable drop in performance.

You can also use a proxy server as a firewall to prevent outside intruders from penetrating your network. Proxy servers block outside access to your intranet, and also prevent your organization's employees from accessing certain Web sites. These restrictions can be based on specific IP addresses or hostnames.

Tip: Most proxy server programs on the market act as a both a firewall and a proxy server. The price for proxy server software ranges from nearly free to several hundred dollars, depending on how many users you need to support and what features you wish to use.

Microsoft Proxy Server 2.0

Microsoft proxy Server 2.0 is a combination proxy server and firewall, and offers the following features:

Distributed and hierarchical caching—Places caching files on multiple computers to distribute the load.

Virtual hosting—Allows computers behind the firewall (those on your intranet) to host Web pages. Virtual hosting is also known as reverse proxy.

Dynamic packet filtering—Determines automatically which TCP/IP ports to open and close, reducing the likelihood of unwanted access.

Alerting and logging—Allows you to monitor specific Web site accesses.

Integrated management tools—The Microsoft Management Console (MMC) allows you to configure Microsoft Proxy Server 2.0. The MMC provides a common interface for most Windows 2000 tools.

Note: Microsoft Proxy Server 2.0 runs on Windows NT 4.0 servers. You can run it on a Windows 2000 server after running the Proxy Server Update Wizard. Information on the update is found at the following Web page: http://www.microsoft.com/proxy

Using Network Address Translation (NAT)

Windows 2000 Server includes Network Address Translation (NAT) that allows you to configure a Windows 2000 computer like a proxy server. NAT works much like a proxy server by using one IP address for external traffic and one IP address for internal traffic. The external IP address is a valid Internet address, while the other IP address configures to match your intranet IP settings.

 Tip: NAT is part of the Routing and Remote Access Service (RRAS) of Windows 2000 Server.

NAT also acts as a scaled-down Dynamic Host Configuration Protocol (DHCP) server, supplying IP addresses to computers on the Intranet.

 Note: The acronym NAT refers to the Network Address Translation (NAT) service, or to the computer that runs the translation service as a Network Address Translator (NAT).

The three components to NAT are as follows:

Translation—NAT acts as the proxy server, translating internal IP address to external IP address and back again.

Addressing—NAT provides IP addresses for the intranet computers. This is a simplified version of DHCP. The default addresses issued by NAT begin with 192.168.0.2, with an internal IP address of 192.168.0.1 for the NAT computer.

Name resolution—NAT acts as a Domain Name System (DNS) server for the intranet. Although it does not actually provide any name resolution, clients are configured to send name resolution requests to the NAT. The NAT then forwards the requests to a real DNS server on the Internet.

There are two advantages to using NAT instead of a proxy server. First, NAT is included with Windows 2000 Server, so you do not need to purchase any additional software. Second, NAT provides basic DHCP and DNS services without having to load either one. Proxy servers do not include this functionality.

Tip: Like a proxy server, NAT can also serve as a firewall, keeping unwanted traffic out of your intranet.

Using Internet Connection Sharing

Internet connection sharing provides another way to attach several computers to the Internet through a single connection. Like NAT and proxy servers, Internet connection sharing uses two connections—one to the Internet and one to the intranet—to act as a passage for TCP/IP messages. Internet connection sharing has the following features:

- Runs on both Windows 2000 Server and Windows 2000 Professional. You do not need to purchase Windows 2000 Server to have a shared internet connection

- Issues IP addresses for your intranet, like a simplified DHCP server

- Does not work on a network that has a DHCP or DNS server

- Requires that each client on the network be configured to automatically obtain the TCP/IP information

Internet connection sharing is available on any Windows 2000 computer that has two or more network connections. For example, if you have a modem and Network Interface Card (NIC) installed, you can share the modem connection. The NIC attaches to the intranet and passes Internet information to the modem.

TCP/IP Technologies

The Transmission Control Protocol/Internet Protocol (TCP/IP) protocol suite is the language of the Internet. All data transmissions on the Internet use TCP/IP. The suite includes numerous protocols, and these protocols provide specific services. For example, the Internet Protocol (IP) handles all addressing and routing, while Transmission Control Protocol (TCP) handles reliable delivery of information. You are already familiar with some other TCP/IP protocols, including DNS and DHCP.

Many of the TCP/IP protocols work at the Application Layer of the Open Systems Interconnection (OSI) model. The Application Layer (Layer 7), which is the top layer of the model, provides a direct connection between the applications we use and the rest of the network protocol suite. The TCP/IP protocol suite includes the following Application Layer protocols: HTTP, FTP, SMTP, POP3, and NNTP.

Understanding HyperText Transfer Protocol (HTTP)

HTTP is perhaps the best-known protocol in the TCP/IP Application Layer. HTTP is the language of the World Wide Web. Web pages (which are written in HyperText Markup Language (HTML)) are transferred using HTTP from the Web server to the client.

HTTP transfers the following types of types of data:

- Text

- Graphics

- Audio

- Video

Note: HTTP is a one-way protocol. It only retrieves information from a server, but does not send data from the client.

Using HTTP Commands

HTTP provides a standard data type and standardizes the basic commands for opening a connection, requesting a service, responding to a request and closing a connection. The process follows these steps:

1. The client requests a connection to the server, using a URL address.

2. Information exchanges between client and server that establishes parameters for the session.

3. Data (a Web page, for example) transmits to the client.

4. The connection closes after transmission of data to the client. A new HTTP connection initiates every time another HTML file is requested.

Accessing HTML Information

HTML documents are sets of instructions that Web browsers understand. The Web page you view is the result of those instructions. A single page may represent a collection of text and files that are scattered across many different computer hard drives.

HTTP is sometimes confused with HTML. HTML is the language that defines the way text and graphics display on a Web page. HTTP is the protocol that controls how you access HTML information. HTML is a subset of a vastly more complicated mark-up language called Standard Generalized Markup Language (SGML).

Using the Secure HyperText Transfer Protocol (HTTPS)

HTTPS transfers Web pages securely. It uses Secure Sockets Layer (SSL) technology to encrypt and protect data sent by the client to the server, and data sent from the server to the client. An example of a Web page that uses the HTTPS protocol is any e-commerce site that accepts credit cards. Using HTTPS, customers enter sensitive credit information without the worry that the information can be intercepted and read.

 Note: You cannot prevent data sent over the Internet from being intercepted, but you can encrypt it to be unreadable to anyone but the intended recipient. HTTPS and SSL encrypt the data.

Using File Transfer Protocol (FTP)

The FTP utility transfers files between a server and client computer. FTP offers platform independence because it is available to any system running TCP/IP. UNIX or Windows NT servers routinely provide FTP services. FTP is an essential Internet service. Anyone who purchases software electronically or downloads a program update uses FTP. FTP is the way most programs and computer files transfer across the Internet.

Using FTP Line Commands

The FTP command-line utility is available on Windows 2000 computers running TCP/IP. Internet Explorer also allows for browsing an FTP site with a graphical interface (making downloading files on FTP servers a point-and-click action). There are also several FTP utilities with graphical interfaces available for accessing FTP servers.

To use the FTP command-line interface, follow these steps:

1.   From the Start Menu, choose Programs, Accessories, and then select Command Prompt.

2.   From the command Prompt, type **FTP** and then press **ENTER**.

     From the FTP> prompt, type **OPEN**, followed by the name or IP address of the FTP server (Figure 9.12). For example, you may type **OPEN ftp.microsoft.com.**

Figure 9.12 Accessing an FTP Server

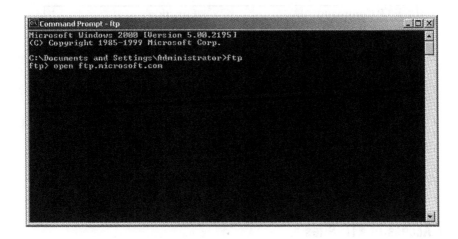

3. From the User> prompt, type your user name. If the server accepts anonymous access (most do), enter **ANONYMOUS** and then press **ENTER**.

4. From the Password> prompt, type your password. If you are logged on anonymously, you can enter anything. Common courtesy is to enter your e-mail address as the password.

Once you connect to the FTP server, you have a wide choice of commands to issue. Table 9.1 lists the four most common FTP commands and their functions. For a more comprehensive list, type **HELP**. For more detailed information on a command, type **HELP COMMAND**, where **COMMAND** is the command on which you want more information.

Table 9.1 FTP Commands

FTP Command	Function
BINARY	Changes file type to binary .
GET	Copies a remote file to a local computer.
PUT	Copies a local file to a remote server.
QUIT	Disconnects from the FTP server and exits FTP.

Anonymous Access of FTP Sites

Many FTP sites are configured for anonymous access to facilitate anyone who has the correct URL to access the site and download files. Anonymous access is a common system for delivering software updates, public files, and shareware applications. However, an anonymous configuration does not allow the FTP administrator to determine the users who actually log on to the site.

Using E-Mail Protocols

There are two TCP/IP protocols that allow transfer e-mail messages across the Internet. The Simple Mail Transport Protocol (SMTP) sends e-mail messages from the client to a mail server, and relays messages between mail servers. The Post Office Protocol Version 3 (POP3) downloads e-mail messages from a mail server to the client.

Simple Mail Transport Protocol (SMTP)

SMTP handles mail delivery to mail servers and between servers. SMTP does not provide local mail services, but does provide remote services. A primary advantage of using e-mail servers is their ability to deliver mail at any time. The recipient, as far as the SMTP is concerned, is the e-mail server.

Post Office Protocol (POP3)

POP3 facilitates local delivery requests for e-mail messages on a mail server. The mail server uses POP3 to send the e-mail to the client computer.

Using Network News Transfer Protocol (NNTP)

Newsgroups are a common and popular way for people to share information over the Internet. A newsgroup is a text-based listing of posted messages from the members of the group. Each newsgroup has a topic or theme, and the members of the newsgroup share an interest in that common theme. Many newsgroups have moderators who are responsible for monitoring the posts and removing inappropriate and off-topic messages.

 Note: Most newsgroups are public, permitting anyone to read and post messages to the newsgroup. However, some professional organizations have newsgroups that require a username and password.

NNTP is a TCP/IP protocol that transfers articles among newsgroup servers, and between a newsgroup server and a client. Originally, NNTP used a command-line utility. Now, very few people read and post newsgroup messages through a command line. There are numerous graphic newsgroup readers on the market, and many e-mail client programs also serve as newsgroup readers.

Using Telnet

Telnet is a command line utility that uses the local computer like a network terminal to connect to a Telnet server. Telnet allows you to work on a remote computer and remotely perform some file and directory management as well as run remote applications. With this type of connection, all processing occurs on the Telnet server.

Note: Telnet is both a command-line utility and an Application Layer protocol in the TCP/IP suite.

Running Telnet

To run Telnet, follow these steps:

1.   From the Start Menu, choose Programs, Accessories, and then select Command Prompt.

2.   From a command prompt, type **TELNET** and then press **ENTER**.

3.   Type **OPEN   SERVERNAME** (where SERVERNAME is the name of the Telnet server), and then press **ENTER**.

4.   Depending on the Telnet server, you will get prompts asking for a username and password. Type a valid username and password.

Once connected to the Telnet server, you can issue a number of commands. Most commands pertain to file and directory administration (like copy, move, ren (rename)). For a list of available commands, type **HELP** or **?** from the Telnet server's prompt.

Connecting to Servers

When you use the HTTP or FTP protocol to connect to a Web or FTP server, you use a Universal Resource Locator (URL). A typical URL looks like this:

http://test.lightpointlearning.net/downloads/test.html

Or this:

ftp://ftp.lightpointlearning.net/downloads/answers.txt

The URL contains the following three parts:

Protocol—The first part of the URL defines the protocol to use (http:// or ftp://).

DNS address—The Fully Qualified Domain Name (FQDN) for the Web or FTP server (test.light-pointlearning.net, for example).

File path—Defines folder path on the server to the requested file and the file type (for example, /downloads/test.html).

Client Configuration

Internet clients access Web pages from Web servers, send and receive e-mail messages, read newsgroups, and download files using FTP. Configuration of the client computer involves changing settings in Web browsers, e-mail clients, and newsgroup clients. Windows 2000 ships with Internet Explorer Version 5.0, a Web browser and FTP client, and Outlook Express, which is both an e-mail and newsgroup client.

Configuring Internet Explorer

There are few settings you need to configure for Internet Explorer. Of primary concern is setting Internet Explorer to use a proxy server. If you are using a proxy server, a NAT, or Internet connection sharing (all simply referred to as a proxy) on your network, Internet Explorer must know how to contact the proxy. Otherwise, Internet Explorer attempts to send requests for Web pages directly to the Web server, which will not work.

You can also configure cache and security settings in Internet Explorer.

Configuring Internet Explorer's Proxy Server Settings

To configure the proxy server settings in Internet Explorer, follow these steps:

1. From the desktop, right-click Internet Explorer, and then choose Properties.

    The Internet Options Windows opens (Figure 9.13).

Tip: If you do not have a shortcut to Internet Explorer on your desktop, open Internet
Explorer. From the Internet Explorer menu bar choose Tools, and then select
Internet Options.

Figure 9.13 Internet Options

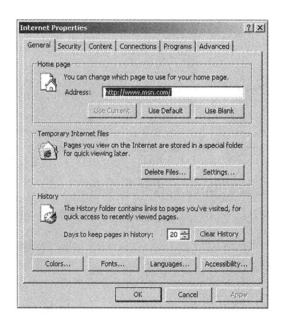

2.   From the Internet Options window, choose the Connections Property page (Figure 9.14).

Figure 9.14 Connections Property Page

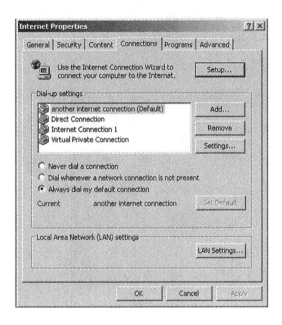

3. From the Connections Property Page, choose LAN Settings.

4. From the Local Area Network (LAN) Settings window, choose Use a proxy server (Figure 9.15).

Figure 9.15 Local Area Network (LAN) Settings

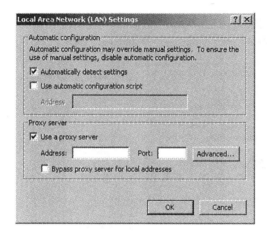

In the Address box, type the IP address for the proxy server (the local intranet IP address, not the Internet IP address) and the port number. Also choose Bypass proxy for local addresses (Figure 9.16).

Tip: Rather than risk a typographic error when entering this information, you can choose Automatically detect settings. Most of the time, Internet Explorer successfully detects the proxy or NAT server and sets the configuration information properly.

Figure 9.16 Proxy Server Address

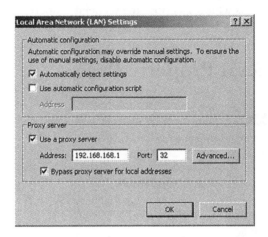

Setting Cache Size in Internet Explorer

Web browsers store recently downloaded files in a local cache. The cache is a folder on the hard drive. When you re-visit a Web page, Internet Explorer first checks the cache to see if the file already exists locally. This speeds up overall Internet use, since you can view a page without actually sending additional data on the Internet.

Tip: In Windows 2000, Internet Explorer stores cached files in the C:\Documents and Settings*Username*\Local Settings\Temporary Internet Files folder, where username is the name of the user currently logged in.

You can set the cache size to better reflect your network needs. If you have a very fast Internet connection, or a very small hard drive, you may wish to decrease the cache size. If you have enough hard drive space and a slow Internet connection, you can increase the cache size. To set the cache size, follow these steps:

1.   From the Internet Options window, choose the General property page (Figure 9.17).

Figure 9.17 General Property Page

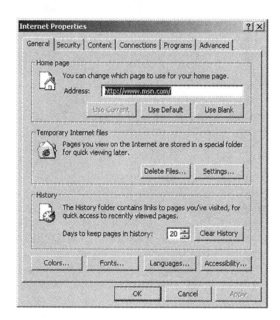

2.   From the General property page, choose Settings under the Temporary Internet Files section.

3.   From the Settings window, you can make several changes (Figure 9.18). These changes are outlined in Table 9.2.

Figure 9.18 Cache Settings

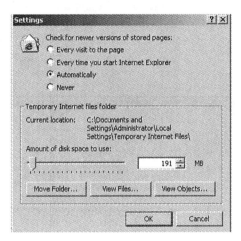

Table 9.2 Settings Options

Option	Description
Check for newer versions of stored pages	Defines how often Internet Explorer checks the original Web page to make sure the content has not changed from the cached version.
Amount of disk space to use	Adjusts the maximum amount of local hard disk space to be used for the cache. You can use the slider to adjust the value, enter a value, or use the arrow keys to choose the amount you wish to use.
Move Folder	Allows you to choose the folder that holds the cached files.
View Files	Allows you to view the currently cached files.
View Objects	Allows you to view any programs that have been downloaded and stored in the Downloaded Programs folder.

Cookies

Cookies are text files a Web server places on the client computer's hard disk. The main purpose of a cookie is to identify a visitor to a Web site. The information in cookies changes depending on the areas of a Web site entered by a user. Cookies are not executable and do not pose a security threat to the operation of your computer.

 Note: When you visit a Web site, the Web server you visit places information in a cookie. The Web site may read and update the cookie each time you visit, but unless you visit the site again, the cookie does not actively send out information.

Cookies are often used to create customized Web pages for visitors that contain their name and particular items of interest. Visitors to a Web site often fill out forms to sign up as a free member of the site or to purchase items. This kind of personal information stores in a cookie and saves to the visitor's hard disk through the Web browser. The next time the visitor goes to the same Web site, the browser sends the cookie to the Web server that updates the file. Web marketing and sales departments use this information to help determine the focus and effectiveness of their Web site and to plan new features or services.

Enabling and Disabling Internet Explorer Cookies

You have the option to allow or deny the storage of cookies on your computer. Although cookies are not executable programs, they can prevent some features of a Web site from functioning when disabled. Some people, however, are willing to forego certain features to preserve privacy. You have the ability to configure Internet Explorer to accept none, all, or only certain cookies. To do so, follow these steps:

1.   From the Internet Explorer menu bar, choose Tools, and then select Internet Options.

2.   From the Internet Options window, choose the Security property page (Figure 9.19).

Figure 9.19 Security Property Page

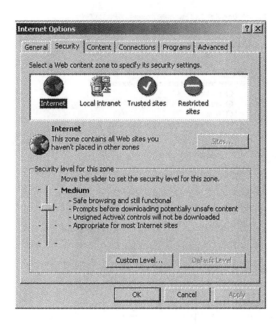

3. From the Security property page, choose Custom Level.

4. From the Security Settings window, scroll down through the list of options to find Cookies (Figure 9.20).

Figure 9.20 Security Settings

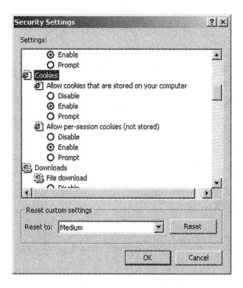

5.   You have three options for two types of cookies. Regular cookies persist—they stay on your computer indefinitely. Per-session cookies do not store on the computer after you leave the initiating Web site. For either of these cookie types, choose one of the following three options (Table 9.3).

Table 9.3 Cookie Options

Option	Description
Disable	Denies the use of all cookies.
Enable	Allows all cookies.
Prompt	Informs you that a Web server is trying to place a cookie, and lets you decide whether to permit or deny the request.

6. Choose OK to save the changes.

Using Outlook Express 5

Microsoft Outlook Express Version 5 is the e-mail and newsgroup client included with Windows 2000. Originally designed as a less powerful version of Microsoft Outlook, Outlook Express is now widely used.

Configuring an E-Mail Account

To configure an e-mail account in Outlook Express, follow these steps:

1. From the Start Menu, choose Programs, and then choose Outlook Express.

2. When Outlook Express opens, the Welcome screen displays in the right pane (Figure 9.21). Choose Set up a Mail account.

Figure 9.21 Outlook Express Welcome Screen

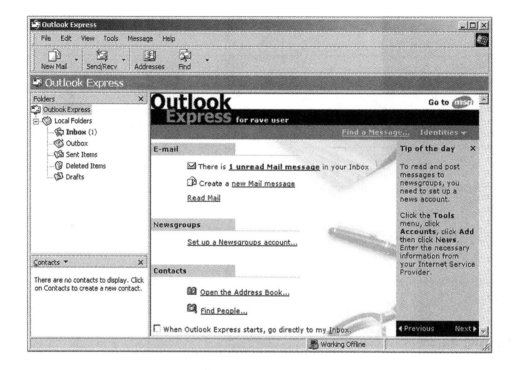

Tip: If you do not see the Welcome screen, from the Menu bar, choose Tools, and then select Accounts. From the Accounts window, select Add, and then choose Mail.

3.   From the Internet Connection Wizard, type the name that people will see when receiving an e-mail from you, and then choose Next (Figure 9.22).

Figure 9.22 Display Name

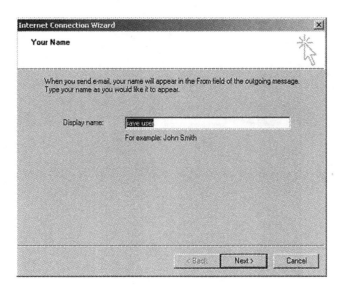

4. If you already have an e-mail account, choose I already have an e-mail address that I'd like to use, and then enter the e-mail account (Figure 9.23).

 Note: You can set up a new Hotmail e-mail account in Outlook Express Version 5.

Figure 9.23 Account Selection

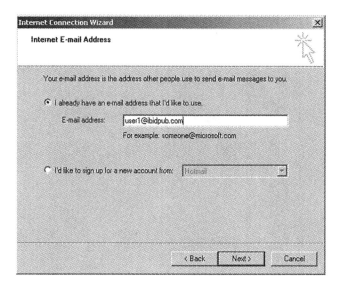

5.   From the E-mail Server Names window, type the full name or IP address for the POP3 and SMTP servers, and then choose Next.

6.   Type the account name and password used to access your e-mail, and then choose Next.

Tip: You can elect to have Outlook Express remember your e-mail password so that you are not prompted to enter a password each time Outlook Express checks mail. However, this poses a potential security problem on shared computers because it allows anyone can read your e-mail.

---

7.   Choose Finish to save your changes.

Configuring Newsgroups

To configure Outlook Express to serve as a newsgroup client, follow these steps:

1.   From the Start Menu, choose Programs, and then select Outlook Express.

2.   From the Welcome screen in the right pane, choose Set up a Newsgroups account.

Tip: To display the Welcome screen, from the Menu bar, choose Tools, and then select Accounts. From the Accounts window, select Add, and then choose News.

---

3.   From the Internet Connection Wizard, enter the name that will be attached to each of your newsgroup posts, and then choose Next.

4.   Enter an e-mail address people can use to reply to your newsgroup posts, and then choose Next.

5.   Type the name of the NNTP server you will use. If you are connecting to a private newsgroup that requires a log on, also choose My news server requires me to log on, and then choose Next (Figure 9.24).

Figure 9.24 Internet News Server Name

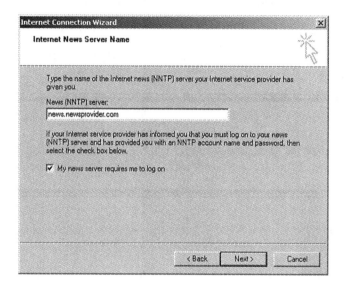

6.   If you selected My news server requires me to log on, type an appropriate username and password, and then choose Next.

7.   Choose Finish to save your changes.

Internet Information Services (IIS)

In order for all of the Internet technologies discussed in this lesson to work, there must be servers on the Internet to provide the services. Windows 2000 Server includes Internet Information Services 5.0 (IIS), a comprehensive package that allows a Windows 2000 server to act as a Web server, FTP server, Telnet server, and Newsgroup server.

IIS is incorporated into the Windows 2000 operating system. Like most other Windows 2000 utilities, management of IIS is done through the MMC. Furthermore, full integration with Windows 2000 allows Web and FTP servers to use the built-in security of Windows 2000. IIS supports NTFS permissions, file encryption, and Windows authentication.

Note: You can remotely manage the IIS server using Internet Explorer or another Web browser on any computer. This allows you to manage Web pages without being physically present at the Web server.

Understanding IIS Features

Although IIS is shipped essentially free with every copy of Windows 2000, IIS supports many of the advanced features available on any Web or FTP server. Some of those supported features are as follows:

Multiple Site Hosting—IIS supports multiple Web and FTP sites using a single IP address.

Web Distributed Authoring and Versioning (WebDAV)—WebDAV allows users to collaborate on a single project by placing the file on the IIS server. ISS monitors changes and handles version control, so that no duplicates of the file are created. Authorized users can access the file with nothing more than a Web browser, expanding the possibilities of intranets and Virtual Private Networking.

Secure Sockets Layer (SSL)—SSL provides a means of securely transmitting data across the Internet by encrypting the data.

Indexing Service—The indexing service allows users to search Web pages for specific text.

Windows Media Services—IIS supports sending live-streaming audio and video information from Web pages.

Active Server Pages (ASP)—ASP allows you to develop platform-independent scripting on Web pages, so that users of all client computer types can receive the information. IIS fully supports ASP.

Scripting—IIS supports VBScript and JavaScript languages in Web pages.

Vocabulary

Review the following terms in preparation for the certification exam.

Term	Description
Application Layer	Layer 7 at the top of the OSI model provides direct connection between applications and the other layers of the network protocol suite.
cache server	Servers that store frequently used Web page s and components to speed up client Web page access.
cookie	A text file that Web servers place on client hard disks to identify them as visitors at Web sites.
default name server	Also called local name server, resolves hostnames to IP addresses using its database file of LAN computers.
DHCP	Dynamic Host Configuration Protocol is a service for automatic IP address and settings assignment.
DNS	Domain Name System is a record-keeping service for the database that holds information about computers on a network; it converts IP address es to host names and host names to addresses.
DNS server	A Domain Name System server runs the DNS service.
domain	A logical grouping of computers that share a common directory database.
domain namespace	A hierarchical organization of groups of computers on the Internet from the root down through top and second level domains and subdomains.

Term	Description
dynamic update	A new feature of both DNS and DHCP that allows DHCP to update the DNS database as changes occur on the network .
extranet	A collection of private intranets to which authorized remote users can log on to over the Internet .
firewall	A hardware or software implementation that protects computer and network systems from unauthorized access.
forward lookup zone	The portion of a DNS database file in a server that maps FQDNs to IP addresses.
FQDN	A Fully Qualified Domain Name is the name of a computer (host) plus the full name of the domain where the computer exists.
FTP	File Transfer Protocol is an Internet essential utility that transfers files between servers and clients, regardless of client types or operating systems.
host	Any object on a TCP/IP network and other domains.
HTML	HyperText Markup Language is language that defines the way text and graphics display on a Web page . It is a subset of SGML.
HTTP	The HyperText Transfer Protocol controls how HTML information, Web page display instructions, is accessed and retrieved over the Internet.
HTTPS	The Secure HyperText Transfer Protocol transfers Web pages using encryption technology to protect data sent to and from servers and clients.

Term	Description
IIS	Internet Information Services 5.0 is a utility incorporated into the Windows 2000 operating system that allows a Windows 2000 server to act as a Web, FTP, Telnet, and Newsgroup server.
Internet	The Internet is a public global collection of thousands of networks connected by routers.
internet	A collection of two or more networks connected by routers.
InterNIC	A joint effort among AT&T, Network Solutions, Inc. (NSI), and the National Science Foundation to ensure no two computers have the same IP address assignment.
intranet	A TCP/IP-based network that belongs to a single organization with access restricted to authorized users; separated from the Internet by a firewall.
IP	The Internet Protocol is the part of the TCP/IP protocol suite that handles information addressing and routing to network computers.
IP address	A number that identifies a computer on a TCP/IP-based network.
iterative request	A request to a root-level DNS server for the best answer, even if it is partial, for the zone that is configured as the default name server.
LAN	A Local Area Network consists of typically fewer than 100 computers all within the same area.
lookup zone	A DNS server contains information in an area used for mapping FQDNs and IP addresses called a lookup zone.

Term	Description
MMC	The Microsoft Management Console provides the foundation for most administrative tools in Windows 2000.
modem	Modulator-demodulator is a device that converts digital signals into analog signals by using a variation of tones to represent ones and zeros.
name server	A computer running the DNS that translates IP addresses into FQDNs.
NAT	The Network Address Translation service allows proxy server and/or firewall-like configuration for Windows 2000 computers, and acts like a scaled-down DHCP server to supply IP addresses to computers on the intranet. The Network Address Translator (NAT) is the computer that runs the Network Address Translation service.
NIC	The Network Interface Card, also called network adapter, is a hardware device inside a computer that allows a computer to access a network, and is manufactured with a MAC address.
NNTP	Network News Transfer Protocol is a TCP/IP protocol that transfers articles between newsgroup servers, and between a newsgroup server and a client.
OSI	The Open Systems Interconnection network model is a seven-layer model that provides a foundation for all network communication. Each layer is responsible for and addresses one part of network communication.
POP3	The Post Office Protocol Version 3 downloads e-mail messages from a mail server to a client.

Term	Description
proxy server	A network server that has the only direct connection to the Internet, which other computers must go through to send and receive information.
recursive request	A request to the DNS server for the zone that is configured as the default name server.
reverse lookup zone	The portion of a DNS database file that resolves IP addresses to FQDNs.
root-level domain	The top of the domain namespace hierarchy, represented by a period (.), of which all domains on the Internet are members.
router	A router is a device that forwards and routes data from its source to the destination.
RRAS	The Routing and Remote Access Service configures routing and remote-access features on the Windows 2000 domain member servers.
second-level domains	The level in the domain name system after root-level and top-level, that consists of host names, which are typically company, agency, or university names.
SGML	Standard Generalized Markup Language, from which HTML was derived, provides Web page structure definitions.
SMTP	The Simple Mail Transport Protocol sends e-mail messages from a client to a mail server, and relays messages between mail servers.
SSL	Secure Sockets Layer is a protocol that encrypts and protects data sent by the client to the server, and from the server to the client.

Term	Description
subdomains	Domains below the root-level domain in the domain name hierarchy.
TCP	The Transmission Control Protocol part of the TCP/IP protocol suite handles reliable information delivery.
TCP/IP	Transmission Control Protocol/Internet Protocol is a network protocol and the standard protocol for all Internet data transmissions.
Telnet	Command line connections utility that uses local computers like network terminals to remotely run applications and manage files and directories. Telnet is both a utility and an Application Layer protocol in the TCP/IP suite.
top-level domains	The level in the domain name system after root-level, that consists of two- or three-letter names that define domain type, such as com to indicate commercial.
URL	A Universal Resource Locator is the address that connects to hosts and resources over the Internet with a Web browser.
VPN	Virtual Private Networks use the Internet to transfer private information.
Web browser	A program that finds and displays Web pages, based entirely on the TCP/IP network protocol, which uses numbers, not names, to identify computers.
Web page	A page displayable in a Web browser.
zone	Also known as zone of authority, the portion of the domain namespace for which a domain name server is responsible.

In Brief

If you want to...	Then do this...
Simplify network use and make Web browsing and Internet-related communication activities possible among your networks	Implement DNS on your intranet.
Keep your DNS server's zone of authority updated with the most current IP addresses and hostnames for computers	Use Windows 2000 DNS and DHCP servers to allow dynamic updates of the DNS database.
Connect an intranet to the Internet with secure and cost effective connection methods	Make sure your network activities are not visible to the Internet when users access the Internet by using a firewall.
Understand the language of the Internet and how various types of information is accessed and transmitted through the Internet	Learn the TCP/IP protocols and technologies that support and provide Internet connectivity and communication, such as HTTP, FTP, e-mail protocols, and other protocols such as NNTP and Telnet.
Connect to HTTP or FTP servers with the HTTP or FTP protocol	Remember to use the three parts of a URL, the protocol, DNS address, and file path, to access an HTTP or FTP server, as follows: ftp://ftp.lightpointlearning.net/tests/one.txt
Set up Windows 2000's tools to access the Internet through a proxy.	Configure the clients' Web browser, Internet Explorer Version 5.0, to use a proxy server, and configure the e-mail and newsgroup tool, Outlook Express.

Lesson 9 Activities

Complete the following activities to better prepare you for the certification exam. \

1. Every computer or network on the Internet is based on the TCP/IP addressing protocol, which is entirely numerical. Describe the system in place for using alphabetic addresses.

2. Name the Internet's alphabetical address naming convention, and explain the hierarchical levels within it.

3. Explain why a firewall is necessary, and give the advantages and disadvantages of a firewall for an intranet.

4. Describe how a client uses a proxy server.

5. Name the Microsoft firewall and a proxy server product and some of its features.

6. Name the TCP/IP Application Layer protocol that transfers HTML-based data on the Internet and explain, in general, how it works.

7. List two e-mail protocols and describe their uses.

8. Discuss how Internet Explorer stores cached files.

9. Describe NAT and give two advantages for using NAT instead of a proxy server.

10. Describe the security features of IIS.

Answers to Lesson 9 Activities

1. Because every computer on the Internet is based on the TCP/IP addressing protocol, which is entirely numerical, browsing the Web is very difficult without a more human-friendly address system using familiar names. The Domain Name System (DNS) makes browsing the network easier because it holds information about computers in a database file. The DNS service references this database to match numerical computer addresses to the corresponding alphabetical computer names. A name server (one that runs DNS) translates the numeric IP addresses into Fully Qualified Domain Names.

2. The alphabetical address naming convention for the Internet is called the domain namespace. The domains that make up the domain namespace are divided into three levels: the root-level domain, the top-level domains, and the second-level domains. Every domain in the domain namespace is a member of the root-level domain. The top-level domains include groups like the military, private corporations, and countries, and are given two- or three-letter extensions, like .mil, .com, and .ca. The second-level groups are made up of local groups, like your company, and any subdomains within your company. The Fully Qualified Domain Name for a server includes all domain levels in the name, like this: webby.sales.ibidpub.com.

3. Firewalls block out unwanted intruders from the private intranet, and prevent proprietary or confidential data from leaving an intranet into the public Internet. The firewall, which can be implemented with hardware, software, or both, is helpful in preventing harmful events such as virus attacks or hackers. However, the firewall can also block user access to the Internet in productive or profitable circumstances, causing frustration over time lost while troubleshooting or discovering blocked paths during the course of regular research business. Firewalls can give no guarantee that computer information will not be leaked out of a company on other media such as floppy disks or CD-ROM.

4. Proxy servers are much like firewalls on a network. However, they allow a network to hold only one IP address visible to the Internet on the proxy server, and share the address connectivity with computers on the local area network. Clients on the network send Internet requests to the proxy server's local area address. The proxy server takes the clients' Internet requests and places the proxy's Internet IP address on the request, and sends it out to the Internet. The client receives Internet messages back from the proxy server in the same manner.

5. The Microsoft Proxy Server 2.0 is both a firewall and a proxy server, and is configured through the MMC. Its firewall-like features allow you to monitor Web site accesses, and it automatically opens and closes TCP/IP ports. The proxy server features allow intranet Web site hosting and supports file caching for faster Internet access performance.

6. The TCP/IP protocol responsible for HTML (Web page) data communication is HTTP. All Web pages are transferred from the Web server to the client using the HTTP protocol. The Web pages can include text, graphics, audio and video data. The HTTP protocol basic commands include opening a connection by entering a URL address into the Web browser. The client and server connect, and the data is sent to the client. The HTTP connection closes after the client receives the data. Whenever a new request is sent, another session is opened.

7. Two e-mail protocols are SMTP and POP3. Simple Mail Transport Protocol sends e-mail messages from clients to mail servers, and from servers to servers. POP3 downloads e-mail messages from a mail server to a client.

8. You can set the cache size in Internet Explorer to help increase Internet access speed, or decrease hard drive space. The cache is a folder on the hard drive, where Web page files are stored. This makes viewing pages faster, since you can see the page without having to send any data over the Internet. You can set options to make sure that Internet Explorer checks the cache version of a Web page against the original Web page, to make sure you view the latest version.

    The Windows 2000 Internet Explorer stores cached files in C:\Documents and Settings\Username\Local Settings\Temporary Internet Files by default.

9. NAT works like a proxy server in that it uses two IP addresses, one for the intranet and one for the Internet to transfer information. It can also function as a firewall. Windows 2000 Server provides NAT as a DHCP server on a lesser scale. NAT, however, is much less expensive than a proxy server. Since NAT comes with the Windows 2000 Server package, there is no need to purchase additional proxy server software or load DHCP or DNS services.

10. IIS is fully integrated with Windows 2000, and takes advantage of the built-in security. ISS supports NTFS permissions, file encryption and authentication through Windows 2000. In addition, advanced security features for Web or FTP servers are also available, including SSL. SSL is a protocol that encrypts data for secure transmission over the Internet.

Lesson 9 Quiz

These questions test your knowledge of features, vocabulary, procedures, and syntax.

1.   What is the term for the shift of responsibility to a higher-level name server when the DNS's zone of authority is exceeded?

   A. Manual update

   B. Forward lookup query

   C. Dynamic update

   D. Reverse proxy

2.   A Virtual Private Network uses which network type to connect a remote user to a LAN?

   A. Intranet

   B. Extranet

   C. Internet

   D. Subnet

3.   What is responsible for resolving an FQDN to an IP address?

   A. Name server

   B. DNS

   C. URL

   D. DHCP

4.   Which of the following is the best way to share an Internet connection without noticeable performance degradation?

   A. Use a dial-up connection

   B. Install large amounts of RAM in the proxy server

   C. Configure the client to not cache files

   D. Use a firewall

5.   Which of the following allows you to configure a Windows 2000 computer like a proxy server?

   A. GNAT

   B. Network Address Translation

   C. Routing and Remote Access Service

   D. Network Address Topology

6.   Which of the following are components of NAT?

   A. Name resolution

   B. Translation

   C. Addressing

   D. Security

7.   Which of the following describes Internet connection sharing on a   Windows 2000 system?

   A. It will not work on a network that has a DHCP or DNS server

   B. It does not need to run on Windows 2000 Server

   C. It issues IP addresses for the intranet like a DHCP server

   D. It supports better caching than Microsoft Proxy Server

8.   Which of the following protocols are used to encrypt data?

   A. HTML

   B. HTTP

   C. HTTPS

   D. SSL

9.   The FTP utility transfers files between a client and server. What is most often used for the user-name to access an FTP server?

A. E-mail address

B. Anonymous

C. Bob

D. Get <username>

10. You can choose to set options to enable, disable, and prompt for two kinds of cookies. Which of the following are types of cookies?

A. Persistent cookies

B. Per-session cookies

C. Fortune cookies

D. Treat cookies

Answers to Lesson 9 Quiz

1. Answer B is correct. If a request for a hostname is not within the zone of authority for a DNS server, the server will perform a forward lookup query.

   Answers A and C are incorrect. DNS servers may be manually or dynamically updated, but these do not affect the zone of authority.

   Answer D is incorrect. Reverse proxy allows computers behind the firewall to host Web pages.

2. Answer C is correct. A user builds a VPN over the Internet to connect to a private LAN.

   Answers A and B are incorrect.

3. Answer A and B are correct. A name server uses the Domain Name System to resolve an FQDN to an IP address.

   Answers C and D are incorrect. A URL is an address, and DHCP is responsible for automatically assigning IP addresses to computers.

4. Answer B is correct. The best way to share an Internet connection without noticeable performance degradation is to install large amounts of RAM in a proxy server so that the server can cache more files.

   Answer A is incorrect. Dial-up connections are the slowest way to access the Internet.

   Answer C is incorrect. You should increase caching on both the proxy server and the client.

   Answer D is incorrect. Although many proxy servers act as firewalls, a firewall itself does not increase shared connection speed, and may actually slow the connection a bit.

5. Answer B is correct. The Network Address Translation (NAT) feature in Windows 2000 allows you to configure a Windows 2000 computer like a proxy server.

   Answer A is incorrect. GNAT is a fictitious acronym.

   Answer C is incorrect. RRAS allows users to connect to a server from remote locations.

   Answer D is incorrect. Network Address Topology is a fictitious term.

6.   Answers A, B, C, and D are all correct. Name resolution is a component of NAT. It functions as a Domain Name Server even though it doesn't provide name resolution; clients see it as a DNS. It then sends the name resolution on to the DNS. NAT provides addressing services for the entire intranet, with addresses beginning 192.168.0.2. Security is inherent in the NAT firewall characteristics, such as keeping unwanted traffic out of the intranet.

7.   Answers A, B, and C are correct. Internet connection sharing on a Windows 2000 system will not work on a network that has a DHCP or DNS server. It does not need to run on Windows 2000 Server, and issues IP addresses for the intranet like a DHCP server.

Answer D is incorrect. None of the internet connection sharing technologies mentioned in this lesson surpass Microsoft Proxy Server in file caching capabilities.

8.   Answers C and D are correct. HTTPS and SSL encrypt data.

Answers A and B are incorrect. HTML and HTTP don't encrypt data. Web pages are written in HyperText Markup Language (HTML), and are transferred using HTTP protocol from the Web server to the client.

9.   Answer B is correct. Most FTP servers are designed to accept anonymous access. For example, companies provide anonymous access to support files on their FTP server.

Answer A is incorrect. Visitors to an FTP site leave their e-mail addresses as a password for common courtesy.

Answers C and D are incorrect.

10.   Answers A and B are correct. Persistent and Per-session cookies are both common.

Answers C and D are incorrect. It is said Web site cookies were named after Fortune cookies because little pieces of text are left behind.

Lesson 10: Remote Access

Many companies have mobile employees who travel from one office to another, or travel away from the office. These employees need access to the company's Local Area Network (LAN) and their personal files. Using Windows 2000, you can implement remote access to the network in order for mobile users to effectively participate in network activity.

You install the Routing and Remote Access service on Windows 2000 Server computers to provide a connection to your LAN for remote users. Windows 2000 supports numerous protocols and security features to ensure flexibility and security for data transmissions.

After completing this lesson, you should have a better understanding of the following topics:

- Remote Access Overview

- Remote Access Protocols

- Remote Access Physical Connections

Remote Access Overview

Remote access is the ability of a computer to remotely connect to LAN. A remote access system includes the client computer (the computer connecting to the network), a remote access server (a computer running remote access software), and the hardware necessary to connect the client computer and remote access server. This hardware typically includes a modem, telephone lines, or other communications lines (Figure 10.1).

 Tip: The connection to a remote access server on Microsoft Windows clients is called dial-up networking.

Figure 10.1 Remote Access Overview

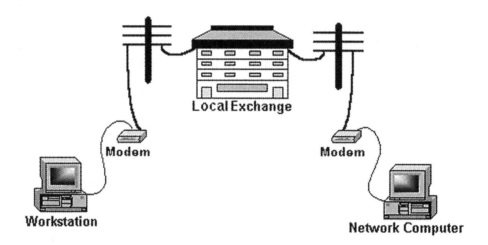

Windows 2000 Server includes Routing and Remote Access Service (RRAS) that allows you to support remote access connections to your network. The RRAS server performs two tasks. It establishes and terminates the remote access connection, and acts as a gateway through which data passes between the LAN and the remote client.

Connecting Remotely

The most common form of remote access requires the use of a modem. A modem converts the digital signal inside a computer to an analog signal that is carried over telephone lines. The modem at the receiving computer converts the analog signal back into a digital signal. The term modem is an abbreviation for MOdulator/DEModulator, where a modulator converts a digital signal to analog, and a demodulator converts an analog signal to digital (Figure 10.2).

Figure 10.2 Digital and Analog Signals

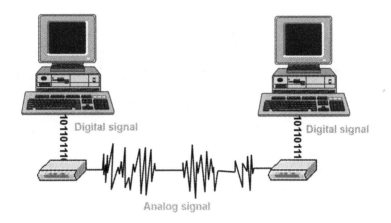

 Note: Many remote access connections today use digital lines that do not require modulation or demodulation, and, therefore, no modem is necessary. However, the term modem has become a generic term for any device that connects a computer to a line. You may even hear the oxymoronic term digital modem.

A remote access connection usually follows this procedure:

1. The client connects to the RRAS server. This may be through a dial-up connection using a modem and telephone lines, or may be through the Internet using a Virtual Private Network (VPN).

2. The client contacts the RRAS server using a protocol both computers support.

Tip: RRAS supports the Transmission Control Protocol/Internet Protocol (TCP/IP), NetBIOS Enhanced User Interface (NetBEUI), and Internet Packet Exchange/Sequenced Packet Exchange (IPX/SPX) protocols.

3.   Data transmits between the RRAS server and the client. The data first formats using the agreed-upon protocol, and then encapsulates using one of the remote access protocols.

4.   The RRAS server unpackages (removes the remote access protocol) from the data sent from the client, and passes the data on to the LAN. Likewise, when a computer on the LAN sends information to the client, the RRAS server encapsulates the data and sends it on.

Understanding Remote Access Types

RRAS for Windows 2000 supports two connection types between the client and the LAN, dial-up connections and Virtual Private Networks (VPNs). Dial-up connections require the use of a telephone or other public line system and a modem. A VPN connection uses the Internet to transfer information. Typically, the client still uses a modem and telephone line to connect to the Internet, but the connection to the RRAS server is indirect.

Dial-Up Connections

With a dial-up connection, the RRAS server answers the incoming call and authenticates the client computer. With Windows 2000 RRAS, you can configure the server with the following options:

- Use caller ID technology to identify the phone number from which the client is calling

- Hang up and call the client back before authentication occurs. This saves the client the long-distance phone charges and adds a level of security

- Require the client to call from only a specified phone number

- Use several different security protocols to ensure safe transfer of logon information and data

Virtual Private Networks (VPNs)

For long-distance remote access, connect to a LAN through the Internet. Usually you can access the Internet with a free local telephone call. Once on the Internet, you have access to any server in the world at no additional long-distance charge. However, remember the Internet is accessible to everyone, making the transfer of data across the Internet risky. VPN technology creates a virtual tunnel on the Internet, through which encrypted data travels securely (Figure 10.3).

Figure 10.3 Virtual Private Network

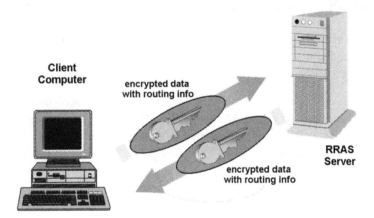

 Note: The name Virtual Private Network means that you are creating what appears to be a private network when, in fact, you use the publicly accessible infrastructure of the Internet.

Both the client computer and the RRAS server agree upon a common tunneling protocol. This protocol encapsulates the data with routing information. The routing information directs the data packets from source to destination. The data also encrypts for security. Consequently, if the data is intercepted on the Internet, the intercepting computer cannot decipher the contents.

You can join VPNs to LANS and create an extranet. An extranet is a private network that allows authorized users to access the company's LAN. For example, if your company wants to allow another company some access to their network or a branch office, establish a VPN between your LAN and the branch office LAN. Then, Information passes securely between the two locations using a tunnel in the Internet.

Remote Access Protocols

Connecting a client to a remote access server involves deciding upon which remote access protocol(s) to use. If you are using a dial-up connection, you have a choice between two remote access protocols. If you are implementing a VPN, you choose between two additional protocols.

The remote access protocols encapsulate the data. You use these protocols in addition to the LAN network protocol. For example, if your LAN uses TCP/IP, the client computer also uses TCP/IP. Before transmission, the TCP/IP-formatted data is formatted with one of the remote access protocols. Upon receipt, the remote access protocol information is removed, and the TCP/IP data passes on to the LAN or the client computer itself (Figure 10.4).

Figure 10.4 Data Encapsulation

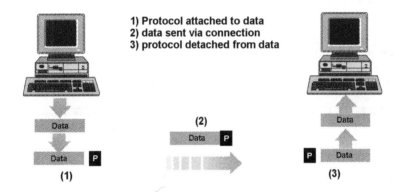

1) Protocol attached to data
2) data sent via connection
3) protocol detached from data

Using Dial-Up Connection Protocols

When establishing a dial-up remote access connection, both the server and the client must use the same dial-up protocol. If you are using a Windows 2000 client, use the Serial Line Internet Protocol (SLIP) or the Point-to-Point Protocol (PPP). If you are using a Windows 2000 server running RRAS, you can only use PPP.

Serial Line Internet Protocol (SLIP)

SLIP was the original standard for serial connections over telephone lines. UNIX and Windows NT 4.0 servers support SLIP, and Windows 2000 clients can use SLIP to connect to these servers. Other Windows and Apple Macintosh clients support SLIP. Although SLIP has been a standard for many years, there are several drawbacks to using this remote access protocol that include the following:

TCP/IP requirement—SLIP only works with TCP/IP. Although TCP/IP is the most common protocol, if your LAN uses NetBEUI or IPX/SPX, you cannot use SLIP.

Static IP address—SLIP requires the client computer to have a static IP address (the IP address identifies computers on a network). If you wish to dynamically assign a dial-up client an IP address when the connection occurs (for example, by using the Dynamic Host Configuration Protocol (DHCP)), you cannot use SLIP.

Security protocols—SLIP does not support many of the newer security protocols and sends the user password in clear text. Anyone monitoring the transmission can easily obtain a user's password during the remote logon process.

 Note: Windows 2000 RRAS servers do not support SLIP because it is less secure and less efficient than PPP.

Point-to-Point Protocol (PPP)

PPP is a newer remote access protocol standard that builds upon SLIP. PPP is more flexible and secure than SLIP, and addresses the major limitations of SLIP. For example, PPP supports the following:

Multiple protocols—PPP supports TCP/IP, IPX/SPX, NetBEUI, and supports the simultaneous use of multiple protocols.

Dynamic IP addressing—PPP allows clients to receive an IP address after connection. For Internet Service Providers (ISPs), this allows using IP addresses on an as-needed basis, and makes them available again after disconnection.

Security—PPP supports data encryption and logon information cannot be read if intercepted.

Connecting with VPN Protocols

When you connect remotely to a LAN through the Internet, you create a secure tunnel through which data passes. One of two VPN protocols creates this tunnel. Windows 2000 supports both the Point-to-Point Tunneling Protocol (PPTP) and the Layer 2 Tunneling Protocol (L2TP).

The data that transmits through a VPN actually formats three times. The data is first formatted for the LAN protocol (TCP/IP, IPX/SPX, or NetBEUI). Then data is encapsulated using PPP. Finally, one of the VPN protocols is applied to create the virtual tunnel (Figure 10.5).

Figure 10.5 VPN Data Encapsulation

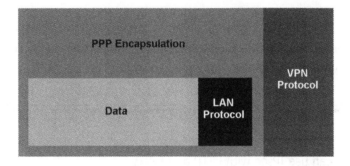

Point-to-Point Tunneling Protocol (PPTP)

PPTP was developed as an extension to PPP and uses PPP data packets to encapsulate and then encrypt the data. Because PPTP uses PPP, all of the benefits of PPP remain, including multiple protocol support and dynamic IP addressing.

Tip: Although PPTP can carry data formatted in several different network protocols, it requires TCP/IP to travel between the client and the VPN server.

PPTP uses the Extensible Authentication Protocol (EAP) to provide enhanced data security. EAP supports several of the newer security protocols, including public-key authentication using certificates and smart cards.

Layer 2 Tunneling Protocol (L2TP)

The L2TP standard provides similar functions to PPTP. Like PPTP, L2TP uses PPP data packets to carry information. L2TP uses Internet Protocol Security (IPSec) to encrypt the data and authenticate users.

IPSec creates more overhead because a larger data packet transmits each time, requiring both the client and server more possessing time to send and receive information. However, when data security is of utmost importance, use IPSec.

 Note: You can use IPsec with L2TP and PPTP.

Unlike PPTP, L2TP works over a number of Wide Area Network (WAN) links, not just the TCP/IP-based Internet. Table 10.1 summarizes the features of PPTP, L2TP, and IPSec.

Table 10.1 VPN Protocol Summary

Feature	PPTP	L2TP	IPSec
User authentication (Who is trying to connect?)	X	X	
Computer authentication (Can this computer connect to our network?)			X
Multi-protocol support	X	X	X
Packet authentication (Is the data valid?)			X
Header compression	6-byte header size	4-byte header size	
Multicast support	X	X	X
Data encryption	Uses EAP or IPSec	Uses IPSec	X

Remote Access Physical Connections

You achieve remote access to a LAN through several possible connections. Already you have seen that remote access takes place through a dial-up connection or through a VPN. Dial-up connections use standard telephone lines, while VPN connects are made through the Internet or through WAN links. This section describes these connection types.

Public Switched Telephone Network (PSTN)

The Public Switched Telephone Network (PSTN) is a collection of copper wires that carries voice. The system transmits analog signals and the wires in the system only handle a limited range of frequencies (our voices are not digital and we speak in a rather limited frequency range).

 Note: PSTN is also known as the Plain Old Telephone Service (POTS).

The limited range of frequencies PSTN supports means that these wires cannot carry data very quickly. Data transmissions are classified by bandwidth, the rate at which data travel across the medium. PSTN data transmissions exceed about 40 Kilobits per second (Kbps). The maximum bandwidth PSTN supports is 56 Kbps. Despite this drawback, the major advantage of using PSTN is that these lines are available globally. No other network provides such extensive coverage. Another advantage is that PSTN hardware (modems) is readily available and very inexpensive.

Because PSTN is analog, there must be conversion from the digital signals inside the computer to analog signals and back again to digital. A modem at each end of the PSTN modulates (converts digital to analog) and demodulates (converts analog to digital) the signal (Figure 10.6).

Figure 10.6 PSTN Network Connection

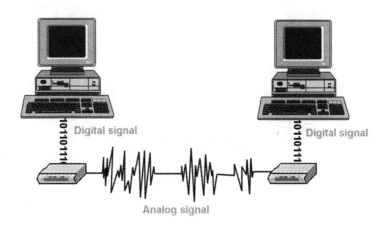

A PSTN connection allows you to dial directly to a remote access server using SLIP or PPP. You can also use PSTN to dial a local ISP through which you connect to the Internet. Once attached to the Internet, you can establish a VPN to your server using PPTP or L2TP.

Integrated Services Digital Network (ISDN)

ISDN uses digital and analog telephone lines to send data, voice, video, and fax signals. ISDN sends information digitally so that a conventional modem is not required on either end of an ISDN connection. However, an ISDN adapter connects the computer or LAN to the ISDN line. This adapter acts much like a modem, and is often referred to as an ISDN modem (Figure 10.7).

Figure 10.7 ISDN Network

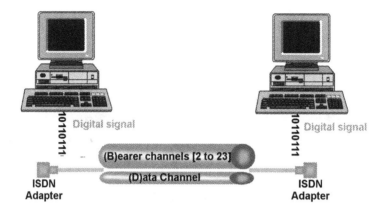

The following are two ISDN available technologies:

Basic Rate Interface (BRI)—BRI uses two B-channels, each with a 64-Kbps bandwidth, and one data D-channel with a 16-Kbps bandwidth. The two B-channels may be combined to create an effective bandwidth of 128 Kbps. The D-channel performs error checking and carries call-control information.

 Note: BRI uses the same wires as PSTN. The telephone company tests and conditions these lines, and verifies they can carry digital signals.

Primary Rate Interface (PRI)—PRI provides almost 1.5-Mbps (megabits per second) bandwidth by using 23 B-channels and one 64K D-channel. PRI uses many more wires and is much more expensive than BRI and, therefore, is rarely used.

Like PSTN, ISDN is readily available in many areas since it often uses the same wires. It does not have quite the same global reach, and is not commonly found beyond urban areas in developed countries.

X.25

X.25 is a network protocol that works at the bottom three layers (the Physical, Data Link, and Network layers) of the Open Systems Interconnection (OSI) model. An X.25 network sends information in discrete packets that travel numerous paths.

Tip: X.25 is one of several network types that uses packet-switching technology.

Computers connect to an X.25 in one of two ways. First, you can connect directly to the X.25 network using an X.25 smart card that is a hardware device that attaches to the computer and provides the physical connection to the X.25 cable. X.25 smart cards are expensive, and commonly used only at the server end of a remote access setup. At the client end, you can attach to an X.25 network using a standard modem. The modem connects to a Packet Assembler/Dissembler (PAD). The PAD converts the analog, serial data from the modem into X.25 packets from the client to the network, and converts the network packets into analog, serial data to the client. In this process, a PAD performs similar to a modem.

Note: X.25 has built-in error-checking and flow control, ensuring good delivery of data.

Asymmetrical Digital Subscriber Line (ADSL)

ADSL uses the same telephone lines as PSTN, but takes advantage of the frequencies that PSTN does not support. ADSL is asymmetric—the bandwidth going from the server to the client (called downstream data) is much faster than the bandwidth going from the client to the server (upstream data). This asymmetry fits well with most personal and business uses. Usually, the remote user downloads information from the Internet or from the corporate LAN, but does not upload much information.

ADSL supports downstream rates between 1.5 Mbps and 9 Mbps, and upstream rates between 16 and 640 Kbps. In addition, since ADSL uses non-voice frequencies, it permits using the telephone line for voice and data simultaneously (Figure 10.8).

Figure 10.8 ADSL Network

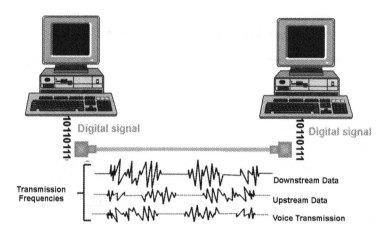

ADSL is not widely available. There are distance limitations on where ADSL effectively works. It requires your computer to be within a certain distance of one of the local telephone company's switching centers. Telephone companies are working on extending ADSL distance and making the service available to more people.

Cable Modem

A strong competitor to ADSL is television cable. Using the same cable connected to many homes in North America for television transmission, cable can achieve downstream bandwidth rates between 3 and 4 Mbps. Like ADSL, cable technology is asymmetric. Upstream rates are typically 500 to 800 Kbps.

The backbone for most of the cable networks in the United States is fiber-optic cable that carries a digital signal. From the backbone to the cable modem, the signal transmits as an analog signal.

The cable modem converts the analog signal back to digital before passing the signal to the computer (Figure 10.9).

Figure 10.9 Cable Modem Network

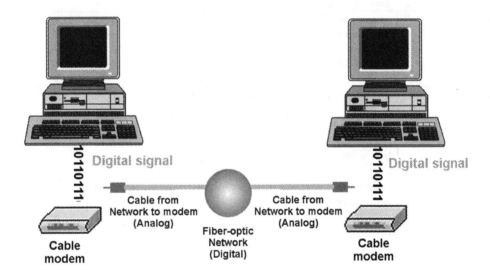

Tip: To learn more about cable modem technology, the following Web page contains an excellent tutorial: http://www.cable-modems.org

Vocabulary

Review the following terms in preparation for the certification exam.

Term	Description
ADSL	Asymmetric Digital Subscriber Line is a broadband device used for high-speed digital communications (including video) across twisted-pair copper phone lines. It supports downstream data at the rate of 1.5 to 9 Mbps and upstream data at the rate of 16 to 640 Kbps.
bandwidth	The rate at which data can be carried across a network connection.
BRI	Basic Rate Interface is an ISDN-available technology that carries voice or data over two B-channels and a D-channel with a maximum bandwidth of 128 Kbps.
cable modem	A device that converts analog signals to digital for transmission over asymmetric fiber-optic television cable.
certificates	A digital attachment to an electronic message that verifies the identification of the message sender but provides the receiver the means to encode a reply.
client	Any computer that connects to a network that accesses resources on a server.
DHCP	Dynamic Host Configuration Protocol is a service that automatically assigns IP addresses and settings on a network.
dial-up networking	On Microsoft Windows clients, the connection to a remote access server.

Term	Description
downstream data	Data that travels over bandwidth going from the server to the client.
EAP	The Extensible Authentication Protocol allows a client and server to negotiate an authentication method before the user logs on to the network.
encapsulation	Construction of data bits into a packet for a specific protocol, such as a TCP/IP packet, to transmit over a network.
encryption	Translating data into secret code.
extranet	A collection of private intranets to which authorized remote users can log on over the Internet.
gateway	A device on the network that changes data from protocols to data suitable to protocols on the receiving network computer, and transfers the data.
IPSec	Internet Protocol Security is a protocol that encrypts data and authenticates that can be used with L2TP and PPTP standards.
IPX/SPX	Internetwork Packet Exchange/Sequenced Packet Exchange are Novell NetWare protocols that work like the TCP/IP protocol suite to handle data delivery.
ISDN	Integrated Services Digital Network uses digital and analog telephone lines to send data, voice, video, and fax signals through an adapter to connect the computer or LAN to the ISDN line.
ISP	An Internet Service Provider is a private concern that offers Internet connectivity to the Internet to individuals or organizations.

Term	Description
L2TP	Layer 2 Tunnel Protocol is a tunneling protocol used with various transmission protocols and provides compression and tunnel authentication.
LAN	A Local Area Network is a small computer network that spans a relatively small area such as a single building or office area.
modem	A MOdulator/DEModulator network device that converts digital computer signals to analog telephone signals, and analog to digital. Also used as a generic term for a device that connects a computer to a line whether or not the line is analog.
multi-cast	A method of simultaneously sending information to several computers over a TCP/IP network.
NetBEUI	A protocol designed by Microsoft, originally designed for small single-segment networks.
NetBIOS	Network Basic Input-Output System is a protocol that uses names to identify computers on a network. It was originally designed as part of NetBEUI.
OSI model	The Open System Interconnection model defines a seven-layer structure upon which network protocols are designed and built.
PAD	A Packet Assembler/Disassembler on the X.25 network is a device similar to a modem that converts analog data into X.25 packets, and X.25 packets back to analog.
PPP	Point-to-Point Protocol provides dial-up connections to TCP/IP-based networks.
PPTP	The Point-to-Point Tunneling Protocol is a tunneling protocol that works with IP-based networks and uses PPP for data encryption.

Term	Description
PRI	Primary Rate Interface is an ISDN-available technology that carries voice and data over 23 B-channels and one D-channel with a maximum bandwidth of 1.5 Mbps. PRI requires more wires and is more expensive than PRI technology and is rarely used.
protocol	A standard or set of rules that computers use to communicate with each other over a network.
PSTN	The Public Switched Telephone Network is the standard copper-wire telecommunication link that carries analog voice communication used for ordinary phone calls and dial-up connections for computer communication with a modem.
public-key authentication	In the security process of using keys to encrypt and decrypt messages, the public key attaches to the encrypted file and verifies the identity of the sender.
remote access server	A computer that runs remote access software and shares resources over the network.
RRAS	Routing and Remote Access Service configures routing and remote access features Windows 2000 domain member servers.
SLIP	Serial Line Internet Protocol transmits TCP/IP data packets over dial-up connections to the Internet or other networks.
smart cards	A credit card-sized attachment for computers that contains its own processor and RAM that stores sensitive information, including security keys.
TCP/IP	Transmission Control Protocol/Internet Protocol is a network protocol and the protocol used for the Internet.
tunneling	The process of creating a secure channel through public lines over which encrypted data travel safely.

Term	Description
upstream data	Data that travels over bandwidth going from the client to the server.
VPN	Virtual Private Networks connect to the Internet with tunneling protocols to transfer private information.
WAN	A Wide Area Network consists of two or more LANS and spans a relatively large geographical area .
X.25	A network protocol that works at the Physical, Data Link, and Network layers of the OSI model to transmit data in discrete packets.

In Brief

If you want to...	Then do this...
Establish remote access connections through a Windows 2000 service that acts as a gateway	Use the Routing and Remote Access Service (RRAS) on a server through either your Virtual Private Network or dial-up modems.
Use different types of communication protocols for remote access	Use RRAS with TCP/IP, NetBEUI, and IPX/SPX LAN protocols for dial-up connections, and the PPTP and L2TP protocols for VPN connections.
Use secure and specific dial-up communication connections	Configure the RAAS dial-up connections with criteria such as caller ID, phone line connection criteria such as authorized phone numbers, and security protocols for logon information.
Remotely access distant sites with no long-distance communication charges	Use a VPN connection technology to the Internet with local phone calls, and tunneling for secure, encrypted communications.
Use a Windows 2000 client or server to establish a remote access dial-up connection	Use the SLIP or PPP protocols for client connections and the PPP protocol for the server connection, with the client and server using the same dial-up protocol.

Lesson 10 Activities

Complete the following activities to better prepare you for the certification exam.

1.   Describe the procedure that a RRAS server usually follows to make a remote access connection.

2.   List two optional dial-up configurations in RRAS that enhance dial-up security.

3.   Explain how VPNs make data transfer over the public Internet secure.

4.   Describe the two protocols you must choose between when building a VPN.

5.   List three disadvantages of the original dial-up telephone line protocol.

6.   Name the only dial-up protocol that can be used with a Windows 2000 RRAS server, and explain how it is different from SLIP.

7.   Give another name for a POTS, and describe how you use it for VPNs.

8.   List the two types of ISDN services and describe their capabilities.

9.   Describe a PAD and where it is used.

10. Explain why asymmetric bandwidth is acceptable for most uses, and name two remote access connections that support it.

Answers to Lesson 10 Activities

1. Remote access RRAS connections usually follow these steps:

    1. Dial-ups:

        The client dials-up to the RRAS server through a modem and telephone lines, or through the Internet via a Virtual Private Network (VPN).

    2. Protocol communications:

        The client contacts the RRAS server using a protocol both computers support.

    3. Transmissions and encapsulations:

        Data is sent between the RRAS server and the client. The protocol formats the data and then is encapsulated with one of the remote access protocols.

    4. De-encapsulates:

        The RRAS server removes the remote access protocol from the data sent from the client, and passes the data on to the LAN. When a computer on the LAN sends information to the client, the RRAS server encapsulates the data and sends it on.

2. Some of the dial-up options to configure RRAS for more enhanced security are:

    Caller ID. Use this technology to identify the phone number from which the client is calling.

    Hang up and call the client back before authentication occurs. This saves the client the long distance phone charges and can be an added level of security.

    Require call-ins from specific phone numbers.

    Use several different security protocols to ensure safe transfer of logon information and data.

3. VPNs use tunneling technology to make private file transfers through the Internet very secure. The tunneling protocol encapsulates or wraps data within special protocol and routing information. This encapsulated data packet then encrypts and transmits through the Internet. The data is secure in the tunneled data packet, and although the Internet is very public, the transmissions are virtually private.

4. You can choose between two tunneling protocols to use with a VPN: PPTP and L2TP. PPTP uses additional data security protocols in the Extensible Authentication Protocol. The EAP supports the tunneling technology with security features such as public-key authentication and

certificates, and smart cards. L2TP is similar to PPTP in its functionality, but it encrypts data and authenticates users with the protocol IPSec. IPSec creates more processing, but is a more secure protocol than EAP.

5.   The original dial-up telephone line protocol, SLIP, doesn't work with protocols other than TCP/IP, it doesn't support dynamic addressing, and doesn't support any newer security protocols to protect user passwords.

6.   PPP is the only dial-up protocol that runs on a Windows 2000 RRAS server. PPP provides features that SLIP does not, which is especially important for secure communications. PPP not only supports protocols other than TCP/IP, it allows you to use several protocols at the same time. PPP doesn't require static IP addresses, and so allows dynamic IP addressing. The most important difference between PPP and SLIP is security. PPP encrypts logon information, and does not allow the actual password to display as does SLIP.

7.   The Plain Old Telephone Service (POTS) is more officially known as the Public Switched Telephone Network (PSTN). The PSTN carries data at a maximum of 56 Kbps, which is the slowest physical remote access medium. But because these phone lines are everywhere, it is an advantage of PSTN. Modems convert PSTN analog signals to digital signals suitable for the computer. You can connect PSTNs directly to a remote access server and configure it to dial-up to your Internet Service Provider. When your server is connected to the Internet, you can connect a VPN configured with appropriate VPN protocols such as PPTP or L2TP to the server. You can have a VPN established using a plain old telephone system.

8.   ISDN physical connections are much faster than PSTN connections. Two types of ISDN services are the Basic Rate Interface (BRI) and the Primary Rate Interface (PRI).

     BRI has three channels. Two channels are combined for faster data transmission, and one channel checks errors. The two B-channels have 64 Kbps bandwidth each, for about 128 Kpbs of bandwidth. The error-checking channel, or the D-channel, allows 16 Kbps bandwidth transmissions. BRI uses the same wire types used for 56 Kbps PSTN, but is much faster.

     PRI provides almost 1.5 megabits per second (Mbps) bandwidth by using 23 B-channels and one 64K D-channel. PRI uses many more wires and is much more expensive than BRI. It is rarely used.

9. Clients can access an X.25 network via modem. However, the modem connects to a Packet Assembler/Disassembler (PAD). Instead of converting analog data to digital data at the modem, the PAD switches the data type to the X.25 protocol format. The data is checked and is delivered free of errors to the X.25 network client.

10. Asymmetric bandwidth means that data flowing through lines transmits faster one way than the other. The data flowing on the bandwidth from the server to the client is called downstream data, and data flowing from the client to the server is called upstream data. This asymmetry is generally acceptable, since most users download far more data from the Internet than they upload.

    Both Asymmetric Digital Subscriber Line (ADSL) and Cable modems use asymmetric bandwidth.

Lesson 10 Quiz

These questions test your knowledge of features, vocabulary, procedures, and syntax.

1.   Which of the following protocols does RRAS support?

A. TCP/IP

B. IPX/SPX

C. NetBEUI

D. X.25

2.   What is the device on an X.25 network that assembles and disassembles packets?

A. Modem

B. Smart card

C. PAD

D. NIC

3.   Which of the following types of remote connections does RRAS support?

A. Dial-up

B. VPN

C. Microwave

D. Radio

4.   Which of the following protocol technologies encapsulates data with routing information and encrypts the data for security?

A. Tunneling

B. Wrapping

C. Multi-homing

D. Multi-casting

5.   Which of the following explains why RRAS does not support SLIP?

A. Because Windows 2000 clients can use SLIP to connect to SLIP-supported servers.

B. SLIP is less secure and efficient than PPP.

C. SLIP sends the user password in clear text.

D. SLIP does not support dynamic addressing.

6.   Which of the following protocols use the tunneling technology?

A. PPTP

B. L2TP

C. IPSec

D. EAP

7.   What is required for PPTP to carry data among clients and servers?

A. EAP

B. L2TP

C. TCP/IP

D. RRAS

8.   Which of the following protocols support multi-protocols, computer authentication, and packet authentication?

A. PPP

B. PPTP

C. L2TP

D. IPSec

9.   Why is ADSL not widely available?

A. Distance limitations

B. Lack of demand

C. Uses non-voice frequencies

D. Non-standard phone lines

10. Which of the following is a strong competitor to ADSL?

A. SSI

B. PRI

C. BRI

D. Cable modem

Answers to Lesson 10 Quiz

1. Answers A, B, C, and D are all correct. RRAS supports TCP/IP, IPX/SPX, NetBEUI protocols, and also supports the X.25 protocol.

2. Answer C is correct. The device on an X.25 network that assembles and disassembles packets is a Packet Assembler/Disassembler(PAD).

    Answer A is incorrect. A standard modem can be connected to a X.25 network, but cannot handle packet switching.

    Answer B is incorrect. A smart card is a hardware device that attaches to the computer and provides security information.

    Answer D is incorrect. A NIC doesn't assemble and disassemble data packets.

3. Answers A and B are correct. RRAS supports dial-up and VPN remote connectivity. Computers and servers must both be configured for RRAS service.

    Answers C and D are incorrect.

4. Answer A is correct. Tunneling is a protocol technology that encapsulates data with routing information and encrypts for security.

    Answer B is incorrect. Wrapping is a fictitious term.

    Answer C is incorrect. Multi-homing involves two NICs on a computer to emulate a router, and does not encapsulate or encrypt data.

    Answer D is incorrect. Multi-casting is a method of simultaneously sending information to several computers over a TCP/IP network.

5. Answers B, C, and D are correct. SLIP is less secure and efficient than PPP because it sends the user password in clear text. Furthermore, SLIP does not support dynamic IP address assignments.

    Answer A is incorrect. Windows 2000 clients do support SLIP, but this is not the reason why RRAS does not.

6.   Answers A and B are correct. The PPTP and L2TP protocols use tunneling technology.

Answers C and D are incorrect. Both IPSec and EAP are involved with VPNs, but neither is a tunneling protocol. IPSec authenticates computers and encrypts data.

7.   Answer C is correct. TCP/IP is required for PPTP to carry data among clients and servers.

Answers A, B, and D are incorrect. EAP and L2TP carries data formatted with these protocols, but TCP/IP is required to carry it among the network nodes. RRAS is required to use TCP/IP as the standard protocol for transmitting PPTP.

8.   Answer D is correct. Only IPSec supports multi-protocols, computer authentication, and packet authentication.

Answers A, B, and C are incorrect. PPTP uses PPP, but it does not support any authentication. L2TP uses IPSec to perform authentication.

9.   Answer A is correct. ADSL not widely available because there are distance limitations. ADSL attenuates at long distances from the telephone switching center.

Answers B, C, and D are incorrect. ADSL uses standard POTS lines, and the use of non-voice frequencies improves the capacity of the lines. There is considerable demand for inexpensive and fast Internet connections.

10.   Answer D is correct. Cable modem is a strong competitor to ADSL. The cabling is in place and is an equally fast medium.

Answer A is incorrect. SSI is a fictitious acronym.

Answers B and C are incorrect. PRI and BRI (ISDN types) are more expensive.

Glossary

Term	Definition
10Base2 cable	A thin, flexible coaxial cable with a 50-ohm impedance sometimes referred to as Thinnet cable.
10Base5 cable	A thick, rigid coaxial cable sometimes referred to as standard Ethernet or Thicknet cable.
10BaseF cable	Uses fiber-optic cable on a star bus topology and can carry an Ethernet signal up to 2 kilometers away.
10BaseT cable	Several pairs of copper wires (twisted-pair cable) twisted around each other that reduce crosstalk and other interference.
802 Specifications	The 802 Specifications define subsets of the Data Link Layer of the OSI model. For example, 802.3 refers to Ethernet using CSMA/CD, and 802.5 defines token ring using token passing.
Active Directory	Active Directory is the new service that defines and supports the organization of a network. In Windows 2000, domain controllers are servers providing the Active Directory service.
ADSL	Asymmetric Digital Subscriber Line is a broadband device used for high-speed digital communications (including video) across twisted-pair copper phone lines. It supports downstream data at the rate of 1.5 to 9 Mbps and upstream data at the rate of 16 to 640 Kbps.
APIPA	Automatic Private IP Addressing is a Windows 2000-supported system that allows client computers to self-assign an IP address if a DHCP server is unavailable.
AppleTalk	A routable protocol for Macintosh-based networks. Macintoshes generate their own network number upon attachment to the network cable.

Term	Definition
applets	Small application programs used to customize other programs or utilities.
Application Layer	The layer of OSI that provides interface among user applications and the network, and passes applications information to the Presentation Layer.
ARP	Address Resolution Protocol is the TCP/IP protocol that resolves or converts IP addresses to MAC addresses, and vice versa.
ARP utility	The TCP/IP diagnostic utility ARP displays the contents of the Address Resolution Protocol cache (the table of MAC and IP addresses).
ATM	Asynchronous Transfer Mode is a standard architecture that uses the point-to-point access method and uses fixed length data packets for increased network speed and bandwidth.
attenuation	Attenuation is signal loss through media and typically occurs at a distance of about 500 meters (1,640 feet).
backbone	A physical cable called a backbone handles network traffic carried between LANs.
bandwidth	The rate at which data can be carried across a network connection.
binary	A numbering system that only uses 1s and 0s to represent all numbers. It is also known as Base 2 because all the numbers are powers of 2.
bit	A single binary digit, represented by either 1 or 0.

Term	Definition
BNC	The British Naval Connector is a hardware connector used between Thinnet and Thicknet cables and computers.
bottleneck	The slowest component in a computer or network.
BRI	Basic Rate Interface is an ISDN-available technology that carries voice or data over two B-channels and a D-channel with a maximum bandwidth of 128 Kbps.
bridge	A network device that works like a switch. It divides a network and isolates traffic, with 80% of the traffic on each LAN segment remaining local. The other 20% or less of the traffic requires bridge processing and forwarding.
broadcast	A broadcast transmission simultaneously sends data to all computers on the network segment.
broadcast messages	Data that simultaneously transmits to all computers on the subnet.
brouter	A brouter is a network device that acts as a router for selected routable protocols, and bridges non-routable protocols.
built-in accounts	Accounts created upon Windows 2000 installation for administrators and guests that provide a way to access local and domain computers and resources.
built-in groups	Groups created by Windows 2000 with pre-assigned configurations for user rights and permissions.
bus	A bus is an internal signal path that passes binary information. Today's computers use 16- and 32-bit parallel buses.

Term	Definition
bus topology	A simple network design that uses a single cable, also called a trunk or backbone, to connect network devices in a single line.
byte	Eight bits equal a byte.
cable modem	A device that converts analog signals to digital for transmission over asymmetric fiber-optic television cable.
CAN	Campus Area Network is an infrequently used term for inte rnetworks used in campus-sized areas.
certificates	A digital attachment to an electronic message that verifies the identification of the message sender but provides the receiver the means to encode a reply.
child domain	All domains that branch from the root are called child domains.
CIDR	Classless Inter-Domain Routing is a new addressing scheme in which IP addresses split at bit level, not byte level, and classes divide within an octet.
CIDR notation	A Classless Inter-Domain Routing notation is a shorthand method for writing the IP address with a subnet mask. The number of bits used for the network ID appends the IP address.
client	A client is any computer that requests a resource from a server.
client/server	A client/server network has one or more central servers that manage users, data, security, and shared resource access. Unlike centralized processing (mainframe) networks, workstations share the processing load with the central server.

Term	Definition
clustering	Clustering distributes network demands to all of the servers in a cluster rather than to just one server.
coaxial cable	A widely used network cable that transmits voice, data, and video information over relatively long distance with reasonable security.
Computer Management Console	The Computer Management console is a module that contains management utilities or snap-ins that work in the MMC to provide a central location for Windows 2000 management. The console has two panes: the Tree pane and the Details pane.
connectionless	Data transmission that doesn't require network nodes to be directly connected. Data packets with addresses pass through nodes until delivery.
console	A module that contains management utilities or snap-ins, designed to work in the MMC to provide a central location for management. The general form of a console includes two panes.
Control Panel	The Control Panel is a collection of applets designed to work in the MMC to provide a central location for management. Each applet addresses a specific Windows 2000 setting or feature.
CPU	The Central Processing Unit is the brain of the computer that processes all actions.
CRC	The Cyclical Redundancy Check is a mathematical calculation of the data portion of a packet. The calculated number adds to the packet trailer for error-checking purposes.
crosstalk	Interference that occurs when data radiates across adjacent unshielded cable and sends energy onto other data paths.

Term	Definition
CSMA/CA	Carrier Sense Multiple Access/Collision Avoidance is a common access method. A computer checks network cable for data. When no transmissions are detected, it sends an intent-to-transmit message. Each computer receives the message and waits to receive the data.
CSMA/CD	Carrier Sense Multiple Access/Collision Detection is the most common access method used on all Ethernet networks. A CSMA/CD computer checks the network cable for signals. If there is no signal, the computer assumes it is safe to send data.
data collision	A loss of data that occurs when two signals are placed on the cable at the same time.
Data Link Layer	The layer of the OSI that defines network access methods. It relies on the Physical Layer to get data onto the network, and relies on the Network Layer to address the data.
decimal notation	The numbering system, also known as Base 10, that uses the digits 0–9 to represent values.
default gateway	A Microsoft term given to Windows devices such as multihomed computers or routers because data passes through them to and from a subnet. However, routers are not actually gateways since they connect two of the same network types.
default subnet mask	A number that contains the values 0 and 255 and includes one, two, or three octets that determines the number of networks and hosts each IP class supports. Subnet masks separate the host ID and the network ID in an IP address.
demand priority	A new access method for 100VG-AnyLAN networks that give certain computers data transmission priority over others.

Term	Definition
Details pane	The right side of the MMC contains the Details pane that displays the contents of folders and information specific to the snap-ins.
DHCP	Dynamic Host Configuration Protocol is a service that automatically assigns IP addresses and settings on a network.
dial-up networking	On Microsoft Windows clients, the connection to a remote access server.
DLC	Data Link Control is a protocol is used to access older IBM mainframe computers and to directly communicate with printers.
DNS	The Domain Name System is a Transport Layer protocol that resolves IP addresses to friendly names called hostnames.
domain	A logical grouping of computers in network that share a common directory database.
domain controller	A computer that stores the Active Directory database on a Windows 2000 domain.
domain user account	A network account that allows permission to access a network domain with most computers in addition to local computer access.
downstream data	Data that travels over bandwidth going from the server to the client.
EAP	The Extensible Authentication Protocol allows a client and server to negotiate an authentication method before the user logs on to the network.

Term	Definition
EISA	Extended Industry Standard Architecture is an extension of ISA architecture that utilizes a 32-bit expansion slot.
EMI	Electromagnetic Interference is the disruption of electrical performance.
encapsulation	Construction of data bits into a packet for a specific protocol, such as a TCP/IP packet, to transmit over a network.
encryption	Translating data into secret code.
ERD	The Emergency Repair Disk is a floppy disk used to rebuild a corrupted installation of Windows 2000.
Ethernet	The most popular network architecture, this IEEE 802.3 Ethernet specification uses the CSMA/CD network access method, and can use the bus or star topology, depending on its cable type.
extranet	A collection of private intranets to which authorized remote users can log on over the Internet.
fault tolerance	The ability of a system to recover from failure. In the case of data, a fault-tolerant system uses more than one physical hard drive to store the same data.
Favorites	Sites that are bookmarked for quick and frequent access.
FDDI	Fiber Distributed Data Interface architecture uses fiber-optic cable, wired as a ring, to transmit data.
fiber-optic	Cable made of glass or plastic fibers that transmit digital data signals using light pulses.
folders	Folders are MMC objects that contain other snap-ins. Folders display with a plus sign (+) next to them.

Term	Definition
frame	Data is called a frame when it reaches the Data Link Layer.
frame relay	An architecture that is used in WAN connections that sends data packets with the point-to-point access method.
FTP	File Transfer Protocol spans the OSI Application, Presentation, and Session layers of the OSI model and is the primary file transfer protocol for HTTP and other files.
FTP utility	The TCP/IP connectivity utility File Transfer Protocol uses TCP for file transfers.
gateway	A gateway works at the Presentation Layer, converts data from on e network type or protocol to another, and then resends the data.
global group	A group scope that may contain users only from the same domain, and may be assigned permission to resources in any domain.
group type	Defines the purpose of the group. The group type is either security or distribution.
groups	A collection of accounts or objects categorized by common characteristics or needs used for organization purposes in Windows 2000 networks.
hardware	Any component on a network that includes cable or NICs that attach computers to the cable, and other devices that help traffic information.
hops	Hops represent steps or instances through which packets travel from a router to another router.

Term	Definition
host	Any object (computer, printer, and so forth) on a TCP /IP network.
host ID	The portion of an IP address that identifies the host.
hostnames	Identify every host (object) on a network. The names are friendly and can be up to 255 characters long; hostnames are entered in World Wide Web browsers.
Hosts file	The Hosts file is a static table of Hostnames and IP addresses. It's a standard text file that must be manually updated, and is used to resolve two different computer names.
HTML	HyperText Markup Language is the programming language of the WWW.
HTTP	HyperText Transfer Protocol, among the OSI Session, Presentation, and Application layers, transfers files written in HTML. WWW files are written in HTML, and HTTP transfers Web pages.
hub	A central connection point for network devices that distributes signals and data, expands networks, and increases th e number of computers in a LAN.
ICMP	The Internet Control Message Protocol sends control messages used for diagnosis of unsuccessful data delivery. Additionally, the PING utility uses ICMP to verify a connection to a remote computer.
IEEE 802.3	The Institute of Electrical and Electronics Engineers 802.3 is a standard Ethernet specification that uses CSMA/CD network access and can use bus or star topology. Ethernet netwo rks today can support 1,000-Mbps transmission rates.
IGMP	The Internet Group Management Protocol performs multicasting, which simultaneously sends one copy of d ata to multiple computers.

Term	Definition
infrared	A light beam that carries network data over short distances and is used as a primary wireless technology for LANs.
InterNIC	A joint effort among AT&T, Network Solutions, Inc. (NSI), and the National Science Foundation to ensure no two computers have the same IP address assignment.
IP	The Internet Protocol is one part of the TCP/IP protocol suite responsible for addressing and routing TCP/IP packets to individual computers. The Internet Protocol is one part of the TCP/IP protocol suite that identifies every object on a network and ensures proper data delivery among all objects on the network.
IP address	A unique 32-bit number that identifies hosts (objects) on a TCP/IP network, written as four octets separated by decimals in the form of aaa.bbb.ccc.ddd, Every host has a unique IP address, and for every IP address there is a subnet mask.
IP datagram	The name applied to data as it travels through the OSI layers when it reaches the Internet Protocol.
IPCONFIG	Internet Protocol Configuration is a Windows 2000 utility that displays TCP/IP settings and administers DHCP client computers.
Ipconfig utility	The TCP/IP diagnostic utility that displays the current TCP/IP configuration information, including the IP address and hostname.
IPSec	Internet Protocol Security is a protocol that encrypts data and authenticates that can be used with L2TP and PPTP standards.

Term	Definition
IPv4	The current version of the TCP/IP protocol is also known as IP Version 4. IPv4 and the next-generation protocol, IPv6, will be used concurrently for several years.
IPv6	The next generation of the TCP/IP protocol after Ipv4, known as IP Version 6, is in draft review and will operate concurrently with IPv4 for several years.
IPX/SPX	Internetwork Packet Exchange/Sequenced Packet Exchange is a protocol suite designed by Novell exclusively for NetWare networks. IPX is a Network Layer routable protocol that uses numeric addresses to identify computers. The SPX Transport Layer protocol provides reliable data transmission.
IrDA	Infrared Data Association sets the standards for infrared use with computers and networks. The IrDA protocol is used to transfer information between a computer (typically a portable computer) and the network.
IrDA-FIR	One of the four IrDA infrared standards that support communication at speeds up to 4 Mbps.
IrDA-SIR	One of the four IrDA infrared standards that support communication at speeds up to a maximum of 115,000 bps.
IrLPT	One of the four IrDA infrared standards that uses the infrared port on the computer as a printer port, and sends information to the printer through this infrared port.
IrTran-P	One of the four IrDA infrared standards that allows a Windows 2000 computer to receive digital images from a digital camera or other digital imaging devices.
ISA	Industry Standard Architecture is a data bus architecture for IBM PCs with either an 8- or 16-bit expansion slot.

Term	Definition
ISDN	Integrated Services Digital Network uses digital and analog telephone lines to send data, voice, video, and fax signals through an adapter to connect the computer or LAN to the ISDN line.
ISO	The International Organization for Standardization is an international organization that creates standards, and designed the seven -layer OSI model from which network protocols are designed.
ISP	An Internet Service Provider is a company that provides IP address es and Internet access to users.
L2TP	Layer 2 Tunnel Protocol is a tunneling protocol used with various transmission protocols and provides compression and tunnel authentication.
LAN	A Local Area Network is a small computer network that spans a relatively small area such as a single building or office area.
lease duration	The length of time a client keeps the same IP address before the address expires and the client must request an address again.
Lmhosts	The Lmhosts file is a static table of NetBIOS names and IP addresses that must be manually updated.
local user account	A network account that allows permission to access files on a specific computer without access to the network.
loopback address	A network ID of 127 that is used to test the NIC.
MAC address	A unique Media Access Control address number is burned into the NIC and cannot be changed. This number identifies each object on the network, working at the Data Link Layer to send and receive data.

Term	Definition
mainframe	A central server that contains all the programs, performs all tasks, and maintains the databases.
MAN	Metropolitan Area Network is a less frequently used term for an internetwork used in a metropolitan area.
MAU	A Multiple Access Unit is the central hub in a token-ring architecture. The wiring inside the MAU forms a ring on which data travels.
MCA	Micro Channel Architecture is an IBM proprietary bus architecture incompatible with ISA buses, and functions as either a 16- or 32-bit bus.
member server	If a network becomes large enough, additional servers called member or stand-alone servers may be required. A member server handles special tasks such as printing or file management on the network.
mesh topology	Multiple redundant paths interconnect network devices in mesh topology. These multiple communication paths to a destination allow selecting the best network route at any time. The topology is commonly used on WANs and the Internet.
message	A message is UDP data at the Transport layer.
MMC	The Microsoft Management Console centralizes management tools in Windows 2000 and provides a common interface for these tools.
multi-cast	A method of simultaneously sending information to several computers over a TCP/IP network.

Term	Definition
multicast transmissions	Multicast transmissions simultaneously send one copy of data to multiple requesting computers, and use Class D and E addresses.
multicasting	The process of simultaneously sending one copy of data to multiple requesting computers. Multicasting messages are routable.
multicasts	A multicast transmission sends a single copy of the data to multiple computers that request the data.
multihomed	A computer with more than one NIC resides, or is at home, on more than one subnet is considered multihomed.
multimaster replication model	In a multimaster replication model, all domain controllers are peers (they are equal). Changes can be made to the Active Directory database on any one of the controllers, and the changes replicate (copy) to the other domain controllers.
multi-port repeater	Also called a hub, this repeater repeats its input signal to all devices or segments that connect to other ports.
namespace	The hierarchical structure of a domain tree where each layer of the tree shares a common DNS domain name.
Nbstat utility	The TCP/IP diagnostic utility Nbstat that displays currently active NetBIOS over TCP/IP sessions.
NBT	The implementation of NetBIOS and TCP/IP is called NBT, or NetBIOS over TCP.
NetBEUI	A protocol designed by Microsoft, originally designed for small single-segment networks.

Term	Definition
NetBEUI/NetBIOS	NetBIOS Extended User Interface (NetBEUI)/NetBIOS is a proprietary Microsoft protocol suite. NetBIOS uses friendly names (called NetBIOS names or WINS names) to identify computers on the network. Combined with NetBEUI, this protocol suite provides a fast, small network protocol that is easy to implement.
NetBIOS	Network Basic Input-Output System is a protocol that uses names to identify computers on a network. It was originally designed as part of NetBEUI.
NetBIOS name	A name assigned to a computer on a NetBIOS-based network to identify it. Also called a WINS name. Names used on networks running NetBIOS over NetBEUI or TCP/IP that can contain up to 15 characters.
NETSTAT	A utility that displays network statistics about the currently active TCP/IP connections.
network	A network consists of two or more connected computers that share tasks and information. Networks provide users with quick and easy access to files and resources, and provide administrators with a centralized system for management.
network access method	Controls that organize when and how users gain access to a network. Four common network access methods are CSMA/CD, CSMA/CA, token passing, and demand priority.
network architecture	The overall structure of a network and its components, including hardware and software that make a network functional.
network components	Devices that facilitate and manipulate data transfer from its source to its destination.

Term	Definition
network ID	The portion of an IP address that identifies the subnet on which the host is connected.
Network Layer	The layer of the OSI primarily responsible for getting data to its intended location, and handles data addressing.
network nodes	Groupings of workstations, hubs, repeaters, bridges, switches, routers, and servers.
network protocol	The language computers use on a network is called a network protocol.
network software	NOS together with protocols make up the network software.
networking model	The networking model refers to the interrelationship of networked computers. The three types of network models (mainframe or central server, peer-to-peer and client/server) each define the interaction between clients and servers in different ways.
NIC	A Network Interface Card, also called a network adapter, is a device that connects a computer to a LAN by accepting the physical connection to the network media. The NIC converts data from a parallel to serial data format
NOS	The Network Operating System is the program that starts or boots the computer and allows you to run programs. You cannot run a computer without an operating system, and you cannot run a network of computers without a NOS.
NTFS	NT File System works with Windows NT and Windows 2000 operating systems and supports advanced features from long filenames to object-oriented files with user and system-defined attributes.

Term	Definition
NTFS permissions	Rights that allow access to files and folders on an NTFS-formatted volume. NTFS permissions apply whether folder access is local or remote.
NWLink	A Microsoft protocol fully compatible with IPX/SPX and usable in Windows 2000.
object	Every network component (for example, a computer, printer, or user) is represented in the Active Directory by an object.
octets	Each number in an IP address is called an octet because it represents exactly 8 bits of data.
OSI	The Open Systems Interconnection network model is a seven-layer model that provides a foundation for all network communication. Each layer is responsible for and addresses one part of network communication.
OSI model	The Open System Interconnection model defines a seven-layer structure upon which network protocols are designed and built.
packet	Data divided into smaller pieces sent across a TCP/IP network.
packet data	The middle section of the TCP/IP packet that contains the actual data being sent.
packet header	The front section of the TCP/IP packet that contains the source address, destination address, and an alert signal.
packet trailer	The end part of the TCP/IP packet that contains error-checking code.

Term	Definition
packets	Units of data divide into smaller pieces when the data is sent across a TCP/IP network. Packets include three parts: the header, the data, and the trailer.
PAD	A Packet Assembler/Disassembler on the X.25 network is a device similar to a modem that converts analog data into X.25 packets, and X.25 packets back to analog.
PAEs	Physical Address Extensions allow an operating system to take advantage of 36-bit memory addressing, rather than the standard 32-bit addressing.
passive technology	Bus topology is an example of passive technology where each network computer listens for transmitted data, checks the destination address, but never actively resends the data.
PCI	Peripheral Component Interconnect is a 32-bit bus architecture found in most PCs and Macintosh computers. Many implementations of PCI are Plug and Play (PnP) compatible that requires minimal user configuration.
peer-to-peer network	A peer-to-peer network does not rely on a central server, but functions with workstations acting as equal peers for handling tasks, data storage, and security matters.
permissions	Authorization settings that determine the level of user or group access to specific objects or resources on the network.
Physical Layer	The layer of the OSI that defines the data transmission conversion from parallel to serial, placement of data on the network, and the conversion of serial to parallel data on the destination computer.

Term	Definition
PING	A utility used to test the network to verify good connections, and diagnose TCP/IP problems.
PING utility	The **PING** utility installs with TCP/IP and works with ICMP to verify the network's remote physical connections by using IP address es.
PnP	The Plug and Play technology automatically detects hardware devices and handles all resource configurations.
point-to-point	The point-to-point or connection-oriented access method sends data packets directly to another computer without other computers receiving or acting upon the data.
port	Ports for TCP and UDP identify individual applications within a computer, and may contain multiple sockets.
PPP	Point-to-Point Protocol provides dial-up connections to TCP/IP-based networks.
PPTP	The Point-to-Point Tunneling Protocol is a tunneling protocol that works with IP-based networks and uses PPP for data encryption.
Presentation Layer	The layer of the OSI that prepares, converts, encrypts, compresses, decrypts, and decompresses data for network transmission. It also converts data from one protocol to another.
PRI	Primary Rate Interface is an ISDN-available technology that carries voice and data over 23 B-channels and one D-channel with a maximum bandwidth of 1.5 Mbps. PRI requires more wires and is more expensive than PRI technology and is rarely used.
profiles	Specifications for certain criteria that define an action, object, or configuration.
protocol	A network protocol is a set of rules that defines how data transmits on the cable, how devices determine the intended destination for the data, and how the device replies to data transmission s. Devices on a network may use more than one protocol, but must share at least one common protocol.

Term	Definition
protocol suite	Several protocols combined together are called a protocol suite or protocol stack.
PSTN	The Public Switched Telephone Network is the standard copper-wire telecommunication link that carries analog voice communication used for ordinary phone calls and dial-up connections for computer communication with a modem.
public-key authentication	In the security process of using keys to encrypt and decrypt messages, the public key attaches to the encrypted file and verifies the identity of the sender.
PVC	Permanent Virtual Circuit acts as a single cable connection between two end points although it uses many different cables.
radio	A primary wireless LAN technology obtained through a radio service subscription.
Registry	The Windows 2000 central database of system configuration information.
remote access server	A computer that runs remote access software and shares resources over the network.
repeater	A network device used to build and extend networks, a repeater restores and repeats a digital signal.
ring topology	A ring topology connects all computers on a single physical circle of cable with no end terminations. The data signal travels the loop in one direction and passes through each computer.

Term	Definition
RIS	Remote Installation Services allows you to install Windows 2000 Professional on client computers across your network from a central server. RIS supports PnP hardware detection, which all ows you to perform automatic installations on computers with different hardware.
root domain	In a tree, the first domain is called the root.
routable protocol	A protocol that carries data across different n etwork segments, uses numeric addresses to identify computers.
Route utility	The TCP/IP diagnostic utility Route displays the local routing table.
router	A sophisticated network device that lo gically interconnects complex network environments on several segments having differing protocols and architectures.
router table	A table that lists computers and their IP addresses the router accesses to redirect messages to the correct segment.
routers	A device that segments networks and passes on data transmission s that have destination addresses.
RRAS	Routing and Remote Access Service configures routing and remote access features Windows 2000 domain member servers.
scope	In Windows 2000, a range of IP address numbers from which the DHCP server assigns IP addresses to clients.
scope	In Windows 2000, the group attribute that defines group member ship in domains.
segment	In data transfer using TCP/IP, a segment is what TCP data is called at the Transport layer.

Term	Definition
serial transmission	A type of transmission where data travels through the network media in a single stream.
server	A computer that has a resource (like a file, a printer, or a Web page) to share on the network.
Session Layer	The layer of the OSI that establishes communication between two computers.
Share permissions	Access rights assigned to a folder that affect what rights users have to the folder and its contents during remote access to the network.
shared folder	A folder on a computer that is available on the network to others.
shielding	A protective layer, such as the braided wire-mesh and outer layer of nonconductive material on coaxial cables, that captures and grounds radiating noise, crosstalk, or electromagnetic energy to prevent interference.
SLIP	Serial Line Internet Protocol transmits TCP/IP data packets over dial-up connections to the Internet or other networks.
smart cards	A credit card-sized attachment for computers that contains its own processor and RAM that stores sensitive information, including security keys.
SMP	Symmetric Multiprocessing is the architecture for computers where several processors share the same memory that has one copy of the operating system, applications, and data.
SMTP	Simple Mail Transfer Protocol works at OSI layers 5, 6, and 7 to provide file transfer services for e-mail message and attachment files.

Term	Definition
snap-ins	Modules that run within the MMC; each snap-in handles a different aspect of Windows 2000 management.
socket	A software object that connects an application to another application on a destination computer. Sockets differentiate TCP/IP streams of data; transmissions end in a software socket.
star topology	The star topology network consists of computers, printers, and other devices connected by cable segments to a central hub in a configuration that resembles a star.
star-bus topology	A topology that combines several star networks linked together with linear bus trunks. A single central backbone connects each star.
star-ring topology	Star networks are connected not by a backbone as in a star-bus network, but by a ring topology.
STP	Shielded Twisted Pair cable consists of two wires twisted around each other with foil and braided mesh for ground shielding.
subnet mask	A 32-bit number that specifies the location of the local or remote segment (or subnet) on which a host is located. It separates the host ID and the network ID in an IP address.
subnets	A method of reducing traffic on a small network is to break it into smaller segments (subnets) that connect to each other through a router.

Term	Definition
superscope	A DHCP scope that contains a collection of two or more scopes used to create logical subnets on the same physical subnet.
switch	A multi-port device that segments a large network into smaller segments to reduce network traffic, increase bandwidth, and reduce collisions.
system state	A collection of files and the Registry that define crucial Windows 2000 settings.
TCP	Transmission Control Protocol TCP is a connection-oriented protocol that works at the Transport Layer of the OSI to ensure data arrives at its destination. If data does not arrive, TCP resends lost packets.
TCP/IP	Transmission Control Protocol (TCP) combines with the Internet Protocol (IP) and several other protocols to create the TCP/IP protocol suite. It includes components from the Network, Transport, Session, Presentation, and Application layers of the OSI model.
TCP/IP Application Layer	This layer corresponds with the Application, Presentation, and Session layers of the OSI model.
TCP/IP Internet Layer	This layer matches the Network Layer of the OSI, and includes IP, ICMP, IGMP, and ARP.
TCP/IP Layer Model	The TCP/IP stack divides into its own three-layer model (Application, Transport, and Internet layers), and maps these layers to the OSI model.
TCP/IP protocol suite	The TCP/IP protocol suite includes numerous smaller protocols that map to specific layers in the OSI model.

Term	Definition
TCP/IP Transport Layer	This layer maps directly to the Transport Layer of the OSI model and includes TCP, UDP, DNS, and WINS.
Telnet utility	A TCP/IP connectivity utility that remotely accesses a server with a command-line-like interface.
TFTP utility	The TCP/IP connectivity utility Trivial File Transfer Protocol uses UDP to transfer files.
Thicknet	Thick, rigid coaxial cable referred to as standard Ethernet or 10Base5 that transfers data over longer distances and is often used as a LAN backbone segment with smaller Thinnet.
Thinnet	Thin, flexible coaxial cable, also known as 10BASE2 cable that carries a signal for approximately 185 meters before attenuation causes data loss.
token passing	A network access method that causes no data collisions and ensures all network computers have equal access rights to send data.
token ring	An IEEE 802.5 standard architecture model that uses token passing on a ring topology, which may be wired as a star, but uses a MAU.
topology	The arrangement of hardware that forms the framework of the network.
TRACERT	A TCP/IP diagnostic utility that traces data and reports the routers that data passes through to reach a destination computer.
Transport Layer	The layer of the OSI that ensures error-free data delivery and handles flow control. It receives data from the Session Layer, re packages it, and sends it to the Network Layer.
tree	A collection of domains that share a common name is called a tree.

Term	Definition
Tree pane	The left side of the MMC contains the Tree pane that contains a list of snap-ins included in the console, and also displays folders.
TTL	Time To Live defines how many hops (through how many routers) a packet travels before it is no longer valid.
tunneling	The process of creating a secure channel through public lines over which encrypted data travel safely.
twisted-pair cable	Several pairs of insulated copper wires twisted around each other. The cable twists prevent unwanted signals from other twisted pairs, and reduces crosstalk and other interference. Twisted-pair cable is also referred to as 10BaseT cable.
UDP	The User Datagram Protocol is connectionless and works at the Transport Layer of the OSI. It is faster than TCP, reduces overhead, and is often used for Internet real-time transmissions.
unicast	A directed transmission where data transmits from one computer to another, and is most efficient when data transmits to only a few computers.
universal group	A group scope that contains users from any domain and who have assigned permissions to resources in any domain.
upstream data	Data that travels over bandwidth going from the client to the server.
user account	An established way for an individual to access a computer, a network, and or resources, with a username and password.
user rights	Settings that determine what a user can and cannot do on a computer or network domain.
utilities	Many of the TCP/IP utilities share the same name as TCP/IP protocols. TCP/IP utilities are user interfaces that allow using the protocols.

Term	Definition
utility	An application or program that solves problems narrow in focus, also known as a snap-in.
UTP	Unshielded Twisted Pair cable consists of two wires twisted around each other with no shielding. It is the most common LAN cable type, and is used for land telephone installations.
VPN	Virtual Private Network technology allows sending encrypted communication over a public network such as the Internet.
WAN	Wide Area Networks are multiple LANs or internetworks that include users in a wide geographical area. A WAN can serve thousands of users and is often referred to as an enterprise network.
WINS	The Windows Internet Name Service works at the OSI Transport Layer, and resolves NetBIOS names to IP addresses. WINS servers support older Windows-based clients that require NetBIOS names.
WWW	The World Wide Web is a complex system of servers that accommodates displaying and linking Web pages written in HTML, and accommodates a variety of files in a variety of formats that may include text, graphics, video and audio files.
X.25	A network protocol that works at the Physical, Data Link, and Network layers of the OSI model to transmit data in discrete packets.

Index

10Base2 cable, 45, 76, 82, 465, 490

10Base5 cable, 76, 465

10BaseF cable, 76, 465

10BaseT cable, 46, 76, 82, 465, 491

5-4-3 rule, 68, 91, 96

802 Specifications, 100, 117, 465

account

user, 6-12, 16, 30-34, 36-37, 43, 87, 103-104, 108, 125, 138, 141, 153, 156, 159-160, 192, 198, 270, 280, 290, 298-299, 303, 310-312, 323-324, 329, 331-340, 342-345, 349-354, 356-358, 364-365, 367-368, 370-372, 386, 397, 405, 408, 426, 428, 431, 436, 440, 447, 458, 461, 463

Active Directory, 12, 15-16, 19, 28, 31-34, 36-37, 266, 268, 301, 337-338, 342, 365, 368, 371

domain, 12-13, 15-20, 32, 38, 133, 139, 154, 156-157, 173, 235, 237, 248, 297, 301, 332, 337-339, 341-344, 357, 365-369, 371-372, 374-378, 380-381, 384, 393, 401, 426, 431-432

Users and Computers, 337-338, 365

Active Server Pages, 417

Address Resolution Protocol, 137, 171, 239

administrative, 5-6, 8, 15-16, 30, 53, 149, 228, 243, 249, 269, 272, 274-275, 281, 283, 287, 302, 323, 331, 335, 337, 339, 342, 365, 368, 371

tasks, 1, 4-8, 15, 30, 101, 133-134, 269-275, 285, 291, 301-302, 323, 329, 335, 342, 351-352, 368, 371, 434

tools, 5, 13, 37, 137, 142, 176, 243, 249, 253, 269, 271, 274-276, 278, 281, 283, 287, 289-290, 292-293, 302, 305, 323-324, 330, 333, 337, 365, 391, 402, 408, 412, 415

Administrator account, 20, 335-336, 368, 371

ADSL, 447-448, 459, 462, 464

alerts, 287, 323, 327, 329

analog signal, 434, 448-449

APIPA, 228-229, 261-262, 264-265, 267

AppleTalk, 64, 97, 104, 106, 109-110, 125-126, 129, 132, 153

applets, 275, 294-295

Application Layer, 98, 102-103, 128, 141, 171, 174, 177, 394, 400, 425

application server, 8, 12, 31, 301